# Entrepreneurial
# Couples

# Entrepreneurial
# Couples

## Making It Work at Work and at Home

Kathy Marshack, Ph.D.

Davies-Black Publishing
Palo Alto, California

Published by Davies-Black Publishing, an imprint of Consulting Psychologists Press, Inc., 3803 East Bayshore Road, Palo Alto, CA 94303; 1-800-624-1765.

Special discounts on bulk quantities of Davies-Black books are available to corporations, professional associations, and other organizations. For details, contact the Director of Book Sales at Davies-Black Publishing, an imprint of Consulting Psychologists Press, Inc., 3803 East Bayshore Road, Palo Alto, CA 94303; 650-691-9123; Fax 650-988-0673.

02 01 00 99 98    10 9 8 7 6 5 4 3 2 1
Printed in the United States of America

**Library of Congress Cataloging-in-Publication Data**
Marshack, Kathy
Entrepreneurial couples : making it work at work and at home  /  Kathy Marshack ;
foreword by Dennis T. Jaffe & Cynthia D. Scott
p.  cm.
Includes bibliographical references and index.
ISBN 0-89106-115-0
1. Dual-career families—United States. 2. Couple-owned business enterprises—United States. 3. Work and family—United States.
4. Marriage—United States. I. Title.
HQ536.M3255  1998
306.872—d21                    97-49921
                                          CIP
FIRST EDITION
First printing 1998

*To my mother, Irene Emilie Heil,*
*who encouraged me to be unconventional,*
*and to my grandmother, Louellen Shirley,*
*who loved me unconditionally*

# CONTENTS

# FOREWORD

This book sheds light on a growing phenomenon: more and more couples are choosing to *not* have two independent jobs, but rather to join forces and create something new—a special place to work in which their dreams are made real right alongside the accountability and pressure of getting results in a competitive world. Entrepreneurial couples have chosen to take on risk, and to live with pressure, for highly personal reasons. This book is their story.

As an entrepreneurial couple, we are featured players in a work revolution. We have been working together, while simultaneously raising a family, for over a decade. The challenges are tremendous, and it is only because the rewards are so clear to us that we are willing to continue. It has been and still is a difficult balancing act. Today, for example, we got up and got our son ready for school, dropped him off at the bus stop, and sped in to work. We honored our agreement to not talk about work until Colton is on the school bus, but then the floodgates opened and a torrent of mixed business and family concerns gushed in. Appointments, dinners, fixing the roof, baby-sitters, who should do what professional presentation, and the ultimate challenge—When are we going to get some quiet time for ourselves, and to be together?—were all discussed during the twenty-minute drive to the office. The boundary between personal life and work life was nowhere to be seen.

With this book, Kathy Marshack does entrepreneurial couples an incredible service. She gives us a voice and an identity, and lets us know that we are not alone. She identifies the challenges we all face, using real-life examples based on the experiences of our peers to offer sound advice about how we can make it all a little bit easier. She doesn't oversimplify and offer magic cures for our ailments. Her book is complex because it deals with an intricate array of choices and actions within a sphere limited by the amount of time in a day.

We know this book can help us—and who knows how many others like us—manage our unique lives. We also hope it will be a beacon, a magnet, to draw more of us together to explore how to balance our conflicting demands and to discover how to make it work at work and at home.

DENNIS T. JAFFE, PH.D.

CYNTHIA D. SCOTT, PH.D.

COPRINCIPALS OF CHANGEWORKS SOLUTIONS

COAUTHORS OF *REKINDLING COMMITMENT*

# PREFACE

This book is for career-minded couples who are self-employed or who aspire to be self-employed. If you are married or living together or otherwise in a committed relationship *and* if you are also partners in a joint business venture or each of you owns your own enterprise, or your spouse is supporting you while you promote your solo business, this book will help you to balance and integrate the competing demands of love and work.

Frank and Louise are such a couple.[1] Frank started his electronics business in his late twenties, several years after marrying Louise, a physical therapist. Although he had a successful career in a corporation and was climbing the executive ladder, Frank developed a chronic illness and was unable to commit fully to his career. He decided to make a career move that would allow him the flexibility to accommodate his schedule to the days (and even weeks) when he was so ill that he could not get out of bed. Louise helped part-time, and together they made the business so successful that in five short years it was booming. The success of the business was also mirrored in Frank's return to robust health.

Still, problems plagued the couple. Louise never intended to work full-time with Frank in the business. She had her own career, except now that career was not so appealing. The electronics business needed her more and more at a time when Louise desired another type of creative outlet. Now in her mid-thirties, she wanted children. Frank and Louise spent many long hours discussing, arguing, and crying over their situation before finally seeking my help. The problem seemed to be, simply, that this couple did not know how to create a life where they could have it all. They wanted a successful business, increasing financial rewards, continued good health, meaningful careers, marital intimacy and friendship, and children. They did not want to sacrifice anything, but there did not seem to be enough time, energy, or money to accomplish it all.

You will learn more about Frank and Louise and other couples like them as you read this book. In fact, Frank and Louise were the inspiration for it. I wanted to learn more about similar couples so that I could help those entrepreneurial couples who came to my office seeking marital therapy. I was interested in that special subgroup of dual-career couples who have chosen entrepreneurship as their career,

---

[1] To thoroughly protect the privacy of the entrepreneurial couples I describe in this book, I have changed superficial details, such as the nature or location of their business or home, and of course their names. For the purpose of illustration, I have also sometimes created composites by combining details about different couples.

whether they share ownership of a business or one is supportive of the other's entrepreneurial venture or they are each owners of separate enterprises. However, when I researched the field, I found very little—some anecdotal reports, a case study or two, and a few interviews with experts. There was very little real research, the kind of research that digs deeply and discovers what entrepreneurial couples are made of.

As a result, I launched my doctoral dissertation with a study of entrepreneurial couples. The title of that dissertation is *Love and Work: How Co-Entrepreneurial Couples Manage the Boundaries and Transitions in Personal Relationship and Business Partnership.* In addition to my research, I have over twenty years of experience as a marriage and family therapist and a consultant to family-owned and couple-owned firms. In this book you will read about many of the couples I have worked with. And you will learn the lessons I have learned as a result of getting to know these couples on an intimate level.

# Entrepreneurial Couples and the Twenty-First Century

*Dual-career couples* are a phenomenon of the 1970s. In 1969 Rapoport and Rapoport first defined these couples and noted the trend. They said that dual-career couples are a special case of "families in which both husband and wife pursue careers (i.e., jobs which are highly salient personally, have a developmental sequence and require a high degree of commitment)." *Entrepreneurial couples* are a subgroup of dual-career couples in that each partner is committed to a meaningful career and to the relationship, but unlike other dual-career couples, one or both members of an entrepreneurial couple are self-employed.

Rapoport and Rapoport predicted that women entering the workforce would change the shape of corporate America and family life. Almost three decades later, we are seeing those changes. For example, half of all law school graduates are women. Women are entering the workforce at a younger age, are better educated, and are utilizing day care for younger and younger children. Men are part of this change also. Today's college-educated man wants a college-educated partner with a career plan. Couples are used to dual incomes and dual career commitments. They have developed (or aspire to develop) quality lives with all the trimmings.

If dual-career couples are a phenomenon of the 1970s, entrepreneurial couples may be a phenomenon of the 1990s and the beginning of the twenty-first century. Two of the most rapidly growing groups of the self-employed are women (i.e., sole proprietorships) and couples (i.e., jointly owned sole proprietorships). Jointly owned sole proprietorships are not necessarily owned by married couples alone.[2] The designation of jointly owned sole proprietorship is primarily a tax term for when two individuals share ownership of a business. Still, the information on jointly owned sole proprietorships suggests that entrepreneurial couple ventures are on the rise.

According to the Small Business Administration (SBA), nonfarm jointly owned sole proprietorships are increasing steadily at about 5 percent a year. In 1985 there were 482,993 jointly owned sole proprietorships, excluding farm businesses, in the United States. By 1994, the most recent year for which statistics are available, the SBA reported 758,743 jointly owned sole proprietorships, an increase of 57 percent. Moreover, the actual number of entrepreneurial couple ventures may be even higher, since the SBA does not keep statistics on corporations and partnerships run by couples.

Much is being written these days about leaving corporate life and striking out on one's own. With the prevalence of downsizing, outsourcing, and the glass ceiling that many women and minorities bump up against, career-minded couples are realizing that the quality life to which they aspire may best be achieved through an entrepreneurial venture. According to business consultant Leon Danco, half of America's gross national product is earned by family firms. And many of these family firms were started by mom and pop. Furthermore, the SBA notes that in 1994 jointly owned sole proprietorships reported $38 trillion in receipts. These facts make self-employment and entrepreneurship look very appealing to many couples.

Many books have been written that speak to this growing trend of entrepreneurial couples. There are books that address the communication styles and differences between men and women. There are time-management books and an array of time-management paraphernalia to make the days of self-employed couples more

---

2 In this book I will occasionally use the terms *married couple, spouse, husband,* and *wife* to refer in a generic way to any two persons living together in a committed relationship. They could be married or unmarried, and they could be two men or two women as well as a man and a woman. I do not intend any bias toward gay and lesbian couples, who cannot in this country legally marry, nor toward straight couples who choose to live together without getting married. I will also in this book use the more strictly generic terms *relationship* and *partner* to refer to any two persons living together in a committed relationship.

efficient. There are books on how to choose the right day-care facility or nanny for one's child or children, or how to organize a day-care plan for one's company. There are career planning books for those weary midlife individuals who desire a change of venue. There are books on how to start a small business. And there are books for women on how to balance the demands of a busy life as a professional, wife, and mother. But until *Entrepreneurial Couples* there has been no book that specifically addresses how *both* partners in an entrepreneurial relationship can balance and integrate intimacy, family life, and meaningful work. *Entrepreneurial Couples* takes a holistic approach. I know of no other book on this subject that combines the practical application of research findings with the commonsense advice of a professional who has years of experience working with entrepreneurial couples. Entrepreneurial couples don't need any more help learning how to do their work faster or more efficiently; they are already masters at this. What I hear in my office as a psychologist, and what I discovered in my research, is a cry for help on how to achieve *balance* in one's life, how to keep both career and life priorities straight, how to stay loving and healthy.

The goal of *Entrepreneurial Couples* is to help these affluent, well-educated, achieving professionals and entrepreneurs to benefit emotionally and mentally from their chosen lifestyle. By assessing your own strengths and weaknesses, planning for the future, improving communication, and reorienting your priorities, you will learn from this book how to design and live a balanced, integrated, and meaningful entrepreneurial life.

## Making the Most of the Entrepreneurial Lifestyle

From my clinical experience and research with entrepreneurial couples, I have learned a great deal about how these couples, without any models or guidelines, negotiate the stressful daily transitions from home to work and back again. By and large these couples are doing a pretty good job. Most entrepreneurial couples would not live any other way. They are stressed, to be sure; they are facing fatigue; they have marital problems; they feel guilty about the little quality time spent with their children; they make personal compromises in order to get ahead in their careers; and they make career compromises in order to keep the family stable. But they also feel as though they are making a real contribution to the community. They are creating a future for their children; they can bring intellectually stimulating conversation to the dinner table; they can afford dream vacations; they can be a force politically.

The problem is that entrepreneurial couples are not the type of people who like doing a "pretty good job." They are not content with just "making do." They are the kind of people who like to excel, or they would not both be pursuing meaningful, demanding careers. And they are the kind of people who like "having it all." It appears, however, that many entrepreneurial couples are just making do. Because many of these couples have no models to guide them in planning and implementing the entrepreneurial couple life, they tend to follow the outdated models of their parents or grandparents. For example, without thinking, some entrepreneurial couples continue to divide home responsibilities along traditional gender lines. Women do the laundry, the cooking, and the cleaning. Men do the yard work, home repairs, and auto maintenance. For entrepreneurial couples, this is especially a problem when they also divide work responsibilities along traditional gender lines, not taking into consideration the training and talents of each partner. For example, some attorney wives are also the office manager for their husband-and-wife law firm.

While most entrepreneurial couples just make do, the purpose of this book is to teach you how to *make the most* of your entrepreneurial lifestyle. This is not just another pop psychology book. Entrepreneurs, by and large, are impatient with well-intentioned but superficial self-help books that apply to the generic person but not to them specifically. I don't want to give you a handful of techniques that you blindly apply. This book does not offer a cookie-cutter approach. Instead, *Entrepreneurial Couples* digs into your beliefs and values, where deep, meaningful change really happens. As you read each chapter you will get to know yourself and your spouse or partner better. In fact, there are fifteen exercises in the book to help you do just that. From these exercises you will not only gain tools and techniques, but you will develop action plans to implement a *Master Life Plan* uniquely suited to yourself and your partner that includes goals for you personally, for your relationship, for the business, for family life, for wealth management, and for stress management.

Each chapter in *Entrepreneurial Couples* could be a book in itself. Although each chapter offers a fairly thorough discussion of the subject, keep in mind that one cannot cover a subject in depth in one chapter. However, I wanted to write one book that covers the major areas of concern to entrepreneurial couples, to give you an overview of the territory needing your attention. Starting from this big-picture point of view makes it easier to compare yourself to other entrepreneurial couples to learn more about your strengths and weaknesses. Later you can isolate for more study the specific topics that apply to you. To really make the most of your entrepreneurial couple lifestyle, continue exploring the territory by reading other books, attending seminars, consulting professionals and talking with other entrepreneurial couples about how they make their lives and relationship work at the business and at home.

In Chapter One, Entrepreneurial Couples: Who Are They? I will introduce you to several entrepreneurial couples as a way of defining the variety of style options. As you read their stories, you will begin to get an idea of the style of entrepreneurship that fits you best. For example, if you enjoy working with family members and want your spouse in the business full-time, you may be well suited to *copreneuring*. On the other hand, if the competition between yourself and your spouse is unpleasant and counterproductive, but you are both entrepreneurial spirits, *dual entrepreneurship* may be a better choice. In all, I have defined twenty different types of entrepreneurial couples, so you are bound to find a model or a blend of models that clarifies your entrepreneurial style.

In Chapter Two, Integrating Lives: Laying the Groundwork to Balance Love and Work, I will introduce you to some new thoughts or new ways to look at why you and your spouse work together the way you do, why you make the choices you do, and how to do it all better. Psychologists have long developed theories to explain human behavior, and in this chapter, I will apply some of these theories to the lives of entrepreneurial couples. You will learn about *dialectical psychology, social exchange theory, life cycle theory,* and *systems theory.* These theories come alive and make sense when viewed from the perspective of the real lives of the couples you are meeting in this book. Furthermore, it is next to impossible to plan for the success of a business, the deepening of a marital relationship, and the future of your children without a *framework.* Each main area of your life—business, marriage, and family—is very complex and makes different demands on you. The theories that I introduce you to in this chapter help you build a framework within which to understand and plan for success in all three areas.

Chapter Three, Communicating with Your Partner: The Nuts and Bolts of How to Talk and Win, is packed with tips to make communication more smooth. Based on the theories learned in the previous chapter, you will learn to take responsibility for your communication and your communication goals. You will learn the importance of *listening.* You will learn how to *fight fairly.* You will learn how to go beyond compromises toward *win-win solutions.* You will learn how to recognize that your spouse has a communication style, too, and that it may be different from your own. You will learn to transcend these differences instead of staying stuck in them. You will learn how to handle the most irrational of arguments. As your *communication flexibility* grows, so will your skill as a businessperson and a marital partner.

Chapter Four, Life Planning: Steps to Achieve Your Business and Personal Goals, is a hefty chapter requiring that you get out a pencil and go to work. I will teach you how to *compose a life* instead of just winging it, to orchestrate a harmonious symphony from the interacting domains of business, marriage, and family life. It isn't good enough to have a successful business with a marriage on the rocks. It is time to develop a *holistic plan* that treats with respect all areas of your life. In this chapter I will teach you the *seven ground rules* for successful life and business planning. Then I will guide you through each important area of your life while you develop a specific plan that fits the unique personality and needs of your particular entrepreneurial couple style.

I take you into the world of my research in Chapter Five, Equality or Equity: How to Find Fairness in Your Partnership. Do not be alarmed by the word research, however, because this chapter is anything but dry ivory-tower psycho-babble. This very important chapter will challenge your beliefs about acceptable roles for husbands and wives. Through studying entrepreneurial couples I have learned of the struggle these couples face in creating a business partnership out of the same cloth from which they have created a personal partnership. You will want to examine your roles, too, after reading of these struggles. Both *traditional* and *egalitarian* approaches to marriage will be explored, as well as variations in between. This chapter will present grist for many provocative conversations between you and your partner, out of which should come a clearer definition of equity in your relationship.

Chapter Six, Women Entrepreneurs: Are They Different from Men? rounds out the picture on entrepreneurs. Because the bulk of the literature on entrepreneurs is about men, it is easy to have a slanted view of the personalities of entrepreneurs. A knowledge of the similarities of and differences between male and female entrepreneurs is vital in a relationship where husband and wife are engaging in entrepreneurial activity. Women entrepreneurs are very similar to men entrepreneurs, but there are some significant differences, most important of which is that women cannot separate their roles as wife/mother/business partner as easily as men can. Furthermore, women entrepreneurs tend to view business as a way to extend their friendship network. In Chapter Six, you will have the opportunity to meet some women entrepreneurs and compare them to the women entrepreneurs you know in your life.

Chapter Seven, Parenting and Family Life: Rounding Out Your Life Plan, takes up where Chapter Four left off. After you have worked on the other aspects of your life composition (i.e., your business plan, your personal life plan, and your relationship life plan), this chapter guides you through the steps necessary to encourage healthy, creative independence and resilience in your children. Although this chapter is not an in-depth look at parenting, it focuses on the unique concerns of entrepreneurial couples. Other parenting books simply do not recognize the complications to parenting that the entrepreneurial life creates. Outlined in this chapter are seven *basic principles of good parenting* for entrepreneurial couples. Even if you have no children or your children are grown, this chapter will be useful, either as a guide for the future, as a guide in your role with adult children, or even as a guide to reexamining the lessons of your own childhood and how they shaped you.

Chapter Eight, Wealth Management: How to Balance Health and Wealth, is an eye-opening chapter. In it you will read the stories of how wealth has unhinged the lives of many entrepreneurial couples. It may seem a silly problem to some, but there are serious challenges that come from wealth, and these challenges can cause health problems, psychological distress, and interpersonal disaster. Many of the entrepreneurial couples in this book were not ready for the problems associated with wealth, so the purpose of this chapter is to help you be better prepared. You will learn about the *money trap*, the *meaning of money*, why *desire creates desire*, and the difference between *poverty consciousness* and *prosperity consciousness*. You will learn when to choose *collaboration* instead of *competition*. You will learn how to teach your children to use the *American work ethic* to build a life that is a healthy composition of love, work, and wealth.

Becoming the best you can be is the theme of Chapter Nine, Personal and Professional Growth: Beyond Problem Solving. Many of you are reading this book because you are stuck or there is a crisis and you want relief. You may be looking for answers to long-standing problems. The bulk of this book addresses those concerns. However, it is equally important to balance problem solving with proactive behaviors. To paraphrase an old saying, you don't have to be sick to get better. In other words, the key to a successful entrepreneurial marriage is to develop a positive, healthy outlook on life, to be curious about the world around you, and to encourage the personal and professional growth of your spouse as well as yourself. This chapter is not meant as an in-depth look at these issues, but is intended to spur you on to discover those methods that work for you. You will learn how to recognize when change is needed or may be imminent. You will learn how to take advantage of opportunities for growth when the timing is right. And you will learn to recognize the difference between crisis management and purposeful change and growth.

Chapter Ten, Stress Management: Taking Care of the Mind-Body-Spirit Connection, may be a shocking chapter for some readers. Throughout *Entrepreneurial Couples* you will have met many couples and learned of their struggles to balance their complex lives. In this chapter you will learn of the serious consequences of failing to attend to problems soon enough. Not only does failure to pay attention to the signals that change is needed result in health problems, divorce, depression, addiction, and financial disaster, but each of these problems will seep into other areas of your life. This chapter carries forward the theoretical framework introduced in Chapter Two by looking at problem creation and problem solution as a holistic process that affects each individual, couple, and business in all areas of their lives. You will learn that *stress is a sign of imbalance in your entire life* and that coping mechanisms such as alcohol abuse or extramarital affairs only compound the problems. Again, there is only so much that I can say on these topics in one chapter, but my goal is to alert you to the kinds of problems that could be lurking in your life. It is up to you to do further exploration and make a power plan that works for you and your partner and business.

If you have been thorough in your reading and have worked through all the self-assessment exercises in the book, you will be ready for Chapter Eleven, Constructing a Master Life Plan: How to Be Successful in the Twenty-First Century. It is here that you will put the pieces together to create a holistic plan to bring balance to your life as an entrepreneurial couple. Out of your patience and hard work will emerge not only a master life plan and action steps to accomplish that plan, but a mission statement to guide you toward your vision.

Reading a book and getting all pumped up about some new ideas is not enough. I encourage you to work through the self-assessment exercises so that you can make the changes you need and want to make. To make it more convenient for you, I have repeated all the exercises in the appendix and added Self-Assessment Exercise 15, Your Master Life Plan, so that you can bring all your insights and decisions together in one place. Feel free to copy the exercises in the appendix and give a set to your spouse, so that you can work the program together. This puts you much closer to making it work at work and at home.

## Taking the First Step

In spite of the conflicts and contradictions that I note among entrepreneurial couples, these couples consistently report great satisfaction with their entrepreneurial lifestyle. Although there are tremendous risks in entrepreneuring with your spouse, apparently those risks make the rewards that much sweeter. That choice is yours to make. This book doesn't question the validity of the entrepreneurial lifestyle. Rather, in these pages you will learn *how to make the most of your relationship and your business* by striking a more humanitarian balance between love and work. You will learn to think and plan. You will learn to modify your goals to accomplish them all, in time. You will learn to communicate effectively. You will come to view parenting as integral to the long-term success of your business. You will come to value health and personal growth as much as making money. And you will reevaluate the meaning of money so that you can be even more prosperous.

You already know that you are committed to the entrepreneurial couple lifestyle, or at least curious about the possibility. You have spent many years developing your career skills and are ready to start your own business or redefine an existing one. You admire and love your personal partner and want him or her as your business partner too. You want to parent properly so that you can launch secure, resilient children into adult life. You want to balance success in business with success in your personal life. *Entrepreneurial Couples* will help you accomplish these goals and dreams by guiding you through the dynamic process of *making your life and relationship work at work and at home.*

# ACKNOWLEDGMENTS

Many people inspired, encouraged, and supported my efforts to write this book; without them, I literally could not have done it. My supporters recognized that there was a need for this book because no one else had addressed the unique concerns of entrepreneurial couples. They understood how difficult if not impossible it is for entrepreneurial couples to separate their personal relationship from their work partnership. They know that entrepreneurial couples take pride in both the business and the marriage they have created. They realize that entrepreneurial couples want to have the best of both worlds, a successful business and a happy marriage. These supporters encouraged me to write this book to finally give some well-deserved attention to these trendsetters, entrepreneurial couples who value the challenges and rewards of competition in the workplace as well as the security and love of meaningful family relationships.

First among the supporters I would like to thank are the entrepreneurial couples themselves. Their stories, triumphs, and failures inspired me—not just to write this book, but to take another look at restoring my own life to balance, to integrate my work and intimate relationships in a more meaningful way. I cannot name them here, for reasons of confidentiality, but I hope you know who you are. Thank you for sharing your life stories with me so that others might benefit from your hard work and insights.

Among my other supporters are my dissertation committee at the Fielding Institute, Kjell Rudestam, Ph.D., William Yabroff, Ph.D., Eugene Kerfoot, Ph.D., Michelle Harway, Ph.D., and W. Gibb Dyer, Jr., Ph.D. Because of their interest in my research, I developed the confidence to continue this work, despite the criticisms and doubts of others. All of them confirmed that this is a field that needs exploring and that I was the person to do it. Thank you.

Two of my most devoted supporters are my office staff, Kathleen Walko and Kelly Cutter. Kelly and Kathleen saw me through the completion of my Ph.D. When I was finally able to breathe a sigh of relief at graduation, my dissertation oral exam finished just the day before, Kelly said to me, "There's a book in you; I just know it." Although Kelly has moved on to work on her own doctorate, I remember her words daily. Kathleen has been the beneficiary of those words, too. She simply accepted it as a given that my next step professionally was to take those years of professional practice with entrepreneurial couples and combine them with the research I had just completed, to create *Entrepreneurial Couples*. Thank you both for accepting me and believing in me.

At long last in the list of special people to acknowledge are my intrepid family—my husband, Howard, and our daughters, Bianca and Phoebe. Among the many duties of being married to an entrepreneur who works out of her home, the most important is to be unflappable in the face of artistic temperament. There were days when my husband had to pick up one child from Girl Scouts, get the other to soccer practice, put a hot supper on the table for all of us, and proof the latest chapter of my book, which requires just the right combination of constructive criticism and unconditional praise. He is a very together fellow, indeed. Thank you, Howard, for being a rock.

Our daughters, Bianca and Phoebe, never had a choice about their parents. They have come to accept us, I think. However, the other day Bianca told me she wished I were like "other mothers." I asked her what she meant by "other mothers," and she said, "Oh, you know. Other mothers leave home every day and work at a building downtown, not at home like you do." And here I had thought I was doing the right thing being home every day to greet her after school! Still, I appreciate her candidness. She and Phoebe remind me that the life of each entrepreneurial couple is unique and must be balanced according to the needs of everyone who is important to them. Thank you, girls.

To round out the picture, a special thanks goes to Melinda Adams Merino, the acquisitions editor at Davies-Black. Frankly, without you this book would be sitting on my shelf, getting dusty, representing only something that might have been. Thank you for your patience and persistence. I hope by now I have earned your confidence.

# ABOUT THE AUTHOR

Kathy Marshack is a psychologist in private practice whose specialty lies in consultation to family-owned businesses. With over twenty years of experience as a marriage and family therapist and a business consultant, she has been profiled in *Inc.*, *Nation's Business,* and the Wells Fargo Bank magazine *Business '97* for her professional expertise. She is a member of the National Association of Social Workers and the American Psychological Association, and she is a board certified diplomate in social work.

Marshack received her B.S. degree (1972) in psychology from Portland State University, her M.S.W. degree (1975) from the University of Hawaii, and her Ph.D. degree (1994) in psychology from the Fielding Institute. She has presented her research at local, national, and international conferences. A regular columnist for the *Vancouver Business Journal,* she has contributed numerous articles to newspapers and journals on topics relevant to families in business.

*Entrepreneurial Couples* in more than just a professional endeavor: it reflects Marshack's personal life as well as she works to balance her roles as an entrepreneur, a dual-career wife, and a team parent. Marshack lives in Vancouver, Washington, with her husband, Howard, a family law attorney, and their two daughters, Bianca and Phoebe.

# Entrepreneurial Couples: Who Are They?

Trish and Kurt are a college-educated couple in their early thirties. Kurt is a district manager for a national company. Trish is an executive for an international corporation. They live in the suburbs in a new trilevel "French cottage" with their twin daughters, a dog, and a cat. They are affluent, own two BMWs, and can afford vacations to Hawaii or Mazatlán. In spite of their successes, Trish and Kurt are considering a transition to the entrepreneurial life and have been investigating a variety of options.

Trish and Kurt, a quintessential dual-career couple, represent only one of the many types of entrepreneurial couples I will discuss in this book. Just as no two people on the planet share the same fingerprints, no two couples share quite the same work/home style. In this book you will learn about the styles of many different entrepreneurial couples and why their particular style works for them. What these varied entrepreneurial couples *do* have in common are three things. First, both partners are working full-time at careers that are highly meaningful personally, have a path of advancement, and require a high degree of commitment. Second, these couples are engaged in developing an enterprise, either as partners in a joint venture, as dual entrepreneurs, or as a solo enterprise with one partner supporting the entrepreneurial one. Third, although some details have been changed to protect each couple's privacy, these are all real people who have real lives, real successes, and real problems.

Because these couples are real people chosen from my research and my consulting practice, you will be able to identify with many aspects of their lives even if the facts in your own case are slightly different. For example, all entrepreneurial couples struggle with money problems and finding time for privacy and getting household chores done. But there are also concerns that are unique to certain styles of marriage. These unique concerns may not apply to you in every case, but I urge you to read about other styles. You may get ideas that could be applied to your own situation.

The styles defined in this chapter include the *solo entrepreneur with a supportive spouse*, the *dual-entrepreneurial couple*, and the *copreneurial couple*. I have also included examples of dual-career couples considering entrepreneurship for those of you not quite decided on your style, or even if you are cut out for entrepreneurship at all. See the chart on page 7 for a schematic summary of the different types of entrepreneurial couples.

Bob and Carol used to work together in their successful nursery and garden supply business, but Bob has since returned to his old employer, leaving Carol to manage the business on her own as a *solo entrepreneur*. Bob has become the *supportive spouse*. He is employed elsewhere and provides emotional support to his wife's business but is not really involved in the day-to-day management and headaches of running it. Carol, on the other hand, recognizes her talent as an entrepreneur and is much better suited to running the operation on her own as a sole proprietor.

Larry and Dorothy, who for fifteen years have worked side by side building their farming enterprises, are a *copreneurial couple*. Copreneurs share ownership, management, and responsibility for their business as full-time partners. The term *copreneur* comes from the blending of the words *couple* and *entrepreneur* and was coined by the husband-and-wife team of Barnett and Barnett in 1988. Copreneurs are different from dual entrepreneurs in that they operate a joint venture. One partner may have more of the entrepreneurial spirit than the other, but they are both equally committed to the enterprise as owners and managers.

Still another style involves *dual entrepreneurs* like Sharon and David, who each separately run their respective businesses. Sharon is a realtor and David runs several successful small businesses. Dual entrepreneurs are like solo entrepreneurs in that each partner is an entrepreneurial spirit tending to his or her own sole proprietorship (or perhaps a partnership with a non–family member). They also may function as a support person to their entrepreneurial spouse. What distinguishes dual-entrepreneurial couples from the others is that both partners have the entrepreneurial spirit yet they are not in business partnership with each other.

There are few couples who fit neatly into one category or another. Jonathan, for example, owned a multimillion-dollar national advertising company ten years ago when he met Brooke, whom he later married. Now Brooke heads up a major division of Jonathan's company. Jonathan and Brooke are copreneurs but often operate as dual entrepreneurs because of the size of their international business. Anton and Carrie were each solo entrepreneurs before they married and merged their respective businesses to become copreneurs. Nalani and Ross over the years have experimented with all types of entrepreneurship: In some ventures they are

2

copreneurs; in others each operates as an independent dual entrepreneur. All the while they consider themselves supportive spouses.

I will outline several other examples in this chapter to expose you to a variety of entrepreneurial styles. The emphasis is on seeing patterns in these styles, not that any one style is the right one. Styles are chosen or they evolve or they are forced upon people. In this chapter you will begin to get a sense of how to define (or redefine) your own entrepreneurial style. This definition can be a starting place for enhancing your relationship and business development.

## Are You an Entrepreneurial Spirit?

In spite of the multitude of studies on entrepreneurs, psychologists have yet to come up with a reliable instrument to assess the qualities that may lead to successful entrepreneurship. This has led some researchers to suggest that types of entrepreneurs may fall along a continuum depending on the type of business they are in, the current economic climate, personality factors, early childhood, and so on. Others have suggested that the confusion over typing entrepreneurs has come from including small business people in the same classification with entrepreneurs. For example, in 1984 Carland, Hoy, Boulton, and Carland reviewed the literature on small business owners and entrepreneurs and determined that they are very different. The major differences are that the entrepreneur is innovative and interested in profitability and growth, whereas the small business manager does not engage in innovative marketing practices and is only interested in making an income to support his or her family.

Most of the research on entrepreneurs has been about *men* who started their businesses shortly after World War II. As a result, these studies show a consistent profile that may not reflect the wider variety of entrepreneurs who are entering the marketplace today, such as women and entrepreneurial couples. The profile is that of a hardworking, rebellious, antiauthoritarian man, who came from an impoverished childhood and is determined to "make good." He is a loner and works long hours at the expense of marriage and family life. He is insecure but has a high need for achievement to compensate for that insecurity. He is innovative as opposed to creative—that is, he makes use of creative ideas even if they are not his own. He is a moderate risk taker, preferring to trust his own skills and judgment over those of others. He is controlling and thus has difficulty moving his business toward professional management.

More recently two researchers have taken a slightly different approach to developing a typology of entrepreneurs. In a 1991 report, Donckels and Frohlich compared the values and attitudes of entrepreneurs in family-owned and non-family-owned businesses. Using eighty-five value indicators taken from the literature on entrepreneurs, these researchers developed a questionnaire and administered it to European business owners. From this study, they discovered four types of entrepreneurial personalities. The *all-rounder* is the versatile, universally responsive, and adaptive entrepreneur. He (or she) is his own designer, accountant, salesperson, and frontline manager. The *routineer* represents the cautious entrepreneur who is more interested in providing an income for his or her family than in being innovative and taking risks. The *organizer* is the administrator and executive type of entrepreneur, applying rational, analytical, and organizing strengths with empathy. The *pioneer* is the dynamic, creative entrepreneur who is innovative, takes risks, and has visions for the future.

# Is Entrepreneurship a Family Affair?

Donckels and Frohlich also found that style of entrepreneurship varies depending on whether the business is *family-owned* or *non-family-owned*. For example, family business owners are less often pioneers (26.6% of family-owned businesses as opposed to 44.6% of non-family-owned businesses). The family-owned entrepreneurs are more often all-rounders and organizers. As a result, family-owned businesses are risk aversive and less growth oriented. As well, creativity and innovation are considered less important to entrepreneurs in family-owned businesses.

*Family businesses* are defined by the experts in a variety of ways with a variety of names, including *family-owned businesses, family firms,* and *family businesses.* I will use these terms interchangeably throughout the book. Furthermore, defining the term *family business* can be confusing in that it describes a legal identity, a tax identity, a family-systems identity, and an organizational identity. Since in this book we are looking at the psychological aspects of working with a family member, the following qualifiers should help you define whether or not your business is a family firm. Not all of the qualifiers are required, but the more of them that are representative of your situation, the more solidly you can define yours as a family firm.

▶ A family business is one that is founded by a family member and is expected to be passed on to succeeding generations of the family (even through marriage).

▶ Family members own and control the business, as in a *closely held* corporation.

4

▶ Although there may be many family members working part-time in the business, there is at least one family member who works full-time in a responsible
position, other than the founder or entrepreneur.

▶ A family member is a spouse, child, parent, sibling, or cousin, or other relation
of the founder or officers of the company, whether by birth, adoption, or
marriage.

Anton and Carrie are copreneurs. So are Jonathan and Brooke. If you are
copreneurs you are considered to have or be part of a family firm by the very fact
that a committed couple is a family, even without children. Larry and Dorothy
likewise have a family business because they are copreneurs and have a grown child
working for them who is eventually expected to take over the business. Trish and
Kurt do not have a family business because they have yet to embark on an entrepreneurial venture. However, if they start a business and continue to work together
full-time, theirs will constitute a family business. Now that Carol is a solo entrepreneur and Bob works only occasionally for her, her business is not considered
family-owned because Bob is not a full-time partner and because Carol has no
other family members employed. Sharon and David as dual entrepreneurs do not
have a family firm because they are not involved in the day-to-day management of
each other's enterprises.

You will meet in this book other couples who are part of a family business as
a result of having inherited it from a parent, or because they work with a sibling,
or because they are grooming a child to inherit or buy the business, or because they
are providing employment for a variety of extended kinfolk, or because family
members are on the board of directors.

It may seem complex enough already to assess whether or not you are an entrepreneurial spirit, as well as to assess and categorize your entrepreneurial personality
(i.e., all-rounder, routineer, organizer, or pioneer). Now the distinction of family-
owned or not is added to the mix. However, because the framework for this book
is a holistic one, it is important to be aware of all the significant elements of your
entrepreneurial venture, including the personality characteristics of you and your
partner, the type of business you have chosen and the industry you work in, and
the influence of your family system on the relationship and business. The research
is showing that those firms that have a strong family influence do function much
differently than other entrepreneurial ventures. Therefore, you will want to consider these differences as you design and refine your entrepreneurial partnership.

# What Type of Entrepreneurial Couple Are You?

From this review you can see that there are three parts to determining the type of entrepreneurial couple that best suits you and your spouse. First, you must determine whether you are a solo entrepreneur with a supportive spouse, a dual-entrepreneurial couple, or a copreneurial couple. Second, you must determine if you are an all-rounder, an organizer, a routineer, or a pioneer. Third, you must determine whether your business is a family or non-family enterprise. See Figure I for a summary of these various considerations.

These distinctions are important in guiding you to success as a business and as a couple. Knowing that you are more of a copreneurial type than a dual-entrepreneurial type, for example, should be helpful in setting guidelines for decision making in the business and relationship. However, it is important to remember that just as no two people on the planet share the same fingerprints, no two entrepreneurial couples are exactly alike. Therefore, as you assess the styles of entrepreneurship, keep in mind that you may fit a majority of the qualities of one style, but there may be attributes from another style that suit you as well.

Looking more closely at the chart on page 7, you can see that there are twelve basic types of entrepreneurial couples—the three styles of entrepreneurship multiplied by the four personality types of entrepreneurs. For solo entrepreneurs and dual entrepreneurs, there is another distinction to be made: whether the business is family-owned or non-family-owned. (Copreneurs, by the very fact of being a committed couple who own, manage, and share responsibility for their joint enterprise, are always considered to have or be a family firm.) This brings the total to twenty possible types of entrepreneurial couples!

Although it may seem confusing to determine where you fit among these twenty types, scan the figure and identify the qualities that are most representative of you and your partner. The chart, however, is not all-inclusive. There are many variations on this theme of entrepreneurial couple. See how these variations pan out as you read the following summaries and examples of each type of entrepreneurial couple both in this chapter and throughout the rest of the book.

In addition to the basic types of entrepreneurial couples, I have included in this chapter examples of dual-career couples who are considering entrepreneurship. These examples may be helpful to those of you who are not yet entrepreneurs but think you might be cut out for this lifestyle. As you read about Sheila and Robert, Gail and Nathan, and Kurt and Trish, you will see how the groundwork is laid early in a relationship that may evolve toward the entrepreneurial lifestyle.

# Types of Entrepreneurial Couples

**STYLE OF ENTREPRENEURSHIP**

### Solo Entrepreneur with a Supportive Spouse
- One partner owns and manages the business
- The supportive partner helps out with the business part-time or psychologically
- The supportive partner may be employed outside the business

OR ▶

### Dual Entepreneurs
- Both partners are self-employed
- Each partner owns and manages a separate business

OR ▶

### Copreneurs
- Both partners are self-employed
- Both partners own and manage their joint business

AND
▼

**PERSONALITY**

### All-Rounder
- Versatile, universally responsive entrepreneur
- Highly adaptable to change
- Often a one-person show, handling accounts, sales, design, production, etc.

OR

### Organizer
- Administrator or executive entrepreneur
- Rational, analytical thinker
- Organized yet empathetic boss who delegates responsibility

OR

### Routineer
- Cautious entrepreneur
- Small business goals
- Wants secure income, not risk

OR

### Pioneer
- Dynamic, creative entrepreneur
- Risk taker
- Innovator
- Visionary

AND
▼

**FAMILY FIRM**

### Family Firm
- Firm founded by a family member
- At least one family member works in the business in a responsible position
- It is a closely held company
- Business is expected to be passed on to family member(s)

OR ▶

### Non-Family Firm
- None of the guidelines in the previous box apply

If after reading about the different styles of entrepreneurship, you are still unclear about where you fit in, there are a few questions at the end of the chapter that should help in your self-assessment.

# Solo Entrepreneur with a Supportive Spouse

## Carol and Bob

Carol and Bob thought of themselves as copreneurs in their nursery and garden supply business. However, it was really Carol who was the founder. For years she had been developing skills that she would later use in her business. First, she had already been self-employed before she met Bob. As a hairstylist, she was well aware of the rigors of self-employment, including an uncertain and inconsistent income. After leaving this career, she returned to college to study horticulture and eventually earned a certificate as a master gardener. She took a position in a nursery, thus expanding her knowledge of horticulture. Advancing from a staff position to manager of the nursery gave her the business background for starting or taking over her own nursery and garden center when the opportunity arose.

Carol had the opportunity to buy the business she had worked for when the owners wanted to retire. She approached Bob with the idea, and he was enthusiastic. He was tired of his job and looked forward to the independence of self-employment. Although gardening was his wife's interest, he thought he could be helpful with maintenance and miscellaneous business issues. Within a short time, however, Carol and Bob began to realize that the garden center was really Carol's business and that Bob was merely along for the ride. Carol was constantly disappointed that Bob did not put as much of himself into the business as she did. Meanwhile Bob was frustrated that he did not have an outlet for his talents. Eventually the couple realized that they were not truly copreneurs, and Bob left the business to pursue his own career as an employee in a large company. Now Carol operates as a solo entrepreneur with a supportive spouse.

Now that Bob is no longer Carol's partner in the business, theirs cannot be defined as a family firm, although his support is still invaluable. Bob's regular income from his job has helped ease the couple through difficult times. Also, Bob's employment provides other benefits such as health insurance and a retirement plan, things that Carol as a small business owner cannot yet afford. And when Carol gets swamped with work at the garden center, Bob has the flexibility at his job to leave and help her out.

Carol is a classic all-rounder since she has skills in many areas. She has the technical knowledge of horticulture and the business experience needed for managing the company. Though she desires business expansion, she wants it to proceed at a pace she can manage herself as owner/manager.

## Stan and Rhonda

Stan and Rhonda started their business venture after a great deal of research and planning. For years Stan had worked as a controller, transferring to a new company whenever he felt he needed a new challenge. He was good at his chosen career, so his moves always bettered his situation. Still, he was restless and, at midlife, tired of helping others make their businesses more successful. He wanted to try his hand at running his own successful business.

Rhonda had married Stan after his divorce from Pat, with whom he had three children. Rhonda had no children of her own, nor had she been married before. However, Rhonda was well established in her career when she met Stan at work. As an accountant, Rhonda had always found excellent jobs and was quickly promoted. When Stan began talking about starting his own business, Rhonda agreed that they made an excellent team, not only because of their love for each other, but because of their combination of professional skills. She was excited to get started on the venture.

Clearly, though, this was Stan's venture. True to his organizer style, he researched the marketplace to discover the most advantageous industry and location for his new business. He was not so concerned with the type of business but with whether it would be profitable. And he was willing to move to a new town where there was a need for his business. Unlike the entrepreneur who pursues a business because of a passion for a particular industry or product, Stan is the type of entrepreneur who can take any good idea and make it into a profitable venture.

When Stan discovered the right business for him, a store that specializes in a variety of environmentally friendly products for the home remodeler, the couple began the second phase of their business development. The plan was for Rhonda to keep her job for the steady income and benefits it provided. Stan quit his job and threw himself into the work of getting the business funded and off the ground. Rhonda helped in the evenings and on weekends with whatever odd jobs Stan could not get to. In this manner their business grew from one retail outlet to two within three years. At this stage the couple needed to reassess Rhonda's role. Stan could no longer manage alone and still achieve his dream of building a franchise business. Although Rhonda was ready to quit her job and come to work full-time with him, Stan had other ideas. He was not emotionally ready to share entrepreneurship with Rhonda. Their relationship worked fine when Rhonda was a supportive spouse, but when she left her job, Stan felt that she was usurping his territory. After a tumultuous year of trying to work together as copreneurs, Stan and Rhonda realized that Stan needed to hire professional management and that Rhonda should continue working in corporate America. They just were not cut out for the challenges of running a family business. Rather, what best suited this couple was the model of solo entrepreneur with a supportive spouse.

## Don and Marla

Don is an orthopedic surgeon. His wife, Marla, is a homemaker. Although the couple's three children are nearly all grown (one is in high school and two are in college), Marla has not returned to paid employment, preferring to devote her time to community activities, her church, and charity work.

As so many physicians have done, Don parlayed his professional career into other investments and now owns apartment buildings and part interest in three small medical-related businesses. He has been quite cautious in branching out as an entrepreneur, which is characteristic of the routineer. He has a formula that works for him, which is hard work, long hours, and conservative investing. For her part, Marla has never been interested in entrepreneurial activity. She has been content to allow her husband to earn the family income while she took care of hearth and home. She has always been proud of her husband's accomplishments. Her way of supporting him has not been to work in his office, nor to handle the books at home, but to provide a loving home for him to come to at the end of a long, arduous workday.

Don and Marla have a traditional marriage defined along stereotypic gender lines. Although the couple is quite satisfied with this division of responsibilities, there are disadvantages. Often children in this type of marriage do not get to see much of their father. Second, there is the danger of husband and wife growing apart because they do not share enough of each other's world. Third, there is great pressure in our society to place a dollar value on one's accomplishments. So when a wife does not earn an income, her husband can assume her contributions are valueless.

Don and Marla represent another type of solo entrepreneur with a supportive spouse. Don is a routineer. Marla's support is emotional rather than physical or monetary. Because she takes care of all duties at home, Don is free to develop his enterprises according to his own individual plan. While family values are very important to Don and Marla, the family is essentially kept out of the business. Perhaps as the children mature, one or more of them may come to work for their father, either as a partner in his medical practice or perhaps as the office manager, in which case the business would evolve into a family firm.

## Tom and Karen

Tom and Karen were in their early thirties when they met at work at a major oil company in Texas. Tom fell in love at first sight, but Karen needed time to warm up to this aggressive guy. He was always dropping in on her unexpectedly, leaving her notes and flowers, but she kept refusing his offers to take her out until he wore her down. To get him to leave her alone, she agreed to one date if after that he would stop pestering her. However, in that first date, Karen came to see the same charisma that would catapult Tom into millionaire status as an entrepreneur.

At about the same time that the two of them planned to get married, Tom was also maneuvering to leave the company and venture out on his own. He had backing and a great new idea to revolutionize the oil-refining industry. So instead of going on a honeymoon, the couple set up a new business in the basement of Karen's house. In three years, Tom sold his new company for a few million dollars and took his wife to Europe for a vacation.

Always restless, Tom could not sit still for long and soon began developing new business ventures. Karen has been along for the ride but also grown restless herself. She wants a more calm existence than Tom seems to need. They have a gorgeous new house, a preschooler and a newborn, a vacation condo, new cars, and money to burn. But somehow the instant wealth is overwhelming to Karen, and she is having trouble keeping her life and family stable. Karen loves her husband dearly, even though he is very different from her, but she is having trouble being the supportive spouse of a solo entrepreneur and a pioneering entrepreneur at that.

## Summary

Carol and Bob, Stan and Rhonda, Don and Marla, and Tom and Karen are examples of the style of entrepreneurial couple known as a solo entrepreneur with a supportive spouse. Clearly, Carol, Stan, Don, and Tom are the founders of their respective businesses. As founders they are better suited to the leadership of the business because it is their vision that guides business decisions. Bob, Rhonda, Marla, and Karen are involved in their spouse's business because they are needed at various times when the business is in a growth phase. Their help comes in the form of financial backing, part-time or temporary labor, and emotional support. However, they do not have the entrepreneurial character to take charge. Bob, Rhonda,

Marla, and Karen see themselves as temporary helpers in the business, though they are of course full partners with their spouses in life.

Even though these couples are all representative of the same style, each couple is still unique. For example, each entrepreneur brings his or her own character to the business. Don as a routineer would be uncomfortable with the risks that pioneering Tom takes. While Carol likes to do a little of everything as an all-rounder, Stan as an organizer would become impatient with this kind of inefficiency. Likewise, each supportive spouse has qualities that balance with the qualities of their entrepreneurial spouse to create a specific relationship style. I will discuss these relationship styles further in Chapter Five; for now you can imagine that the marital style that works for Don and Marla is quite different from the style that works for Carol and Bob.

As is often the case with solo entrepreneurs, the slower growth and development required of a family business is not appealing. However, as businesses mature, solo entrepreneurs may begin looking to family members to help them expand or to take over the business as they retire. If a business founded by a solo entrepreneur successfully makes the transition to the next generation of the family, it becomes a family firm.

# Dual Entrepreneurs

## Sharon and David

Sharon and David started out as dual entrepreneurs. Their business interests have never overlapped, but they have each functioned as a supportive spouse. David has always been self-employed. He resembles more than she does the entrepreneurs of the 1940s, those insecure men from impoverished childhoods who desire to make a fortune to prove themselves as adults. He has a fire and a curiosity about how things work that is always pushing him to new conquests. As a result, he owns several small businesses, all of them successful.

When David met Sharon, all she wanted was to get married and raise a family, and for a few years she did just that. Eventually, however, David's energy rubbed off on her and she too wanted to try her hand at an entrepreneurial venture. Her love of houses and of decorating led her into real estate. Little did she know that she had a tremendous talent for sales. She could match the buyer and seller in record time, and she was soon setting new sales records for her company and the county in which she worked. Eventually, Sharon was not satisfied being only a realtor, so she became a broker and started her own realty and property management company.

David is an aggressive pioneer, while Sharon is more of an all-rounder. Because they keep their businesses separate, this difference is not a problem. In the past, they have attempted to collaborate on a venture with disastrous results. David is impatient with his wife's slow style. Because she likes to be part of everything, David feels that Sharon wastes time with unnecessary meetings and spends money on extras like a huge cellular phone bill. Sharon, for her part, is unnerved by the risks her husband takes. She sees him as ruthless when it comes to making money because he can be so single-minded and thoughtless when he has a goal to accomplish.

## Earl and Crystal

Earl and Crystal were both solo entrepreneurs when they met each other fifteen years ago. Both were divorced with children. Crystal's children were of middle school age, and Earl's were in high school. Their relationship was rocky in those first few years: Blending a family with children from previous marriages, coordinating parenting with ex-spouses, and running two businesses kept them busy and tired. In fact, the consequences of those early years are still being sorted out.

To compound the situation, both Earl and Crystal are pioneering entrepreneurs. They are adventurous risk takers in their respective fields. What has held their relationship together all these years is a deep love and sincere respect for each other. However, they are often at cross-purposes because of their dogged determination to succeed at business. When I first met this high-energy couple, they were deeply distressed by the state of affairs in their family. Although Crystal and Earl had amassed great wealth, they were estranged from their grown children.

## Charlene and Ted

Ted and Charlene think of themselves as copreneurs, but their different business interests are moving them in the direction of dual entrepreneurs. Although Charlene founded the business, her husband has equally helped shape its destiny. In midlife, after the children were raised, Charlene took the real estate exam and began selling houses. She enjoyed her new career so much that she quickly became quite successful. Within five years, she had become a broker with her own real estate company and had hired several sales associates.

When Charlene talked with Ted about further business expansion, Ted showed a strong interest in joining her. Although Ted enjoyed his work very much, the economic climate was dealing his company a heavy blow. Nearing retirement, Ted decided that it was time to reshape his destiny and forge a new career to carry him into the next stage of his life. Building upon his wife's real estate successes, Ted decided to get his real estate license as well, but focused his attention on investments and property management instead of residential sales. Although Ted and Charlene consult with each other about their respective divisions of the corporation, each runs their own division with separate staff and are even housed in separate buildings.

Like Sharon, Charlene is an all-rounder. She is skilled in many areas and likes to keep her hand in all of them. Her staff adore her for it. Ted, on the other hand, is more of an organizer. His move to entrepreneurship was made of necessity due to a decline in his industry. He saw an opportunity in the business with his wife and took advantage of her connections to develop his own enterprise. However, Ted's goal was never to develop anything unique such as a pioneer might do, but simply to build upon his wife's proven formula.

### Jay and Celia

Jay and Celia developed a dual-entrepreneurial style gradually over time. It was never anything either of them openly desired but evolved as a result of needing to provide income for the family. This is very typical of routineers. Some experts do not even consider routineers entrepreneurs, preferring to call them small business people, because they do not have the same spirit as other entrepreneurs and because their business ventures seldom grow large. However, entrepreneurial ventures are not measured only by wealth accumulated but also by the ability to take charge of a business and make a go of it.

Jay had become disenchanted with trying to work his way to the top of a major auto maintenance chain. He had achieved moderate success as a shop manager, but it was clear that he would probably go no further unless he was willing to move his family to another state. The family had strong ties to the area, so moving was not desirable. Until this time, Celia had been a homemaker with full-time responsibility for the children. But seeing her husband's disappointment with his career, she was willing to brainstorm options. The couple could not afford a career change for Jay that would decrease his salary. Celia had been out of the workforce since she married at nineteen, so it was unlikely that she could earn enough at a job to support the family during a transition. Self-employment at a business that required a small investment and few skills seemed a likely option for Celia. It did not take long for her to discover the espresso business. A coffee cart, conveniently located in a shopping mall, was the ideal vehicle for a working mom who needed to make money but also work flexible hours. At first, the money only trickled in, but as Celia's reputation grew, so did her business. She is a hard worker and thorough. She developed a following over time because she is reliable, if not creative.

With Celia launched on a successful career, Jay began to get serious about buying his own auto repair shop. Although he did not have the capital, he did have the skill. It took a year, but he found two business partners willing to enter into the venture with him. He knew that he would have to develop a niche market if he were to compete with the larger chains. He felt confident that being a hometown boy could be an advantage in promoting his auto repair and maintenance shop. His partners had some ideas to diversify as well.

## Summary

As with the dual-career style in general, the dual-entrepreneurial couple faces many stresses and challenges. They work long, hard hours and they do it alone. In the case of the solo entrepreneur, the couple has only one business to support. With copreneurial couples, they have each other to work with and one business to promote. But the dual-entrepreneurial couple has twice the workload. It is not easy to face the uncertainties of an entrepreneurial venture, but it can become frightening and discouraging when your partner is facing the same uncertainties with his or her career.

Timing is important. Starting two businesses at the same time is like having twins. Anyone who has had twins knows that raising two babies at once is not simply twice the work but much more. Most dual-entrepreneurial couples who achieve success in their businesses and marriage do not attempt to develop both ventures at the same time. On the other hand, dual entrepreneurship is highly recommended for two pioneering competitive partners who need space to do their own thing.

Usually dual entrepreneurs are not involved in a family business. Although Charlene and Ted were copreneurs at one time, and still function that way superficially, they consider themselves as operating separate businesses. Because dual entrepreneurs are actually two solo entrepreneurs who happen to be in a committed relationship with each other, they can get emotional support and understanding from their spouses but not the actual full-time physical or material support of a business partner. As with solo entrepreneurs, however, their venture may evolve into a family business as children or other family members come to work for them. For example, as David and Sharon's children and their cousins have grown up, they have come to work after school and during the summer for both David and Sharon. Should one of these offspring desire to try working at one of the businesses full-time, he or she may offer either Sharon or David the opportunity to expand the venture into a family firm.

# Copreneurs

## Rick and Chris

Rick and Chris are more typical of copreneurial couples. Rick's family has been in the restaurant business for three generations, so it was a family business even before Rick married Chris. After finishing college, Rick returned home to work with his father and eventually bought out his father's interest. Although Rick's father and grandfather are still advisors to the business, Rick and his wife are now the sole owners.

Rick met Chris after he took over his father's business. She was an employee in one of the restaurants and had her eye on advancing into management. Chris had a stnathang background in business and accounting, and Rick quickly saw the possibilities both personally and professionally. He and Chris married at about the same time that she moved into the management circle. Over the years, Rick and Chris have developed a comfortable style of comanaging their expanding restaurant empire. They work side by side in their warehouse/office and consult with each other on all major business decisions. Although Rick technically owned the business before he married Chris, she is now a full partner in every sense of the word. Whenever the receptionist receives a call for "the boss," she has to inquire, "Which one?"

Rick and Chris are a good balance for each other in terms of their entrepreneurial style. Rick is an all-rounder, much like his father before him. He grew up with the business and loves every facet of it. He is equally at home hiring new employees or repairing a broken kitchen vent. Chris, on the other hand, came into the business with an eye for reshaping it and making it more efficient. She is a very competent organizer. Rick recognized this ability and gave Chris room to revitalize the business. Closely held firms, such as Rick's third-generation restaurant business, are often not open to change. But Rick's love for the business and his wife allowed him to advance into the future and to remain competitive in the marketplace.

## Miguel and Phaedra

Miguel and Phaedra entered entrepreneurship as business partners first. They had worked together for several years at a California spa and resort. Phaedra had functioned in several capacities for the resort, working her way up from maid services to manager of the hotel cleaning staff. Miguel was an excellent cook, and he likewise moved up the corporate ladder. Miguel had always had it in mind to run his own restaurant someday. He was just waiting until he had enough experience as a chef and enough money saved. Phaedra, who came from a working-class family that lived from paycheck to paycheck, had never really considered self-employment. She was more than pleased with the progress she had made working at the resort. She had even been able to save several thousand dollars. Nevertheless, Miguel had an intuition about Phaedra. He recognized her managerial skills and wanted to tap into them to make his own business a success. Since Phaedra was single and had few obligations to tie her down, she was game when Miguel approached her with a business proposition.

Miguel had put a lot of thought into his plan. He had researched likely towns to move to that would be supportive of a new delicatessen. Characteristic of a pioneer, he also planned so far ahead that he envisioned the deli expanding into a full-service restaurant. As the chef, Miguel was the creative force. Phaedra's role was to make Miguel's vision a reality. As a practical, down-to-earth type, Phaedra was the perfect manager for Miguel's dream deli. Miguel liked Phaedra's organizational skills, even though her routineer style was a bit too cautious for his liking. So the pair quit their jobs, pulled out their savings, and moved to northern California. Because they were used to hard work, long hours, and low pay, and because they were used to living as young, single adults on next to nothing, the first five years of their business were a breeze. All they did was work and put their personal life on hold.

Then, as success caught up with them, Miguel and Phaedra had to look at reorganizing their lives. In their early thirties, they wanted more from life than just work. They had so much in common, and already felt like each other's family, that becoming sweethearts seemed a natural move.

Whether it was a natural move or not, Miguel and Phaedra were in for a tumultuous time redefining their relationship. It is no easier to move from being business partners to also being sweethearts than it is to move from being sweethearts to also being business partners. In a couple of years Miguel and Phaedra learned a lot about themselves and their relationship as they integrated their roles as business and life partners into the model of a copreneurial couple working in a family business.

### Nalani and Ross

Nalani and Ross are about ready to retire and to either turn their multiple enterprises over to their children or sell out. They were high school sweethearts and have been married for fifty years. They have raised four children together, put each other through college and graduate school, lived through three major

**17**

wars, and built a thriving financial empire. Over the years, they have functioned as solo entrepreneurs, dual entrepreneurs, and copreneurs. Their success as a couple and as business partners is due to their value system: They have always had respect for each other and considered themselves partners first in all endeavors, whether it was raising a family or getting Ross's legal practice off the ground.

Nalani and Ross are routineers. They have been in no hurry to accumulate wealth. Rather, they have been driven by a desire to build a quality life for themselves and their family, which includes their extended kin network as well. If Nalani and Ross can find work for a relative in their family business empire, they always make room.

As a result of these values, Nalani and Ross have done one thing at a time. First, they helped each other complete college so that they both would have good educations to begin solid careers. Next came the children and law school for Ross. These were hard years but well worth the effort because the couple felt they were building something important. Nalani was the primary child-care provider, but she also ran Ross's office when he first set up his law practice. The children were equally at home in the law office as they were at their grandmother's or at the family home.

As Ross's practice began to thrive, the couple felt they could branch out further and began investing in real estate and securities. They were building a nest egg for their retirement and for the children's college educations. When the children completed college, it was Nalani's turn to return to school. Her dream for many years was to become a psychologist. At the age of sixty, she got her Ph.D. and set up a small part-time practice.

Although considering retirement, Nalani and Ross are still a very active couple. With financial security taken care of, retirement really means considering new ventures without any need to plan for their long-term security. For example, Nalani wants to do more traveling and develop a small import-export business, while Ross wants to turn his interest in golf into promotion of celebrity sporting events. At this stage in their lives, Nalani and Ross are able to unleash their creativity and become pioneering copreneurs.

## Summary

Copreneurial couples tend to be all-rounders or organizers because of their need to balance marital and family needs with business demands. However, this is not necessarily always true, as is seen with Nalani and Ross and Miguel and Phaedra.

There is room for the pioneering spirit within a copreneurial relationship, but the less pioneering partner has more work cut out for him or her. For example, Phaedra is frequently overwhelmed by the fast pace and futuristic notions of her partner, Miguel.

Copreneurs are different from other dual-career couples in that they work within the overlapping domains of love and work in a family firm. Because their relationship and their family are so important to them, they tend to fashion their business around the family needs. This is not as true of solo entrepreneurs or dual entrepreneurs, who may not work with their spouse or employ family members. With the latter types of entrepreneurial couple, the business domain and the family domain do not overlap as much. This results in more clear boundaries between work and home life. As a result, the lure of the business can sometimes outweigh the needs of the family.

I have introduced you to only three of the copreneurial couples you will be meeting in this book. If you do not see yourself in them, there are many more copreneurial couples that I will describe throughout the book. Basically, though, copreneurial couples share these qualities: (1) they both work full-time in a joint venture, (2) they are predominantly all-rounders or organizers, and (3) they usually keep their business small enough to manage it themselves.

# Dual-Career Couples Considering Entrepreneurship

### Sheila and Robert

When I first met Sheila, she was twenty-five and looking for career guidance. With a degree in marketing, she was disappointed that she had been unable to locate a challenging position. She had moved from job to job because she was bored. Now she couldn't even get boring jobs. Employers recognized that this talented and intelligent young woman wouldn't be happy for long in an entry-level corporate position. But with little job experience and only a bachelor's degree, an entry-level job was all she was qualified for.

Finally she took a position as a secretary for a solo entrepreneur. Since this man had no staff other than Sheila, she began to handle many duties outside the range of her job title, eventually operating basically as his business manager. In spite of the greater responsibility and the chance to prove herself, Sheila became disenchanted with this job too. She didn't approve of her employer's shady business practices and general inefficiency. Sheila called my office for a consultation because she was depressed and had given up on herself. She had come to believe that there was something innately wrong with her, that in spite of her education and intelligence, no employer would want her.

Over the next few months as we worked together, Sheila's depression lifted as she realized that perhaps she had been looking in the wrong place for a job. She is a dynamic, creative leader. She had many ideas for developing her last employer's business, and he benefited greatly from these ideas. Eventually, Sheila began to think of herself as an entrepreneurial personality herself. Although her parents were not entrepreneurs and her husband held a steady job as a chemical engineer, Sheila had developed the entrepreneurial spirit on her own.

Sheila again quit her job in search of just the right vehicle for her entrepreneurial venture. Several more months of networking and researching the marketplace brought her into the travel and vacation industry. With very little effort and using the skills she had developed in acquiring her marketing degree, she began to develop a modestly successful business. All of this time, Robert, Sheila's husband of two years, was very emotionally supportive. His income was more than enough for this young, childless couple, as well. He loves his wife dearly and wants the best for her. He has always been amazed at her intelligence and creativity but never encouraged her to pursue an entrepreneurial venture, probably because it was nothing that interested him and did not "run in the family." Yet, when Sheila announced her intentions, he told her to "go for it."

Unlike the typical male entrepreneur of the 1940s, Sheila did not have a difficult childhood with a distant and abusive father. She isn't especially antiauthoritarian either. However, like those earlier entrepreneurs, she is frustrated by the limitations most employers place on her. Gifted intellectually, she resents being held back from the more creative and prestigious jobs because of her youth and inexperience. While most people will accept that they have to pay their dues, Sheila wants to prove herself on her own without anyone's help or hindrance.

There are a number of reasons why Sheila did not recognize her entrepreneurial spirit before she came into my office. First, there had never been any self-employed people in her family, so she didn't have any models to follow. Many entrepreneurs have self-employed parents who have already shown them an alternative to typical employment options. Second, when Sheila entered college she believed—wrongly, it turned out—that she was entering a job-training program that would prepare her for immediate employment in a satisfying position after graduation. Even in college she found her course work tedious. Sheila's interests were always extremely diverse; sticking with just one thing bored her. Nevertheless, she bravely hung in there and completed her degree in marketing. Third, Sheila's husband is content to be an employee. He is a calm, laid-back sort of fellow who has a hard time understanding his wife's need to achieve and conquer. He is amazed that she can tinker with the computer and install new programs without a manual. He can understand why she might be interested in taking an adult-education class at the community college just for fun, but Sheila takes an advanced math class, not photography or ceramics. All of these reasons taken together present an environment wherein Sheila is different. And being different sometimes makes people fear that they are inadequate or defective in some way.

Sheila and Robert are a dual-career couple just venturing into the territory of entrepreneurship. Although Sheila has just started her business and it is too early to tell if she is an all-rounder, organizer, routineer, or pioneer (although she is leaning toward a pioneering style), and it is too early to tell if Robert will join her in the business, at this stage, Sheila and Robert are representative of the solo entrepreneur with a supportive spouse, and do not yet have a family firm since Sheila has no employees or partner.

Interestingly, Sheila is still not satisfied with the business she has founded. She may have underestimated herself again and chosen an industry in which it is too easy for her to succeed. This is characteristic of entrepreneurs. They are not lazy people; they want to make their mark. So they keep pushing themselves to reach their maximum potential. Often they are involved in several ventures before they settle on the one that is just right for them. Whether she sticks with this business or not, Sheila no longer doubts herself. She doesn't worry as much about fitting in. Rather, she has learned to assess her individual talents and interests and design the "job" that fits her best.

### Gail and Nathan

When Nathan met Gail, she was working as a cashier in the bookstore where he frequently browsed. Gail had recently returned to college after four or five years working as a clerk in a department store. Nathan was still adrift after his tour in the Navy, but he admired Gail's determination and secretly wished some of it would rub off on him. The young couple began dating and within a year had fallen in love.

By this time Nathan was also considering returning to college to pursue his dream of becoming an artist and designer and one day owning his own shop. Gail's positive attitude had indeed rubbed off on him. The couple began planning how to accomplish both of their career goals. Since Gail had one more year of college, they reasoned that she should finish. But then she wanted to attend graduate school to pursue an M.B.A., a degree she felt she needed in order to break into the entertainment industry as a producer. For his part, Nathan had veteran's benefits that could defray some of his college costs. In the end they decided that both should go to school at the same time and see where it would lead them.

Although only in their mid-twenties, this couple is mature. They are already independent adults who do not rely on anyone except themselves to make their way in the world. One reason that Gail and Nathan were attracted to each other is this independence. More like the entrepreneurs of the 1940s, Gail and Nathan grew up in impoverished homes with serious neglect and childhood abuse. They had absent or ineffective fathers. Rather than let this slow them down, Gail and Nathan developed resilience. As children, somehow they learned that they were still valuable even if their parents did not think so. This resilience grew into the drive and confidence they demonstrate today, which will lead them to succeed as entrepreneurs.

Because their career goals were so clear and because there were no real constraints on them, Gail and Nathan moved ahead at a quick pace. Before graduating with her bachelor's degree, Gail was already receiving offers to produce concerts for the college and other agencies in town. Nathan had such natural talent as an artist that he was already designing promotional materials not only for Gail's concerts but for other local merchants. These opportunities are the building blocks for their future entrepreneurial ventures.

Gail and Nathan still have much work ahead of them, not only to plan for their respective business ventures, but to thoughtfully plan their personal lives together. At present they cannot really be considered a dual-career couple since they are both still in college. And with full-time self-employment still a dream, there is no evidence of whether their respective empires will be built along the lines of a family business. However, it is clear that they have the personalities and the determination to be entrepreneurs and will probably be dual entrepreneurs with a pioneering flair.

## Kurt and Trish

Kurt, who is thirty-two, was in tears when he first came to me. His wife, Trish, also thirty-two, whom he adored, was threatening him with divorce. It seemed that everything he had worked so hard for over the last ten years was going up in smoke. All that Kurt ever wanted was a happy marriage, children, and a successful career to support his family. Trish did not really want the divorce, but she was tired of Kurt's career always coming first. Whenever he was offered a promotion that required a move, the couple just assumed that of course he would take it and that Trish would accommodate him. Trish's career options were always flexible until now. Working for a large international corporation as she did, Trish could at least make a lateral move within her company each time they had to move geographically. As luck would have it, she actually got a promotion each time, because like Kurt, she was on a fast track to the executive level. This time, however, there was no promotion option and not even a lateral move available. This meant that Trish would have to leave her company and settle for temporary jobs while she followed Kurt's career.

Fortunately, this couple wanted to resolve their problems and agreed that Trish's career development was just as valuable as Kurt's. However, Kurt's company made it clear that if he did not take this promotion, he would no longer be on an executive track. He would be sidelined. Neither Trish nor Kurt wanted to be sidelined, nor did they want that for each other.

Faced with the harsh realities of corporate life, Kurt and Trish considered an alternative—self-employment. Even as they pursued corporate careers, they had always dreamed of returning to their midwestern home and raising their children among the extended kinfolk. Family and roots had always been very important to them. Also true to their midwestern roots, Kurt and Trish always dreamed of independence, owning land, and developing a small business. These dreams were supposed to be in the future, but with the crisis at hand, their dream timetable needed to be pushed up.

Confronting quality-of-life issues brought Kurt and Trish into the world of entrepreneurship. Like Sheila and Robert, they do not have family members who are self-employed to guide them. They are aware, however, that they want to have a life that is not determined by the whims of a corporation. They want to be able to nurture their children and teach them the same solid midwestern values that they themselves grew up with. And they want to be true partners who make decisions by consensus.

Kurt quit his job and Trish kept hers while the couple investigated self-employment options. They have investigated everything from dorothychises to farms. They have even considered a joint venture with a colleague of Trish's. Although they still have not chosen a vehicle for their enterprise, they do know that they will work it together this time, instead of having separate careers. They also know that the business cannot rob them of their family time and couple time. Finally, they know that the business will be well planned and organized because they will use the tools learned from their years in corporate life. All of this leads Kurt and Trish into the world of copreneurial couples with an organizer style, built upon the foundation of a family firm.

## Summary

These three couples represent only a few ways that dual-career couples enter entrepreneurship. However, there are commonalities among these couples. First, there is a need to be self-employed, whether this need is innate, as with Sheila, or born of childhood insecurities, as with Gail and Nathan, or the function of being eased out of corporate life, as with Kurt and Trish. Second, there is emotional support from the spouse for the venture. Although these young couples do not know yet what entrepreneurship has in store for them, they are at least supportive of each other's career endeavor. Third, they are young enough to roll with the punches. If one venture fails, they know that there are still others to try and still time to try them.

# What's Your Entrepreneurial Couple Style?

If you are still puzzling about what type of entrepreneurial couple you and your partner are, you might ask yourselves the following questions:

▶ *Who started the business or who wants to start the business?* It's a simple question, but very revealing. In general, copreneurs each contribute a strong desire to develop the business. Solo entrepreneurs are on their own when it comes to envisioning business success, but they do require a supportive spouse. Dual entrepreneurs are both driven to develop their respective businesses but can' t imagine working together. These generalizations are simple, and many couples will represent a blend of styles, but this is a place to start in sizing up your situation.

▶ *Are you an all-rounder, organizer, routineer, or pioneer?* Next, each member of the couple needs to determine how strong his or her entrepreneurial traits are. Most readers have a sense by now if they have what it takes to be an entrepreneur. Now take a look at your personality and determine what type of entrepreneurial spirit you are. Are you cautious and looking only for income to support your family, such as a routineer might do? Are you adventurous and content only with creating a new product or service that will revolutionize your industry, such as a pioneering entrepreneur? Are you well liked by employees because you pitch in and work side by side with them, as an all-rounder does? Or are you an executive type who runs an efficient company by hiring responsibly and delegating duties and authority, as an organizer does?

▶ *Can you be a supportive spouse when the need arises? Can you be a supportive spouse over a long period of time?* The supportive spouse is often the unsung hero. As one wife put

**24**

it, "My mission is to showcase my husband's talents." This wife works side by side with her husband in their chain of hardware stores. Her daughter and two sons-in-law are also in the business. While she is vital to the welfare of the business in many ways, her husband operates as the solitary leader. He consults her and the children, but as the founder he has veto power over all decisions.

Not everyone is cut out to be a supportive spouse—at least, not all of the time. Most of us think of marriage as a partnership with give-and-take, where sometimes we are the leader and sometimes our spouse is the leader. In an entrepreneurial venture, however, this may not always be the case. Entrepreneurs are driven people who can become so consumed with their businesses that they ignore their families. A supportive spouse is often the one who must hold the entire marriage and family together, so that the entrepreneurial spouse can devote his or her undivided attention to the business venture's success.

▶ *Do you employ or share partnership with family members? Do family members hold responsible positions within the company?* If the answer to these questions is yes, you already have a family firm. If you would like your business to develop along these lines but do not yet hire family members, you may want to consider how hiring family will change the focus of your enterprise. Obviously, copreneurships are family firms by the very nature of spouses working full-time together in the business and sharing in the ownership, management, and responsibility for it. Solo entrepreneurs and dual entrepreneurs may or may not be involved in family firms. Sisters may work together in a joint venture while their husbands work elsewhere. A solo entrepreneur may have a supportive spouse and hire his son as marketing manager. Siblings may inherit their parents' business. There are infinite combinations. The significant defining factors are (1) that there are at least two family members who work in the business in responsible full-time positions, (2) that the business is intended to be closely held, and (3) that there is an intention to pass the business on to descendants of the founder(s).

By now you should have a good idea of your entrepreneurial couple style. In Self-Assessment Exercise 1, identify the qualities that are most applicable to you, your partner, and your situation, so that you can make the most of the rest of the book. As you read about the styles of other couples, you will be in a better position to utilize your new learnings if you can define your own style. This is not to say that your style may not change over time. By the end of the book, you may even wish to renegotiate the terms of your partnership and business. And it remains to be seen whether it is the type of business or the personalities involved that contributes most strongly to the style an entrepreneurial couple eventually chooses.

# What's Your Entrepreneurial Couple Style?

Check the boxes that apply to yourself and your partner. Choose just one box to check in each category, even if you have a blend of styles, because you probably have one dominant style. It is easier to plan around your dominant style. You may also wish to note your less dominant style and determine what that message is all about.

**Type of entrepreneurial couple**

❏ Solo entrepreneur
with a supportive spouse      ❏ Dual entrepreneurs      ❏ Copreneurs

| **Your personality** | **Your partner's personality** |
| --- | --- |
| ❏ All-Rounder | ❏ All-Rounder |
| ❏ Organizer | ❏ Organizer |
| ❏ Routineer | ❏ Routineer |
| ❏ Pioneer | ❏ Pioneer |

| **Family firm** | **Names of family members (if a family firm)** |
| --- | --- |
| ❏ Yes | 1. _____ |
| ❏ No | 2. _____ |
|  | 3. _____ |

## Evaluating Your Responses

Take note of the style you have chosen. Does your partner see it differently? Has the style changed over time? Why? Is your personality compatible with that of your partner? What are the strengths and weaknesses of your respective styles and as a team? Now that you are consciously aware of your style you are in a position to make the most of it for the success of your business and your partnership.

## Summarizing Remark

In one sentence or a brief paragraph, summarize (1) What is your style?, and (2) Who are the significant players?

# Intregrating Lives:
# Laying the Groundwork
# to Balance Love and Work

We humans have always known that we are part of something greater than our-selves, and recently there is astounding evidence of our interconnection as a species and even as individuals with our environment. Trees cut down in the Amazon rain forest can destroy the habitat for an entire species, possibly leading to its extinc-tion. Out of all the babies in the nursery, a mother knows the distinctive cry of her own infant. Each year we get flu shots to protect us from the discomfort of this winter illness, yet we catch the flu anyway because the virus has mutated.

As fuzzy as these connections may seem, they have been explained by a system of psychology known as *dialectical psychology*, first defined by Klaus Riegel in 1976. The term *dialectical* is related to the word *dialogue*. According to Riegel it is the dia-logue between people and between systems that produces conflict, chaos, change, and ultimately growth. In essence, dialectical theory explains the dynamic interac-tions or dialogues between subsystems such as husband and wife, parent and child, career and personality, home life and work life. Each element or system in our life is affected by every other element and cannot be fully understood independent of those others. Further, with each evolution in a subsystem, the entire ecology changes forever. As Riegel puts it, each of us must be seen as a "changing individ-ual in a changing world."

Out of the dialectical system of psychology, come three theories that will help explain entrepreneurial couples. These three theories are *social exchange theory, life cycle theory,* and *systems theory.* Taken to the practical level, this chapter will show the dynamic, recursive interaction among the individual, the couple, the family, the career or business, and many other systems that touch the lives of the couple. The goal is to learn to appreciate these interactions, to anticipate them, and to modify and grow from them.

Take your time reading this chapter. Read a section and perhaps reread it. Then allow yourself to digest the content. I will be presenting examples once again of entrepreneurial couples, but this time I am examining how the various facets, stages, and systems of their lives interact. This is a dense chapter, of necessity, in order to give you a thorough understanding of the complexity of the entrepreneurial lifestyle. But if you muscle your way through this chapter, you will not only gain an understanding of *why* we are the way we are as human beings, but you will also gain an understanding of *how* we do the things we do. After the brief theoretical outline, the remainder of the book will make more sense because you will have a context or framework within which to relate the practical application. Ultimately, you should have a better grasp of how to work with change to balance the competing demands of marriage, family, and business.

## The Myth of Separate Domains

The two worlds of love and work have long been acknowledged as fundamental to an adult's psychosocial development. To some, these two worlds are inextricably intertwined. In fact, early writers believed that the institutions of society (among which are marriage and family) and work are highly interdependent. In 1939 Karl Marx argued that the advent of capitalism resulted in alienating conditions, which in turn produced alienating behavior among workers, both on and off the job. In 1947 Durkheim suggested that basic work-related divisions of labor produced interdependence among institutions, thus integrating members of society. However, Durkheim also warned that extensive division of labor carried the risk of fragmenting institutions and individuals, thus leading to a breakdown of social norms and a loss of roots and connection between people. Looking at the non-work domain, Weber in 1947 suggested that the *Protestant work ethic* has led to work behaviors that made a capitalistic economic system possible.

Yet in spite of this common sense, there is a myth in modern American society that the domains of family life and work life have always been discrete and separate subsystems, and thus can influence each other only in a linear, cause-and-effect manner. So, for example, industrial analysts, when studying an organization, will take into consideration the composition of the workforce, including family status and sex. And family theorists will consider social class, as measured by income level and occupational status, when studying families. However, rarely has either group considered the operation of the world studied by the other, or looked at the dynamic interconnections between the two worlds.

Taken to a practical level, entrepreneurial couples represent the dynamic inter-action or the dialogue of love and work. It is obvious with copreneurs that there is little distinction between home life and work life and that these two worlds pro-foundly affect each other. However, even with solo entrepreneurs, personal and professional worlds overlap and interact. Don and Marla provide an example of very well defined boundaries between home and work, and between husband and wife. Don is a routineer solo entrepreneur, and Marla is his supportive spouse. Don as a surgeon and the breadwinner works at the hospital and clinic all day, while Marla manages the home front. Don provides the material goods for the family. Yet without Marla to manage the household and children, Don would not be free to develop his entrepreneurial interests. As Elizabeth Kanter pointed out in her 1977 essay on families in business, there is the simple interdependency that family is defined by its consumption of the resources provided by work.

Carol, Sharon, and Nalani show us the impact of the interactions of family and work lives. Carol's desire to share her work with her husband, Bob, moved her in the direction of copreneurship at first. After Sharon mastered the challenges of being a mom, she wanted to find out what her husband, David, knew about entre-preneurship. Nalani worked for years with her husband, Ross, to develop their empire and keep the family healthy. These women represent the impact that work-ing women have had on our society.

Rapoport and Rapoport were the first researchers to publish studies on dual-career couples. In 1965 they suggested that in spite of civilization and all of its industrialization and specialization, family values have flourished. Further, they suggested that increasing numbers of women entering the workforce, and increas-ing numbers of these women entering the professions, have contributed to a return of stronger family values. Not only the feminine influence in the workplace but also the higher commitment to career seen among women professionals and execu-tives are factors that bring family values into the workplace. In other words, the commitment that women professionals make to their careers is quite similar to the commitment women make to their families. Because Carol, Sharon, and Nalani have laid the groundwork, Sheila and Gail, who are just considering entrepreneur-ship, have models to follow in developing their own entrepreneurial ventures.

Recognizing that the worlds of love and work are not separate but are in dynamic interaction with each other is extremely important. Over the years I have met many adults who grew up with entrepreneurial parents. Many of these grown children have vowed *never* to be self-employed themselves, because they felt deprived of a childhood by the demands of their parents' business. On the other hand, I have also seen situations where the entrepreneurial parents insisted that their child go to college and graduate school to become a physician or lawyer, in order to avoid the hard work of entrepreneurship, when all the child wanted was to follow in the footsteps of his or her parents.

In both such situations, the solution is the same: At this very moment, acknowledge that whatever decisions you make regarding your work will have an impact on your spouse and family. And acknowledge that whatever modeling you provide for your children today will influence them for a lifetime. Just what the nature of that impact or influence will be depends on the factors of any particular system, such as personalities, timing, history, and so on.

For example, copreneurs Mike and Karla were not at all prepared for the overnight success of their family business, which specialized in the production of bicycle accessories. A young couple still in their twenties, they found themselves moving to larger warehouse space every six months. They couldn't hire employees fast enough for the factory. Mike, a pioneer, worked long hours at the office, while Karla, a routineer, tried to juggle her responsibilities as the personnel manager and the mother of two small children. Still, the money rolled in, and Mike and Karla had plenty of desires to fulfill. They bought new cars and a boat, and built a new million-dollar house.

Now with a nanny to watch the children, Karla could devote even more time to the business. But the more time she spent at work, the more time Mike poured in, too. One evening at about eleven o'clock another fight erupted between the couple. Their fighting had become a regular, almost nightly event, especially after the children were fed and put to bed. With no dinner themselves, Karla and Mike would try to relax and talk. They each had a drink to facilitate the relaxation, but instead it facilitated a fight. When Mike, in a fit of rage, threw a bottle of liquor at the mirrored family room wall, shattering glass all over the room, Karla realized that their lives were out of control.

Mike and Karla had a lot of work to do to restore sanity to their lives. Through their pain, they learned that work and home life are *not* separate, but more to the point, they learned that you cannot make one more important than the other. The lure of money and the ever-increasing demands of the business blinded them to the needs of their children, their relationship with each other, and their own individual health.

## Do the Costs Outweigh the Gain?

The question I always ask myself in cases like Mike and Karla's is, What does it take to finally tip the scales so that an individual will take action to change his or her situation? Why did that particular fight wake Karla up to the problems in front of her and move her to action?

The answer lies in a dialectical theory known as *social exchange theory*. Kelley and Thibaut defined the basic propositions of social exchange theory in 1978: (1) costs being equal, individuals choose alternatives from which they expect the greatest rewards; (2) rewards being equal, individuals choose alternatives from which they anticipate the fewest costs; (3) immediate outcomes being equal, individuals choose alternatives that promise better long-term outcomes; (4) long-term outcomes being equal, individuals choose alternatives providing better immediate outcomes.

These basic propositions of social exchange theory can be used to describe the essential features of exchanges in married couples. They can also be used to predict relationship satisfaction, relationship progress, and relationship decay. For all married couples, the exchange context includes trading with one's partner for love, sex, status, and life support. However, entrepreneurial couples—especially copreneurs because they work together—must also trade with their spouses for self-esteem, mastery, and achievement. Whereas other couples have a wider variety of resources from which to negotiate exchanges (i.e., colleagues, employers, fellow workers, as well as their spouse), copreneurs must negotiate their love and work needs only from one another. Therefore, the potential for stress is heightened.

In other words, Mike and Karla got locked into getting all of their rewards from work and spending money (i.e., immediate rewards). And they had only themselves to compare to, so no way of knowing that they were heading into a major problem. As long as those rewards (i.e., work and money) outweighed the costs, the couple did not notice the other rewards or benefits of marriage and family life that were slipping away. When that liquor bottle hit the mirrored wall, the immediate costs to Karla's quality of life no longer outweighed the long-term gain of business wealth. At this point she was willing to risk shame, divorce, and loss of wealth in order to restore health to herself and her family.

At first, Mike wouldn't listen to Karla about their problems. Since the business was successful, he reasoned that their home problems would iron themselves out in time. This is when Karla sought professional help. Talking it over with me, she learned that Mike was probably in denial about his alcohol abuse. Before he could recognize the other problems in their life together, Mike had to face his alcoholism first. Although Karla loved Mike very much, her love for him did not outweigh the costs of continuing the self-destructive pattern of their lives. Karla arranged to take Mike to an alcohol treatment program for an evaluation. Because Karla had been firm in her commitment both to Mike and to no longer living in the unbalanced way that had evolved, Mike got the support he needed to face his fears and accept his abusive drinking. After an interview with the intake worker, Mike agreed to enter the hospital for treatment.

Rick (an all-rounder) and Chris (an organizer) have worked hard to maintain balance between love and work. As copreneurs of a third-generation restaurant business, they face the same dilemmas as Mike and Karla. They derive most of their rewards for both home and work from their spouse. However, Rick and Chris have a well-developed system for maintaining a healthy balance in their lives. First, they never talk about work at home. And although they have desks side by side in their office/warehouse, they discuss only business at the office. They reserve relationship issues and family talk for after work hours, and preferably discuss these things at home. Keeping discussions separate like this actually insures that the important issues get discussed. Second, Rick and Chris are equal business partners, thus giving each other full credit and respect for their separate contributions. Although each of them handles different aspects of the business, they each feel that the business would not be successful without the full participation of the other. Third, they insist on developing individual private lives. Chris is working on a college degree by taking night classes. Rick has a group of childhood buddies that he regularly skis with, and he is president of a local charity board. With these outside contacts, the couple have other people in their lives with whom they can trade for feelings of self-esteem, mastery, and achievement.

## The Human Life Cycle

When my daughter was twelve months old, she took her first step. When she was two and a half, she was toilet trained. When she was six, she started losing her baby teeth. These are developmental milestones familiar to all parents. Most of us view the human life cycle as unfolding in predictable stages much as children grow from babies to toddlers to preschoolers to school-age children, and so on. This-com-monsense view is supported by theorists such as Freud, Piaget, and Erikson, each of whom developed a *stage theory* regarding a certain aspect of human development.

These theories share a common set of assumptions about how change and growth occur over time. Stage theory implies that all people pass through a hierarchy of qualitatively different stages of organization. These stages are sequential and invariant in their order. Development is seen as discontinuous, and there are irreversible consequences for not evolving through a stage properly. Each stage has its unique developmental tasks. Adult development is seen as an extension of child development, which in turn is tied to biology.

While stage theories are useful in that they map out the predictable stages of growth of the generic human being, they are not particularly helpful for those who do not fit the rule. Most children start walking around twelve months. Most six-years-olds are entering first grade and learning to read for the first time. However, similar generalizations cannot be made about most thirty-year-olds or fifty-five-year-olds. As we enter adulthood, the life cycle takes on a decidedly different look: There is no clear biological timetable unfolding, and major life events occur in an unpredictable order. Therefore, adult development is best understood from the dialectical perspective that consists of *continuing changes along several developing progressions at the same time.*

To be sure, there are still stages that adults go through, though they are not as directly tied to biology. These stages have a pattern in that they follow a sequence and the sequence is hierarchical. However, the stages are not linear and can be both continuous and discontinuous, depending on the evolution of the individual in interaction with other developing progressions. The *midlife crisis,* for example, is a stage that most adults experience between the ages of thirty-eight and forty-three. It is a time for reevaluating one's direction in life. Often people feel the need to catch up on parts of their life they have not yet experienced. There is a tug to know oneself at a deeper level. This transition at midlife can transform an individual, block the person from moving ahead altogether, or merely reinforce his or her basic values. How such a crisis affects each individual depends on myriad factors in the individual's life and the developmental levels of the other people the person lives with.

A dialectical interpretation of human development focuses on concrete human beings and their interactions with biological and cultural-sociological shifts and changes. Human development is codetermined by these inner and outer changes. Riegel describes four dimensions of human development: (1) inner-biological, (2) individual-psychological, (3) cultural-sociological, and (4) outer-physical. Whenever two sequences are not synchronized, a crisis takes place, which produces development. If the development is a major reorganization, then the individual has moved into a new stage or period of development. Therefore, development is seen as consisting of continuous changes along several dimensions at the same time.

Out of all of this comes a startling discovery. Because human transformation is a product of conflicting developmental progressions, human beings are motivated by discordance and upheaval rather than stability, equilibrium, and rest. Of all the entrepreneurial couples described so far, you can certainly see that for many of them their decision to start a business was motivated by a conflict or disagreement of some kind with reality. For Sheila (a dual-career wife considering entrepreneurship), the conflict was her inability to be hired as an employee. For Sharon (an all-rounder and dual entrepreneur), it was a curiosity about all the fun her entrepreneurial husband was having. For Frank (a solo entrepreneur and all-rounder), entrepreneurship was a way to reduce his fears about how to make money when he had a chronic illness.

This dialectical perspective on individual human development can be applied to couple development, family development, business/career development, and organizational development as well. For example, copreneurs Phaedra and Miguel are at a crossroads in their relationship. If you recall, Miguel and Phaedra are not married, nor had they even dated before they joined forces for the sole purpose of starting a business. Until now they have been business partners only and turned a blind eye to the potential for romance between them. They were so busy getting their business going that they did not have time for a personal life anyway. However, as life events proceeded, the business provided them with time and money to interact with each other in new ways. The conflict for the couple is whether they want the changes that are being offered. Can they continue as business partners only? Can the business partnership handle the involvement of outsiders if either Miguel or Phaedra should marry someone else? If they do accept the budding romance between them as an opportunity to be both love partners and business partners, are they capable of constructing a life in which two such important domains overlap?

The situation of Miguel and Phaedra demonstrates the interaction of at least three major developing systems: individual, business, and couple. Phaedra and Miguel are developing human beings, both of whom are just turning thirty. They have both accomplished many of the tasks of becoming an adult, such as finishing school and establishing a career. But they are feeling the pressure to find a mate too. This is another task of early adulthood. At the same time that Phaedra and Miguel are maturing, their business is also growing. It is out of the infant and toddler stage, when it required all of their attention, and is now more independent. The business is starting to give back to its founders in the form of freeing up their time and providing income. As a couple, the developmental imperatives are to move past a casual relationship and make a *choice* to either be good friends and business partners or to be lovers. The couple relationship needs to evolve too or stagnate. Even if they remain as business partners only, the relationship has to mature to prepare for the growth in Phaedra, Miguel, and the business.

# The Family Life Cycle

If it is difficult to apply linear stage theory to adult development, it is even more so with the complex system of a family. A family is composed of several developing individuals in interaction with each other and a developing family system. If one attempts to use stage theory alone, the family system degenerates into a group of developing individuals or subsystems, whereas dialectical psychology views the family as a whole.

In 1981 Hoffman asserted that development is not a continuous process but one characterized by transformation, *second-order changes,* and the sudden appearance of more functionally organized patterns that simply did not exist before. *First-order changes,* as they relate to development, are those increments of adaptation and mastery made by individuals within the system. *Second-order change* is the family's adaptation to the individual's changes, resulting in the transformation of status and meaning within the system and the evolution of new elements of structure.

According to Hoffman, it is not possible to predict the timing or nature of developmental shifts, though we may predict the issues and the direction of organization that will take place. At the level of evolution of the family system, the elements of change may be too complex to analyze, and the change that takes place is discontinuous. Therefore, the family life cycle is not a linear progression. It does not begin with one stage, nor does it end with the deaths of a particular generation. Rather, the family life cycle is a developmental progression in dynamic interaction with the developmental progressions of the members who form the family. The family life cycle is like a spiral that gets wider with each developing stage of each generation. In fact, it is like a spiral of spirals because of the interconnected developing progressions of each member of the family. There are predictable stages that each family member will probably pass through, and as they do, they reframe the dimensions of the family.

The situation of copreneurs Larry and Dorothy is an example of the dialogue of life cycles of the individual, couple, family, and even business. Dorothy and Larry have been looking forward to retirement even though it is still five to ten years away. Although they never discussed directly with their son the fact that they wanted him to take over the family business (three orchard farms located in the fertile Willamette Valley of Oregon), they had assumed he would want to. And indeed the son had worked for his parents since he was a child. However, as the couple approached retirement age, it was becoming painfully apparent to them that their son was not mature enough to handle the business. What this couple failed to consider as they grew their business was that their son would have to mature also.

At the age of thirty-two he had never worked for anyone other than his father, had never had to face any major financial crises, had never had to prove himself in the adult world. Now instead of being groomed for leadership he often acted rebellious and defiant, much like a young teenager searching for an identity instead of the thirty-two-year-old married father of two that he was.

In this case, the developmental needs of the family business interfered with the developmental needs of the son, such that he was unprepared for adult life, or at least for taking over the family firm. Larry and Dorothy, like so many entrepreneurial couples, failed to plan ahead for retirement. That is, they failed to develop a succession plan for the business. Instead, they poured all of their energy into *developing* the business. At the same time that Larry and Dorothy were growing a business, they were also raising two children. However, the developmental needs of the children always came second to the business; the only way Larry's son could have any time with his father was to hang out with him at work. Larry and Dorothy were bewildered that their son was so immature. But is it really surprising that he failed to grow up, when he had so little parental guidance? Although the business thrived as a result of the hard work and determination of Larry and Dorothy, the children and family system stagnated miserably.

In another family, the birth of a child was the crisis that would lead to transformation. Kevin and Lana were at the point of divorce when they came into my office. Both are well educated and have successful careers. Kevin, who is a pioneering solo entrepreneur, owns several small businesses, including a family enterprise with two siblings. Lana works in commission sales and supports her husband's entrepreneurial endeavors. Their young son, age two, is the light of their lives. However, they were totally unprepared to manage the change in their relationship that would come from bringing a new baby into the world of Kevin's large Italian family. All of a sudden Lana was overwhelmed with the "interference" she was getting. For his part, Kevin thought his wife ungrateful because his family was only trying to help.

In the case of Kevin and Lana, the various interacting developing progressions needed readjusting as life changed. But instead of expanding the space to incorporate some status changes, Kevin and Lana and perhaps the extended kinfolk kept on following the old rules, rules that were destined to fail since they were designed for a family without a baby. On the *individual* level, Kevin and Lana were adjusting from their old identities as a carefree childless couple to their new identities as parents. The extended kinfolk were making similar adjustments in their identities. On the *couple level*, Kevin and Lana were no longer free to focus just on themselves; they had new challenges and responsibilities. Finding time for each other now required more planning. On the *family level*, Lana learned that she had married not just Kevin but his extended family and their beliefs and values as well. Kevin's commitment to his extended kin is as great as his commitment to his wife and young son. For Kevin and his family, a baby *belongs* to all of them.

Kevin and Lana and their extended family can use this conflict and crisis to grow and change. Dialectical psychology would predict that something must change as a result of this crisis. However, the change may or may not move the individuals, couple, and family along the path of healthy development. If Kevin and Lana divorce, for example, their baby may never develop Kevin's values. If Lana holds fast to her desire for noninterference, she and Kevin will have unresolved tension between them. If Kevin ignores the fact that his wife was raised differently than he, Lana may come to feel like an outsider in the family. If, on the other hand, all parties recognize the crisis for what it is, an opportunity to reorganize the family, they may assist each other in progressing developmentally. For example, instead of being so *helpful*, Kevin's mother may recognize that a young mother wants to feel *competent* with her baby. Grandmother can then give the new mother plenty of room to develop and demonstrate her skill.

# The Business Life Cycle

The development of an organization is not as easily defined as that of an individual or even a family since there are many different types of organizations and cultures in which they grow. However, several theories have been postulated, and they suggest that there are predictable stages of development for an organization just as there are for people. One model, described by Quinn and Cameron in 1983, proposes four stages of development: (1) the entrepreneurial stage of early innovation, niche formation, and creativity; (2) a collectivity stage, where there is high cohesion and commitment; (3) a formalization and control stage, where there is stability and institutionalization; and (4) a structural elaboration and adaptation stage, where the business expands and decentralizes.

I would like to again venture away from pure stage theory and add a dialectical perspective. The entrepreneurial couple will have a business that reflects their own individual, couple, and family development as well. Another author, McWhinney, suggests that a family business moves through three stages: (1) the entrepreneurial stage, which is creative, an act of generativity; (2) the ownership stage, when there is a need for stability and security to nurture the family; and (3) the stewardship stage, when the business is well established, the children are grown, and the founder has developed beyond the need to use the business for his or her expression of personal power. Stewardship offers the family business the opportunity to give something back to the community, such as establishing a charitable foundation or employee stock option plans.

We have already seen how Ross and Nalani adapted their various entrepreneurial ventures to fit the needs of their individual developing progressions and those of their family. Now in their late sixties, Ross and Nalani are at the stage of *stewardship*. They have accomplished their dreams. Their children are raised and raising their grandchildren. They have financial security. They have already incorporated two of their children into the family business and have groomed them to take over the empire when they retire. In fact, their son is already really running the show while Ross and Nalani take extended vacations. All that is left is for the couple to discover how to make their next contribution.

Evan and Amy, on the other hand, are just getting started. They are entering the *entrepreneurial* stage. Evan is an organizing solo entrepreneur, and Amy is his supportive spouse. Amy just returned half-time to her job as an elementary school teacher, and takes care of their two toddlers as well. Evan and Amy are struggling emotionally right now because Amy would like more stability than Evan's fledgling business allows. He always manages to pay the bills, but Amy has yet to see the advantages of the entrepreneurial life. All she sees is that Evan works long hours and falls asleep on the couch soon after he gets home. She wants to be supportive, but she is lonely and envious of the time Evan devotes to the business. Evan, to his credit, recognizes his wife's plight and has agreed to take the children one weekday afternoon and one weekend day so that Amy can have some private time. But of course this does not solve the couple's lack of intimacy. At this stage of creativity and generativity, a young entrepreneurial couple needs a lot of stamina and confidence that there will be a payoff in the future.

Anton and Carrie are square in the middle of the *ownership* stage of family business development. They have eight years under their belts of both dual entrepreneurship and copreneurship. The children are in elementary and middle school. Because the business is up and running on its own, Anton and Carrie have time for their three girls and are willing to take an occasional afternoon off to cheer the girls' soccer team.

Anton and Carrie are no strangers to entrepreneurship; in fact, both come from entrepreneurial families. Carrie, an all-rounder, started an electrical contracting business with her first husband. Shortly thereafter, Anton, who is an organizer, and a brother started a heating and air-conditioning business. When Carrie's husband was killed in a motorcycle accident, she continued to run the business as a solo entrepreneur. Although her first husband had been the trained electrician, Carrie had learned a lot from him about bidding and managing the paper flow in the office. So she hired capable electricians and carried on.

Carrie's children were still babies and toddlers when she married Anton. They each had a business to bring into the marriage, but the young businesses required a lot of work too. Anton and Carrie felt they were a good match because they understood each other's entrepreneurial spirit and had complementary businesses. The marriage and the business merger were nearly simultaneous. Because Carrie had been a supportive spouse, a copreneur, and a solo entrepreneur before marrying Anton, she had more insight than he about the challenges facing an entrepreneurial couple. In those first seven years of marriage, dual entrepreneurship, and copreneurship, the couple faced many conflicts and confrontations as they adjusted to "his," "hers," and "ours." Now, however, they are settling into a routine of managing a thriving family business and raising three precocious daughters.

## People Are Relationships

So far you have been introduced to two major theories that help us better understand the nature of the entrepreneurial couple, social exchange theory and life cycle theory. From social exchange theory we have learned that couples evaluate their relationships according to the costs and benefits derived and make decisions accordingly. From life cycle theory, we have learned that each element in a system (i.e., an individual, couple, family, or business) has a developing progression and that these progressions interact to produce conflict, chaos, reorganization, and growth. The third major theory is *systems theory*, which is the theory that links the others into a meaningful whole.

General systems theory was first introduced by Ludwig von Bertalanffy in 1951 in the journal *Human Biology*. In proposing general systems theory, von Bertalanffy suggested that the theory is a *pure natural science*. In other words, general systems theory can be applied to all levels of science, including physical, biological, and sociological. When Riegel later developed dialectical psychology, he was incorporating the concept of systems theory. Dialectical psychology focuses on the interactive changes in common activities and everyday situations. The emphasis is on the social bases of human beings, the interaction between two persons in the form of dialogues. In summing up how systems theory applies to psychology, Riegel says, "Meaning is not something that can be added to the system after it has been analyzed; rather it is the first and most fundamental topic."

One characteristic of general systems theory is that important changes often arise on the boundaries of formerly unconnected domains, frequently creating a synthesis or a new entity. Let's take this idea to the level of entrepreneurial couples who are each individuals with developing progressions. In a couple relationship with a developing progression, in families with developing progressions, engaged in a business with a developing progression, systems theory makes meaning of the interacting boundaries between these developing progressions or subsystems. For example, Lana's developing identity as a mother interacted with Kevin's developing identity as a child in his Italian family in such a way that they both had to redefine their identities in order to stay in the relationship. Kevin had to consider that there might be more than one way to raise a baby, and that he and his wife could decide for themselves whether or not to follow his family's ideas. For her part, Lana had to expand her notion of what it meant to be a wife, in order to remain married to a man so committed to his extended family.

If all of this is beginning to sound circular, it is. The ultimate definition of a system is this circularity. Lynn Hoffman (1981) uses this example in summing up the cybernetic theory of Gregory Bateson: "A brain does not *think*. What *thinks* is a brain inside a man who is part of larger systems residing in balance within their environment. One cannot draw a line indicating one part that thinks and another that is profiting by the thinking." Systems are constantly unfolding and reforming. Instead of seeking stability and homeostasis, people and other systems seek order through fluctuation. That is, as long as the fluctuations in any system are within a normal range, there is little noticeable change. But as the movement gets amplified beyond the stable range, it moves the organism to a new level or direction.

Discontinuous change explains the leaps in evolution that cannot be explained from a static model of error-activated feedback (such as stage theory). Individuals and families sometimes make sudden rapid shifts. They do not make changes in a smooth, unbroken line, but in discontinuous leaps. Complex organizations like families and businesses especially are examples of systems that change through leaps. Not only is the family or business as a whole going through stages of development, but each individual is also developing. As each subsystem changes, they affect the other subsystems, with the result that families are forming and reforming continually. When Kevin and Lana had a baby, the family could no longer define itself as it had without this child. Many parents tell me that they really cannot remember what life was like before they had children. This can be explained by the fact that once the system changes to fit the new circumstances, we move on to the next level of evolution without looking back.

To circle back again, and to risk trying your patience, I want to explain one more element in systems theory because of its relevance to entrepreneurial couples especially. If you view yourself as part of many interacting systems (individual, couple, family, and business at least), then distinctions made about, between, and within each system are based on your point of view at any one moment. The conceptual distinctions we humans make as we experience the world are known as *relational thought*. For example, we understand our *uniqueness* (separation) in *relation* (connection) to others. And we understand our *bond* (connection) to others in terms of our *differences* (separation). In 1992 Flemmons and Cole, two theorists in the field of family systems theory, summed it up nicely: "People *are* relationships."

When couples attempt entrepreneurship, whether they are a solo entrepreneur with a supportive spouse, dual entrepreneurs, or copreneurs, the meaning they make of their relationships (all of their relationships) is the most significant factor in determining the success of the business or marriage. There is not one style that works for all entrepreneurial couples. There is not one right way to do anything. Those couples who *are* successful in balancing the competing demands of marriage, family, and business tend to view *limitations* as *opportunities to learn.* They tend to view *failure* as only *feedback.* And they have confidence in their ability as a team to discover the *meaning* in the most complex and convoluted of situations. Taken together, these three basic beliefs turn crises into opportunities for growth.

# Examine the Dialectic
# of Your Entrepreneurial Relationship

With all of the couples introduced so far, it is clear that the couple bond is a significant element in the success of entrepreneurial businesses. Not only do entrepreneurial couples negotiate with each other for love, sex, status, and life support, but they also each define who they are in relation to their spouse/business partner. These negotiations and identities are further refined by the life tasks each spouse is facing in their unique developmental progressions. As the couple and individual evolve through negotiation and attacking the tasks of development, they are being affected by other developing progressions, such as those of their children and the business. Altogether they create a system of systems that is so unique that there are no two entrepreneurial couples with the same pattern.

Congratulate yourself now for having read this chapter, perhaps the most complex of the entire book. There are no simple explanations here, but a sophisticated interplay of theories that is much more than a simple sum of the parts.

**41**

Entrepreneurial couple life is just as complex as these theories, and it is an injustice to try to explain this lifestyle in two-dimensional terms. If you really want to make sense of your life and use that knowledge to enhance your business and your marriage, then you absolutely have to understand this holistic perspective.

Now take this complex holistic perspective and look at your own situation specifically. You might ask yourself the questions listed in Self-Assessment Exercise 2 to assess the current developmental progressions operating in your life and in your spouse's, your family's, and/or your business(es). Using this dialectical framework to pinpoint the stages operating in your life will make the other lessons in this book more meaningful. In this way you should acquire a clearer idea of the tasks required for this stage of your entrepreneurial life, and a hint of how the next stage may take shape.

## SELF-ASSESSMENT EXERCISE 2

### Examining the Dialectic of Your Relationship

Answer the following questions as honestly as you can. There are no right or wrong answers. The purpose of this exercise is to help you gain insight into yourself and your relationship.

1. **With regard to how you live your life (including your business, your marriage, and your family), what is the single most important thing you learned from your father? From your mother?**

2. **Why did you choose your spouse or partner? Why did he or she choose you? What do you do to keep the relationship alive?**

3. **Where do you want to be in five years? In ten?**

4. **Are you and your partner on the same wavelength when it comes to goals in life? For the business? For the children?**

5. **Are your personal goals, couple goals, and business goals in line with your goals for the children? For the extended family?**

6. **What one accomplishment would you like to be known for after you are dead?**

## SELF-ASSESSMENT EXERCISE 2 (CONT'D)

# Evaluating Your Responses

The answers to these questions will help you determine the stages of development for yourself, your partner, your family, and your business. Perhaps you will notice discrepancies in developmental goals among the systems. Some of your current values may be different from those you held when you started the business or the relationship. Take note of these discrepancies and differences and discuss them with your partner. You will take the insights from this exercise into the next few chapters of the book as you revamp your entrepreneurial couple lifestyle to fit your unique personalities and developmental requirements.

# Summarizing Remark

Summarize in one sentence or a brief paragraph what you learned in this chapter and in this exercise. Then use that summary as a lens through which to view each succeeding chapter and exercise.

# Communicating with Your Partner: The Nuts and Bolts of How to Talk and Win

To paraphrase my sister, who is a realtor, the three keys to a successful marriage are "communication, communication, and communication." Without good communication skills and quality time dedicated to communicating, relationships soon flounder and fail, especially among couples with the stress of two careers, or a joint enterprise, and a full family life. Moreover, the potential for a breakdown in communication grows as the number of interacting systems increases. As well, these systems are evolving so that what once worked may not work anymore. Couples need to learn that their relationship is not a *thing*, but a *process*.

In this chapter I will discuss how to communicate effectively—meaning that the receiver actually gets the message and in such a way that the couple can move toward win-win solutions to their conflicts. This chapter is not intended to be all-inclusive. There is so much to cover and so much to learn when it comes to improving communication skills, that I would recommend starting here and continuing your study by reading more in-depth materials as well as taking seminars and workshops with your partner. In this chapter I will provide an overview of some *truths* or *presuppositions* that facilitate healthy communication. I will start with some *basic truths* and move on to more *advanced truths* fairly quickly. Take your time and absorb the knowledge. Then make some notes about what you would like to pursue further.

## The Three Basic Truths of Healthy Communication

**1.** People are relationships.

**2.** Listening is at the heart of quality communication.

**3.** Conflict and confrontation are natural and healthy components of any relationship.

## People Are Relationships

The first basic truth is that *people are relationships*. I discussed this basic truth in Chapter Two when reviewing systems theory as applied to family/firm development. Psychiatrist Milton Erickson once said that mental illness is the breakdown of communication between people. What he was referring to is that we know ourselves (our similarities and differences) only in relationship to others. When we are not able to communicate with others, we become confused, can begin to doubt ourselves, or build impenetrable defenses against change. (A good summary of Erickson's work and philosophy was published by Stephen and Carol Lankton in 1983.)

Trish and Kurt (a dual-career couple considering entrepreneurship) were at an impasse when they came to my office. Their two careers had matured along with their marital relationship and developing family. They had moved three times in their ten years of marriage to accommodate promotions for Kurt. But the moves had been good for Trish, too, since her company had her on a fast track. She had been able to move into a new job at a higher level with each of Kurt's promotion/transfers.

Then the day came when this ideal synchronicity shattered. Kurt was offered another promotion, this time to company headquarters, but there was no comparable position for Trish within her own company. Kurt accepted the new job without discussing it with Trish, assuming that she would follow him as she had always done before. When Trish refused to move to Kurt's new location, the couple's communication system ground to a halt. They had no mechanism for dealing with this kind of conflict.

As it turned out, Trish was tired of moving and wanted to raise their daughters in one community. She was even grateful that her company had no options for her in the new town. But she was equally committed to Kurt and wanted to stay married. So for six months Kurt commuted 2,000 miles every other weekend to be home with his family and to consult with me on how to redesign their marriage to accommodate a new career agenda.

Ultimately, this couple had to look outside their current reality to discover what marriage, family, and career advancement meant to them. In order to move toward a win-win solution, they had to develop a plan that provided for (1) a rewarding career with potential for growth for each partner, (2) a parenting plan that provided stability for their daughters, and (3) a way for the couple to stay connected and loving. The solution that surprised them was to leave both their jobs and start their own business, something they dreamed of doing only when they were older and had achieved their maximum level of success in corporate life.

After a lot of hard work, Trish and Kurt recognized that they were part of several interacting systems that contributed to their identities. As these interacting systems began to interact in a conflictual way (i.e., an employer's need conflicting with a spouse's need), their identities started to undergo strain. Because they did not know how to communicate about the changes going on within each of them, the marital system broke down. At first, they proceeded to blindly solve problems the way they always had, which only made matters worse. Eventually, they realized that the solution was an expanded level of consciousness or identity for each of them. For example, Kurt could still be a husband, a father, and a breadwinner in a family firm if not in a corporate setting. And Trish could still be a mother, a breadwinner, and a supportive spouse even if she did not follow her husband's corporate ambitions.

## Listen, Listen, Listen

The second basic truth is that *listening is at the heart of quality communication*. If you learn nothing else about communicating more effectively, at least learn this truth. Without listening skills, you do not have rapport with your partner and you cannot even stay on the same subject. The next time you are having a discussion with your spouse, instead of planning your next comment, just listen and try to understand where your partner is coming from. Just understand; do not comment; do not judge. Listening goes a long way toward developing trust between marital partners.

Don and Marla were at an impasse and considering divorce when I first met them. In spite of the great deal they had in common, in spite of the love for each other that they had once felt, in spite of having three beautiful children and a successful business, Don and Marla were incredibly poor communicators when it came to listening to each other. Their lives were so full that they had little time to listen; they seldom made time even to fill each other in on the day's events.

Don and Marla are representative of the solo entrepreneur with a supportive spouse. If you recall, Don, a routineer, is a surgeon, and Marla a homemaker. Because they spent so little time together, they rarely communicated about anything. Each took care of their own responsibilities, Don as breadwinner, Marla as homemaker. Unfortunately, when conflicts arose, the couple had no mechanism for solving them and retreated to their own separate worlds.

The first step in bringing Don and Marla back together was to teach them how to listen and to make time for listening. When they scheduled fifteen minutes each day for uninterrupted listening to each other, they began to rekindle their friendship. Marla learned that Don felt very left out of the family because she handled all of their children's affairs without consulting him. Don learned that Marla felt devalued because he handled all of their financial affairs without consulting her. Furthermore, by just listening, this couple began to recognize that they had more in common than they had realized. Even though they handled separate responsibilities, the values underlying their work were the same. One of these underlying values is that "Whatever I do is for the benefit of the family as a whole."

Arthur and Leslie found themselves in a similar situation; that is, a nonlistening mode. Arthur and Leslie are copreneurs, although the business was founded by Arthur and he is the lead decision maker. Leslie, who is a routineer, enjoys her role as a specialist in the business and is supportive of Arthur's decisions. She views him as a visionary who has made the business successful through his ability to stay one step ahead of the competition. Arthur, on the other hand, has pressured his wife to be more like himself. He wants her to assume more of the responsibilities of leadership. He would like to branch out and create additional business entities, leaving his wife in charge of those he is moving away from.

Arthur's failing has been to ignore the personality of his wife, and as a result she feels unappreciated. She interprets Arthur's pressure to be a leader to mean that her contributions to the business are not valuable. Leslie enjoys the team effort of copreneuring; she is not interested in being a leader. Unfortunately, Leslie and Arthur never had any time to discuss this issue because both were overwhelmed by work, which was taking them further and further away from each other. Only in my office did they finally make the time to talk.

It took Arthur a while to learn to listen. Pioneering entrepreneurs like Arthur are good at talking and directing but sometimes quite poor at listening. Arthur felt that he was encouraging his wife when he suggested these changes for her. He had the best intentions for both of them when he began developing new business ventures without first discussing them with her. What he learned through listening is that his way of doing things might not always be the best way.

Leslie had a fully developed personality and was a successful adult when she married Arthur. She is not a pioneer and does not care to be. While Leslie wants to be included in the discussions regarding all of Arthur's plans, she recognizes that he is in a better position to make the final decision. But she feels disrespected when Arthur fails to discuss things with her and pressures her to change because he feels it would be in her best interest. Arthur and Leslie have had to learn to listen to respect the differences between them.

Listening took on a different strain for Mike and Karla. If you recall, Karla and Mike are a young copreneurial couple whose nearly overnight success overwhelmed them and erupted into alcohol abuse. In this case, what saved them, the marriage, and the business was that Karla confronted Mike about his substance abuse problem. Fortunately, Mike listened and sought treatment.

Another facet of being a good listener is appreciating that there may be a grain of truth in what the other person is saying about you. If you dismiss the communication, you may miss important information about yourself or the other person. With drug and alcohol abuse, the addict is seldom a good listener. They do not want to hear that their life is out of control. They do not want to accept that they have a problem that is damaging not only their lives, but the lives of those around them. They are quick to point a finger at others, noting their numerous flaws. But in this case, Mike was willing to listen, because Karla approached him with both love and firmness. He trusted her and knew that she meant business. No matter how ashamed of himself he was for his past actions, he could no longer continue shaming himself.

There are three basic steps to being a good listener and therefore a good communicator, as these couples learned:

1. You must stay on the subject.
2. You must listen to be sure you are staying on the subject.
3. You must be flexible enough to adapt your behavior if you are not staying on the subject.

If two people are not focusing on the same subject, they cannot have a successful communication. Arthur and Leslie were not on the same subject for years. Arthur thought he was doing what was best for both of them, while Leslie thought Arthur was trying to control her. Before you begin going into any depth on a topic, be sure that you and your partner are discussing the same problem and that there is agreement about just what the problem is. Once there is agreement on the topic, the problem practically works itself out. By listening to Leslie's experience and perception of Arthur, Arthur and Leslie could define the real problem, which was how to move ahead together as a team at a pace that was challenging enough for Arthur. After redefining the problem, Arthur and Leslie had to develop new skills (i.e., be adaptable) to assist them in accomplishing this goal. Instead of fighting about control issues, they could brainstorm ways that Leslie could still be a supportive spouse while Arthur created new business entities.

Similarly, Mike and Karla were faced with redefining their problem in a way they could both agree on. When they realized that they were not fighting about work pressures but about Mike's alcoholism, they adapted their behavior to deal with the problem successfully.

For Marla and Don, new listening skills were not needed as much as simply making time to listen. Once this priority was in place, the problems began to melt away. By listening to each other and getting agreement on their problems, Don and Marla adapted their behavior to create an environment more conducive to listening and problem solving.

## Conflict and Confrontation

There is a common misperception that conflict and confrontation are bad. One of the major reasons entrepreneurial couples have problems is their failure to confront issues head-on. They may fight openly or quietly seethe, but they have a terrible time confronting the real conflict respectfully and honestly. It's as if confrontation and conflict are impolite. However, the third basic truth of healthy communication is that *conflict and confrontation are natural and healthy components of any relationship.* Remember that systems (individuals, couples, families, and businesses) evolve and advance through conflict and confrontation. We are shaken out of our comfort zones by conflicting systems such as marital needs and children's needs. And we need to be shaken out of our comfort zones in order to advance to the next level of development.

You are neither bad nor wrong for causing a conflict or identifying one. Conflict is an opportunity to open up communication on a difficult subject. Karla was sick and tired of the conflict that ensued every evening after the children were in bed and she and Mike began drinking. Yet one more conflict was needed—only with a different confrontation. This time instead of arguing in circles to no purpose, Karla pushed open the door to take a hard look at her husband's substance

### The Four Mistakes Entrepreneurial Couples Make in Handling Confrontation

**1.** Allowing the business to run your life.

**2.** Being too willing to compromise.

**3.** Pushing to win at all costs or acquiescing to the persuader.

**4.** Pursuing consistency to a foolish degree.

abuse. As painful as it was for both of them, they both feel this confrontation saved their lives.

## Do Not Let the Business Run Your Life

Confronting another person responsibly requires training and patience. The entrepreneurial couples I have worked with have typically made one of four mistakes in handling confrontation—usually as a result of seeking to avoid conflict and healthy confrontation. *The first mistake is allowing the business to run their lives.* In my research I found that both dual-career couples who do not work together and copreneurial couples (who do work together full-time) are more willing to take time from home for work activities than they are willing to take time from work for home activities.

My 1994 research on entrepreneurial couples shows an alarming trend. In general these couples are *rarely* willing to leave for work late; very occasionally they may be late no more than fifteen minutes. However, they are willing to be late getting home *one to four times a week* by more than an hour each time. As well, these couples are willing to leave home for work more than thirty minutes early *one to two times per week.* On the other hand, they are willing to leave work early for home only *once a month.* As long as these tendencies prevail, entrepreneurial couples are giving themselves very little quality time to confront the inevitable conflicts that will arise in their personal relationships.

Work is a major source of satisfaction for adults. There are immediate payoffs with work, unlike with relationships. Likewise, there are problems and crises at work that draw our attention away from relationship responsibilities. Most career-minded Americans admit that their families are more important to them than their work, but that they derive more personal satisfaction from work. This obviously poses a serious dilemma, and one that most entrepreneurial couples ignore, because everyone else does.

Conflicts are not avoided by remaining unconscious of the problem. Marital and family relationships need to be individualized to fit the unique needs of the couple, the family, the individual, and the business. In this day and age of pagers, cell phones, and fax machines, it is easy to be drawn along with the crowd and make work your number one priority, especially if you are self-employed. But cultural norms need to be confronted if they no longer serve a purpose or are causing major damage.

I know of one brave sales representative who turned in her pager. She decided that nothing was so much of an emergency that it could not wait until she had time to answer her voice mail. After all, she is not an emergency room physician; her work is not a matter of life and death. To her surprise and pleasure she found that many of her customers were solving their own problems, problems that in the past caused unnecessary phone calls to the sales representative. She also was pleased to have found a way to "turn off" the workday so that she could have some private time and time for her husband. And to top it off, the lack of a pager did not affect sales volume. In fact, her customers admired her more for having the guts to put her home life first.

## Do Not Make Compromises

*The second mistake couples make in order to avoid conflict and confrontation is that they are too willing to compromise.* Most couples are shocked when I advise them to avoid compromises at all costs. After all, isn't compromise a requirement of partnership, both personal and business? The reality is that decisions that are arrived at through compromise usually lack creativity and seldom last. Sure, a compromise now and then may be necessary for the sake of expediency, but if a decision is important, a compromise may cause anger and resistance. Because compromises are usually a result of both people giving up something in order to get an agreement, the decision is a watered-down version of two stronger opinions. While it may be satisfactory to accept compromise decisions for things like choosing a restaurant for dinner, where neither of you gets your first choice but both must accept a third alternative, accepting a third, less-threatening alternative for your business may sabotage your competitive edge.

Compromise is the easy way out when you are trying to avoid conflict and confrontation. It appears that the compromise will smooth ruffled feathers and that both partners can go away happy. What really happens, however, is that each partner leaves feeling as though they have been had. One person may resent having to compromise and will be looking for ammunition to prove that the decision was a bad one. Another person may feel he or she has done the honorable thing by not pushing his or her opinion on the other, only to feel unappreciated later when the compromise plan is dropped. If you stop and think about it, how long have your compromise decisions really lasted?

Copreneurs Susan and Steven had made compromises all of their married life and well into their joint venture when they entered the garment manufacturing business. For over twenty years, Steven, who is an organizer, had modeled his life after what would please Susan, moving and taking promotions to increase the family's income and quality of life. Likewise, Susan, who is an all-rounder, had accommodated several moves for their family of five in order to support Steven's career and eventually put them in a position to buy the business that Steven said he always wanted. But it all came to a crashing halt when Susan confronted Steven about the affair he was having. With Susan's discovery of his infidelity, Steven announced that he wanted a divorce and shortly thereafter moved out of the house.

Susan and Steven are described by friends as "the ideal couple." They never fought, had three great kids, and went camping and waterskiing every summer with their extended family. Even the kids helped out in the family business. What friends did not see, however, was that two decades of compromises had left this couple feeling as if they really had not been living their own lives. They were sick and tired of always doing the "right" thing, which meant never disagreeing with each other. Their fear of disagreement or conflict was so strong that they failed to develop as individuals and to learn to deal with differences between them. Eventually, the differences became overwhelming, and the only way to find themselves again was to separate. Compromise is hardly a virtue when the only thing really compromised is your sense of self.

### Acquiescence and Agreement Are Not the Same Thing

The art of persuasion is an interesting phenomenon. The skills of persuasion are neither good nor bad in and of themselves. However, the skills can be used in an honest and fair way or can be misused in an unethical and harmful way. It all depends on the consciousness and intentions of the user and receiver in the communication.

In seeking to avoid conflict and confrontation, a persuasive person may push his or her partner to acquiesce to a certain point of view, but this does not mean that the partner agrees. It may mean only that the partner actually does not want to fight and so appears to agree, when he or she has only given in. Therefore, the *third mistake couples make in order to avoid conflict and confrontation is either to push to win at all costs or to acquiesce to the persuader.* In either case, whether you are the persuader or the acquiescent partner, the conflict has not been resolved and, what's worse, may have been driven underground.

Larry and Dorothy have used this method to avoid conflict and confrontation in their marriage and their partnership in a farming business. Larry is a driven businessman typical of the post–World War II entrepreneurs. He has succeeded from nothing by sheer willpower and guts. He has not let anything or anyone get in his way, not even his wife and children.

**53**

Years ago, when the children were little, Larry and Dorothy separated when Dorothy discovered that Larry was having yet another affair. The affair went on for years and even resulted in the birth of a child, but after Larry decided to return home to Dorothy and their children, Dorothy acquiesced. She says that at the time she wanted a divorce but could not bring herself to confront Larry. Instead she hoped that he had changed, even though he continued to bully his wife and children. Now that Larry's children are grown, one of them wants nothing to do with him or the business. The other child is willing to work in the family business, but, as I discussed earlier, at the age of thirty-two is ill prepared to take over management because of Larry's controlling nature.

Unfortunately, Larry has confused acquiescence with agreement. Dorothy confuses acquiescence with cooperation. She timidly agrees to every idea that Larry suggests. Behind his back, though, she tells a different story to her children and employees. Rather than confront Larry directly, Dorothy tries to cajole him into considering her opinion. She also operates as the voice of the grown children and other employees who are too intimidated to approach Larry.

Larry has built a successful business, if you measure success in financial terms. However, there is no trust in his marriage, and he has destroyed the self-esteem of his children. His own insecurities are undoubtedly to blame. Making money and needing to win have been Larry's ways of proving that he is a worthy person. Unfortunately, this style has only deepened his insecurities because no one really wants to spend quality time with him. They are too afraid to open up to a man who will use against them any information he uncovers.

If you are a natural at persuasion, be careful to consider the context in which you are using this skill, and consider carefully what your motive or intention is. If you are clarifying difficult points or reframing your partner's position to help move both of you toward a mutually agreeable solution, then by all means use persuasion. But if your motives are not well intended for both parties, do not take advantage of a partner who is quick to acquiesce because she or he is afraid of confrontation. There are other, more rewarding ways to win at love and business than by undermining another person's self-respect.

### Foolish Consistency Is Not a Virtue

*The fourth mistake can be summed up by Ralph Waldo Emerson, who wrote over a century ago, "A foolish consistency is the hobgoblin of little minds."* In other words, it is acceptable to say "I don't care"; or "I've changed my mind"; or "I didn't know that." Holding fast to your position just because that is the way you have always been contributes to a stalemate in the relationship. On the other hand, being flexible and adapting your position in light of new information contributes to a dynamic relationship. Successful business owners are aware that change is the norm. Why then would you cling to outmoded notions in your marriage?

Family business members are notorious for their adherence to outmoded gender roles. For example, male entrepreneurs more typically consider their sons for succession to leadership than they do their daughters. Daughters are only considered if the male entrepreneurs have no other choice. Mass Mutual, a national insurance company, recently conducted a survey and discovered that sons in family firms earn on average $115,000, whereas their sisters earn on average only $19,000. Among American entrepreneurial couples, wives have less decision-making power than their husbands except in situations where the business is more female oriented, such as a nail salon. Even then the wives only have equal decision-making power compared to the husbands.

The risks to your business of carrying on these "traditions" is obvious: Your business suffers because you are not using the best people for the job. Instead you are making decisions on the basis of outmoded cultural values. Consider also what happens when you carry these attitudes into your personal life. One husband-and-wife law team finally crumbled because the husband insisted that his wife carry the full responsibility for the children and homemaking even though she had a professional career as well. While she struggled valiantly to carry on her traditional role at home and her modern professional role at the office, she finally failed. The marriage did not fail, but she abandoned her career to raise her three boys. Oddly enough, it was her husband's idea that she go to law school in the first place. He had no idea at the time that his turn-of-the-century notion of "a woman's place" was not flexible enough to allow for full-time employment outside the home for his wife.

Clinging to outmoded cultural norms is not the only way that entrepreneurial couples get hung up. Evan and Amy struggled with adjusting to entrepreneurial life because of a foolish consistency embedded in Amy's family history. As a teacher, Amy was used to working from eight-thirty until four and could not understand why her husband, Evan, an organizing solo entrepreneur, could not be home sooner. Also, when she had weeklong school breaks in December and April as well as three months off in the summer, she was frustrated that Evan would not leave his business to take an out-of-town vacation with her and the children.

Amy had developed these values watching her parents fail at entrepreneurship. After losing a great deal of money, her parents found modest careers and stuck to them in order to provide a middle-class life for their children. Amy admits that there was no joy in the work her parents did, but they stood by their commitments. Even though Amy had encouraged her husband to pursue his dream of being a professional writer, she really did not want to change anything about her life to accommodate this dream. Somehow Evan was supposed to get a fledgling business off the ground, bring home a steady paycheck, and be available for extended vacations whenever Amy was. I still remember the day in my office when Amy looked at Evan with tears in her eyes and anger in her voice and said, "You are asking me to change!" as if his request was treachery. It may take Amy a while to realize that a foolish consistency can cost her a marriage.

Change is necessary and even the norm among dynamic beings like people, but we resist it nonetheless. This resistance to new information, changed norms, or even entrepreneurship is normal but costly. Take a look at what you are currently angry about. Perhaps your anger is fueled by the fact that a change is due and requires some work on your part, and you just do not want to be bothered. Perhaps you are secretly aware that your spouse is correct about something that needs changing, but you are afraid that you are not up to the change. Stop viewing change as a problem to be avoided, and try to see it as an opportunity to develop new and exciting skills that will help you, your marriage and family, and your business advance to a more productive and creative level of development. It is not consistency per se that is bad; standing by your beliefs makes you reliable. It is *foolish consistency* that creates conflict and potential rifts in your marriage and business partnership.

## Some Advanced Truths

So far I have discussed the *basic truths* of healthy communication. In this section I will discuss more *advanced truths*. These truths will assist you in refining your communication skills so that you can (1) more clearly define the problem or topic of discussion, (2) more accurately listen and understand your partner, and (3) develop even more flexibility and expediency in accomplishing your communication goals.

These advanced truths are quite sophisticated in some ways and yet also right to the point. As you read this material, try to absorb the meaning rather than focus on learning a new skill. Communicating effectively is more of an attitude than having specific skills, and the skills seem to emerge when your heart is in the right place. Keeping these advanced truths in mind will tend to put your heart in the right place so you begin to trust that you and your partner really are on the same side.

## The Four Advanced Truths of Healthy Communication

**1.** The explanation used to describe a person or situation is not the person.

**2.** People do not operate out of sensory experience, but rather out of their interpretation or map of reality.

**3.** All people mean well or have good intentions.

**4.** The person with the most flexibility has control of the system.

# The Explanation Is Not the Person

Actually, these basic and advanced truths of healthy communication are not truths at all, but *useful presuppositions*. Truths imply some absolute facts, when the reality is that there are always exceptions. Useful presuppositions are rules or guidelines to follow that usually prove to be true. The first advanced truth is that *the explanation used to describe a person or situation is not the person*. We all build hypotheses about our partner in order to understand and respond to his or her behavior. For example, Arthur believed that Leslie was just like himself. He believed that she just needed a little encouragement to move into a role of leadership in the company. If he had only realized that he was responding to Leslie according to *his hypothesis or explanation of her*, he may have been able to notice new information that would have allowed him to correct his hypothesis.

Likewise, Kurt assumed that Trish always followed his career moves because she put his career before her own. In reality, Kurt's promotions opened career doors for Trish also. Furthermore, moving to a new town every few years when she was younger and childless was not a problem for Trish. But with twin daughters to care for, a desire to put down roots in a community, and a career of her own that she loved, Trish demonstrated another side of herself that did not fit Kurt's *explanation* of her. As Kurt expanded his consciousness, both he and Trish learned that there is more to their partner than one simple explanation.

# Internal Maps Versus Sensory Experience

Because we build hypotheses, we tend to operate in the world as if our internal maps (i.e., hypotheses or explanations of reality) are the truth. We forget that we developed these internal maps after gathering information with our senses. Once the map is built, we sometimes ignore future sensory experience in favor of our presuppositions. Therefore, the second advanced truth is that *people do not operate out of sensory experience but rather out of their interpretation or map of reality.*

The second advanced truth is closely aligned with the first advanced truth. Knowing that you and others are operating in the world according to your own interpretation of reality releases you to notice what facts or real experience contributed to a specific behavior. For example, if you believe that conflict and confrontation are bad or at best impolite, you will operate in the world *as if* they are bad. You may shrink from confrontation or become defensive or abusive to avoid the situation. If, on the other hand, you believe that conflict and confrontation are signs that there is a problem or that they are an opportunity to move toward a mutually satisfying solution, you will approach conflict and confrontation with more ease and comfort.

Karla and Mike had been ignoring their own senses with regard to Mike's alcohol abuse. They ignored how much he drank. They ignored the irrationality of their fights. They ignored the effects of alcohol abuse on their children, employees, and friends. Chemical dependency is easy to ignore in our society, which supports social drinking. Also, because of the incredible success of their business, and moving into a brand-new million-dollar house, Mike and Karla felt as if they were on top of the world without a care. It seemed a contradiction that they would have a serious problem at the height of their financial and material success. Yet Karla was shaken to notice her sensory experience when Mike shattered the liquor bottle against the living room wall. Then all of the other sensory clues she'd been ignoring fell into place, too. It was time to adjust her map of reality to include the possibility that the husband she loved was an addict. Similarly, Mike's map of reality changed shortly after Karla confronted him.

# People Have Good Intentions

The third advanced truth is often hard for people to swallow. It is that *all people mean well or have good intentions.* Remember that these are *useful presuppositions*, not absolute truths. It is *useful* to believe that at any given moment your partner is doing the best he or she knows how, or making the best choice for him- or herself. If you at least credit your partner for making sense to him- or herself and for operating out of his or her map of reality to accomplish desirable goals, then chances are the person will feel respected. From respect comes trust, followed by the desire to communicate with you to reach a mutually satisfying agreement.

Before Trish was willing to work anything out with Kurt, she had to understand that his taking the promotion without talking with her first was something he did with the best of intentions. He was making a wise choice given the current terms of their relationship and the current requirements of his career. He was not trying to be disrespectful or to sabotage Trish's career ambitions. Only when Trish began to understand her husband's reality was she able to advise him of some missing information, information that he needed to expand his concept of reality. Likewise, Kurt needed to stretch his awareness to understand why Trish thwarted his career move when he was trying to better the family's situation. When he recognized that she was not being stubborn or irrational but simply trying to protect her own career and the well-being of their children, Kurt was able to suggest alternative solutions that would meet both of their models of reality.

It may be difficult to see the good intentions behind Larry's behavior toward Dorothy and his children, since he appears to be so ruthless. However, if you consider that Larry came from a childhood of battering and abandonment, requiring that he virtually raise himself, you may better understand his defensiveness. As a teenager he was out on his own learning to make a living. With no parents to support or love him, he learned how to get admiration through work. The childhood abuse taught him to be wary, an approach that actually has been quite useful to him in keeping ahead of business competition. On the other hand, these behaviors and attitudes also made Larry wary of his own family. Never trusting his son to handle the job right has left Larry in the position of having an immature son who may never be ready to take over the family business.

## Flexibility Builds Strength

The fourth advanced truth is that *the person with the most flexibility has control of the system*. For example, when your child is screaming in the supermarket, it is likely that you will not be able to get her under control by asking politely. Just at that moment when you are begging her to cooperate, she throws herself on the floor or knocks several items off the shelf as you push the cart by. If you become embarrassed by her display, you may be tempted to punish or bribe her. You may also try to leave the store as soon as possible, making apologies as you fly out the door. If you take any of these alternatives, you have allowed yourself to operate according to your child's terms. Therefore, she has become the person with the most flexibility, and she is in control. In other words, whatever she does will get a response from you.

On the other hand, if you ignore the tantrum, continue your shopping, or leave the store immediately without giving your daughter what she is demanding, you are the controlling element in the system. You have remained in your reality and have exercised more flexible options than she has.

Similarly, when you have a conflict with your partner about business or home life, you are at an advantage by remaining flexible. By embracing the basic and advanced truths of healthy communication discussed previously, you have many more options available to you to listen to and understand your partner, and to move both of you toward a mutually agreeable solution. If you make time to communicate, if you refuse to stray off the topic, if you listen to the well-intended meaning behind your partner's words and actions, if you remain open to the prospect that you could be wrong, if you recognize that your partner is so unique that she or he will surprise you daily, if you are willing to change even though you have always done things a certain way in the past, if you refuse to compromise but press for a win-win solution, then you will be better able to guide yourself and your spouse away from conflict and toward appropriate solutions.

Remaining flexible is tricky when tempers flare, but it is not useful to persist in behavior that will get you nowhere. Accordingly, when you are doing something that is not working and you are not sure what else to do, you might as well do *anything* else. Even if the new behavior is not terribly effective, breaking the pattern of conflict is. The following example demonstrates how one copreneurial couple utilized several of the advanced truths, including flexibility, to resolve a problem.

One day Rick got home considerably later than usual, with a serious headache. His wife, Chris, had prepared a nice dinner for the two of them, and the baby was already asleep. If you recall, Rick and Chris own restaurants, the first of which was inherited from Rick's dad. When Chris asked Rick how his day had been, he snarled, "It was awful and I have a terrible headache" as he passed through the kitchen on his way to the living room.

Wanting to help, Chris asked if she could ease the headache by giving Rick a neck rub. He responded rather unkindly by saying, "No! Nothing can get rid of this headache!" He then fell onto the couch, moaning in pain.

Now Chris was at a loss for words. Not only was her husband in physical pain, but he was angry at her for trying to help him. Without thinking this one through more thoroughly than that, Chris blurted out, "Well, I guess I can't help with *that* headache. You really earned it!"

Not two seconds later, Rick was up off the couch and walking into the kitchen, where Chris was still standing. He looked amazed as he tried to make sense of her last comment. It certainly was not what he expected. Anything else from Chris would have been more reason to fight. Then, before he could think of what to say, he realized that his headache was gone.

Although Chris will tell you that she did not consciously attempt to use the truths of healthy communication, she had inadvertently used many of them. She recognized that her husband was trying to tell her something even if it was disguised in argumentative language. She accepted that she is in a relationship with Rick and that he trusts her help. She saw that she needed to remain flexible because Rick was less able at that moment to do so. She understood that Rick was making meaning of his headache and that he did not want her to treat it lightly. In other words, she broke the spell by remaining flexible and offering a solution that pleased them both. She realized that Rick needed recognition for his hard day at work and that she needed to have an agreeable mate for dinner. By honoring the headache, both needs were ultimately satisfied.

## How to Survive When Things Get Irrational

No matter how excellent your communication skills are or how flexible you remain, there will be times when the situation or the persons involved are so irrational that you cannot break the code. That is, you may not be able to discern the meaning or good intention behind the irrational behavior. This does not mean there is not a code or a way to interpret and understand the other person's communication. All of the basic and advanced truths or presuppositions may still apply. It may be only that you are not skillful enough at communicating in this particular situation or with this particular person. Before you draw this conclusion, however, make a valiant effort to try all of the options listed in this chapter.

If after trying all of the options you are aware of, you still cannot resolve the conflict, you can try the next two options. First, quit. Stop whatever you are doing and move away from the situation. There is no sense in allowing conflict to escalate to screaming and physical violence. Second, if there is still some rapport left between the two of you, suggest to your partner that you seek professional guidance. Through the support and education of a neutral professional, you may be able to restore the relationship to its former healthy state and develop yet more new skills to enable the next level of personal, marital, or business development to occur. Many of the couples in this book came to that point. The communication breakdown was so severe that they were unaware of, or unable to achieve, any solutions until they asked me or another professional for help.

There is actually a third alternative after trying professional help, and that is to give up altogether. Obviously you want to use this option sparingly. All too often people jump to the decision to end the relationship when they are just going through a normal transition to another stage of development. Remember, even normal transitions cause conflict. But there are times when two people have made terrible mistakes in choosing each other as marital or business partners. It is not wrong to recognize this and end the relationship. After all, we as individuals are growing and changing daily, and it is not unlikely that these changes may conflict in such a way that the only solution is to set each other free.

Dual entrepreneurs Jay and Celia came to that conclusion. In a nutshell, they married each other on the rebound. Jay was recently divorced from a woman he felt "took me to the cleaners." Celia was also recently divorced from a man who had abandoned her and their young son. When Jay and Celia married each other, they were desperate and lonely. The only thing they really had in common was alcohol and marijuana. After they got older, Celia had outgrown drug use, but Jay had not. A series of business mishaps left Jay angry, depressed, and defeated. As he drank more to escape the depression, he drove Celia farther and farther away. Although Celia had tried repeatedly to get Jay into treatment for alcoholism, he refused. Her only alternative was divorce.

## Confront Your Fears and Talk

I have covered a lot of territory in this meaty chapter on communication skills. First of all, communication is really a *process*, a dynamic, engaging process between two people involved in a developing progression of systems. Communication is not really separate from who we are as people. People are always communicating something about who they are, even when they sleep. We can really know ourselves only in relationship to others through our communication.

Getting to know yourself better and improving your communication skills with others are significant ways to improve your entrepreneurial relationship. Through listening and using healthy confrontation skills, conflicts can usually be resolved in a mutually satisfying way that produces individual, couple, family, and business growth.

The more advanced truths or presuppositions outlined in this chapter can transform your life, not just your partnerships, if you begin applying them today. Developing your flexibility so that you recognize that all people make sense and that all people are doing the best they know how, not only enables you to communicate better with others, but also gives you direction in better understanding your own motives. Changing your own bad habits is a powerful way of intervening in any system, be it a marital or business partnership.

Although improving one's ability to relate to others will reduce and convert pain and suffering to transformational growth, there are times when the best option is to quit or pull out. Remember, the person with the most flexibility in any system is the controlling element. If you allow an irrational person to direct you, then you may both go down with the ship. Failure is not necessarily bad; it may actually be the beginning of the best change you ever made.

You may be asking yourself, "Where do I begin?" The answer to that question depends on your situation, but because you are a member of an entrepreneurial couple, chances are you will need to start by facing your fear of conflict and confrontation. My own informal surveys show that members of family firms would not choose to work with family members if they had to do it over again. Their reason is fear of conflict and the ensuing disruptive consequences to the family. However, conquering this fear opens the path to communicating more effectively with the ones you love—whether at work or at home.

# Life Planning:
# Steps to Achieve Your
# Business and Personal Goals

Gail and Nathan came to me to resolve their interpersonal problems because they were considering marriage. They are a young couple, not yet dual-career or entrepreneurial but on their way. Gail was working on a bachelor's degree in business and Nathan was working odd jobs but wanted to return to art school. They had goals of establishing their own separate businesses as dual entrepreneurs someday when their educations were completed. Gail and Nathan also came into therapy with their own personal histories of childhood abuse. They insightfully recognized that their histories might affect their relationship and their career aspirations. They wanted to develop a plan for life together that was proactive rather than a reflection of survival and denial.

This young couple had already chosen to live together because they were very much in love and saw the potential for a long-term relationship. The crisis developed when Gail announced she was pregnant. While Nathan was thrilled and wanted to get married, Gail stalled. She wondered if the two of them were ready for such a major commitment, especially since they were at the beginning stages of their respective careers.

This chapter is about planning for one's life goals (personal, relationship, and family) and one's career/business goals. While Gail and Nathan were conscientious about planning for their careers, they neglected to take stock of what they wanted personally in their relationship with a long-term partner. With a child on the way, the young couple needed to decide how they would parent, married or not.

Most couples do not plan either their relationship or their careers. They may have some vague notions of what they hope will evolve over time, but things are still usually left to chance. With couples who work together, planning is even more likely to be absent. Entrepreneurial couples often act as if "all you need is love."

Stan and Rhonda fell victim to having no plan except for the "all you need is love" plan. Both were successful executives in their respective careers, when at midlife Stan wanted to leave his corporate job and start his own retail business selling environmentally safe home remodeling products. The couple was well established financially and had reared their children, so they were very excited to start this new venture. The plan for the moment was that Stan would quit his job and put all his energies into starting the business, as an organizing solo entrepreneur. Rhonda was to keep her job to provide a stable income while the business got under way, but as a supportive spouse she would work nights and weekends helping Stan.

Shortly after they opened a second store, Rhonda was ready to quit her job and share ownership and management with Stan of their two stores. However, this is when the marriage and partnership faltered. Much to Rhonda's surprise, Stan did not want her to come to work in "his" business. Stan had hired an assistant to take Rhonda's place. Shortly after Rhonda quit her job to work full-time with her husband, Stan moved out into his own apartment and filed for divorce.

The planning that might have helped this couple would have been to be clear up front about their assumptions and vision. Rhonda assumed that the business venture was a shared one, while Stan assumed that Rhonda was just helping him to get started. Rhonda assumed that the plan was for her to quit her job when the business was more successful, while Stan intended all along for Rhonda to keep her career separate.

During many months of consultation, Stan and Rhonda resolved many problems, which did lead to a reconciliation. To make a long story short, Stan continued to run the business alone. Rhonda realized that she needed a career change, too, but that she had followed her husband into the business because she did not want to do the hard work of personal discovery. After doing the necessary personal discovery process, she learned that she was a corporate executive after all and moved to a company that was more her style.

## Develop a Holistic Plan

If life is a dialectic of interacting and developing systems, then life planning requires a *holistic* approach. By this I mean you must consider that each area of your life—whether personal, relationship, family, or business—will affect the other areas, now or sometime in the future. With Nathan and Gail, and with Stan and Rhonda, we saw that their planning was limited to one or two areas of their lives.

Yet they failed to recognize that a decision in one area would affect results in another until there was a crisis.

Trying to keep these different life systems separate just will not work. Many consultants to entrepreneurial couples and other families in business have suggested that these business owners should leave their family issues at home and leave business issues at the office. Those of you already actively involved in an enterprise with your spouse know the unreasonableness of this suggestion. Try as you might, you are as much a spouse at work as you are a business partner at home. The territories commingle constantly.

This is just as true with your role as an individual, parent, child, and so on. Have you ever had to cut a business meeting short to pick up a sick child at school? Have you ever noticed employees avoiding you because of the tension you brought to work after having had a spat with your spouse? How many times have you tried to make the bedroom off-limits to business discussions? How many vacations have you taken that were not business related? How many times did you come to work dressed in jeans because it was a casual day, only to have an impromptu board meeting or unexpected visit from a client?

Try as you might to keep roles separate, the truth is that your personal life and your work life do indeed interact. In fact, they are not really separate at all, but are elements of one holistic system. At any one moment in time we may address one element of the system or another, but you have not *isolated* that element from the others. It is still in a dynamic relationship to each other element and the whole. The Gestalt concept of figure/ground offers a useful analogy: At any moment in time, one element of the whole may be the figure and the other elements the ground. At the next moment, an element in the ground will become the figure and the first element will fade into the ground. You may be the C.E.O. as you discuss the new industrial park near the airport, but when the phone rings, you become Daddy congratulating your eighteen-year-old on being accepted into Stanford. It was Daddy *and* the C.E.O. who contributed to both endeavors.

# Be Brave Enough to Compose a Life

To be successful as an entrepreneurial couple requires *planning a life*, one that includes your personal goals, your relationship goals, your family goals, and your career or business goals. You probably already have plans and goals, but many of them are outside your consciousness, and therefore you have no idea if all of your life plans are compatible. Bringing them into consciousness is hard work. Most entrepreneurial couples just wing it when it comes to business or marriage. They trust their drive, intelligence, and savvy to get them through life's roadblocks. But as life becomes more complicated by marriage, children, and an expanding business, the weaknesses in this style begin to emerge. Without a plan for the evolution of your marriage, family, or business, you may be very unprepared for the consequences. It is no surprise that most family-owned businesses never make it to the second generation. The business often dies with the founder.

*Composing a life* may be a better euphemism than life planning because it implies that life is art. The artist understands that the picture is more than the sum of its parts. The artist knows that when all of the elements are woven together, the tapestry takes on a life of its own. When you think about the business you have chosen to run with your spouse or partner, is it a representation of both of you or of some family history? How did you choose the name for your business? Does the name reflect a value or interest of yours? The answers to these questions reveal that it is not by chance that you are precisely at this point in your life.

It would be a lot easier to compose a life if you had a clean slate to start with. Unfortunately, you have probably been wandering around in life for a few decades already. You made decisions years ago that are still affecting you today. Some of these decisions can be changed; others are more permanent. Still others are perfectly good choices and are the foundation of the life you will begin composing today.

The first consideration in composing a life is to *be brave.* You may have to do radical surgery on yourself. You will probably find that your basic values as a human being are sound, but that their expression in the real world will have to change. Rhonda and Stan, for example, discovered that their values had not changed. They still believed in supporting each other as marital partners. It was even possible for Rhonda to help out at the business once in a while. However, support was redefined from copreneurship to Rhonda being the supportive spouse of a solo entrepreneur.

Other necessary changes may require that you expand your consciousness to include higher-order values. Because you have never been pressed this far before, these values did not have an opportunity to develop or emerge. As an employee you may have had many thoughts about how the boss should change. As an employer yourself, you may have a better understanding of the difficulties there are in managing employees. Before your children were born you probably had notions about good parenting. After the children came along, and with each stage they go through, you probably gain a new appreciation for how well your own parents handled such a complicated task. When you were a young adult in your early twenties, developing a relationship with your new spouse was based on the needs and goals of youth. Your marriage today, as an older, wiser couple, may require revamping to keep up with individual, family, and business development. Even the business in which you chose to involve yourself may have been suited to you at thirty, but at forty-five has lost its appeal.

When people face a crisis or even just an ordinary problem, they are tempted to try a simple change. They change jobs, change spouses, build a new house, and so on. These simple changes are supposed to make them feel better—and sometimes they do, for a while. But in the long run the new job fizzles, the new spouse presents problems remarkably similar to those the previous spouse presented, and the new house is still not quite big enough. Rather than waste your time with pointless changes, *compose* a life, and plan for *meaningful change*. Change your map of reality to include the possibilities that you (your spouse and your family) are capable of, even if this involves painful and difficult work. In other words, composing a life that works this time probably means changing your concept of the interdependence of love and work.

# The Seven Ground Rules for Successful Life Planning

Before composing your life plan, it is important to understand the ground rules. If you jump into a new plan too quickly, you may be repeating the mistakes of the past. Take your time. Follow these ground rules. After you have thoroughly explored the territory, assemble the pieces and weave the new tapestry.

1. *Plan with your spouse and others who are significant in your life.* Getting others' feedback is imperative. It keeps you aware that you are not in this life alone. Even when you are planning a life goal that seems so personal that it could not possibly be relevant to anyone but yourself, ask others for their opinions. Many of your personal goals can be thwarted by the unexpected demands of other areas of your life.

2. *Develop the communication attitudes and skills discussed in Chapter Three.* Becoming an excellent communicator will assist you in communicating with yourself as well as others. As important as these skills are in learning about the ones you love and work with, learning to listen to yourself (i.e., to trust your intuition) will move you toward the most powerful decisions in your life.

3. *Brainstorm.* Be open to new understandings about the interdependence of love and work. Look at different models than what you are used to. Brainstorm as many options as you can think of for redefining your relationship, yourself, your family life, and your business structure.

**69**

4. *Be open.* Let go of all the reasons you should not or cannot do something. Do not turn away any option while you are brainstorming. Later, as you develop a plan to integrate these new notions, you can discard the unworkable ones. But remember, even the unworkable option today may prove workable sometime in the future.

5. *Shoot for the moon.* Allow yourself and your significant others to dream. Plan for the optimum in all areas of your life. A common mistake is settling for the average when with a little extra effort you could produce something extraordinary. You may not get to the moon in all cases, but you are certain to fail if you never try.

6. *Plan for the worst.* This sounds a little pessimistic, but the value is in planning. If you have contingency plans, you feel less threatened by the unknown. However, it is important to not be guided by your thoughts of the worst possibilities. Then your plans take on the shape of fear and failure.

7. *Be flexible.* Ultimately, the life plan you develop will encompass as many areas of your life as you are aware of, but no plan is perfect or permanent. Life is full of surprises. Be prepared to change the plan with the evolution of yourself as an individual, as a marital partner, as a parent, and as a business owner or partner.

# Your Personal Life Plan

As selfish as it may seem, the place to start in composing your life is with your own personal goals. The key ingredient of a good life plan for an entrepreneurial couple is that it meets the needs of both partners without compromising their individual integrity. This requires that you be aware of the composition of your integrity. How can you be a good spouse, business partner, or parent if you do not know yourself very well? You cannot. Therefore, the first step in making your life plan is to build a plan for you personally. Remember to keep the ground rules for successful life planning in mind: Discuss your ideas with others, practice communicating, brainstorm, be open, shoot for the moon, plan for the worst, and be flexible.

### Brainstorm Your Personal Life Plan

There are a number of ways to begin this process of personal life planning. The questions and suggestions included in Self-Assessment Exercise 3 should get the brainstorming process started. As you continue your life planning, you may adapt the suggestions to fit more with your own personal style of problem solving.

## Your Personal Life Plan

Answer the following questions as honestly as you can. There are no right or wrong answers. The purpose of this exercise is to help you identify your personal values and goals, so that you can plan for yourself a life that is consistent with them.

1. Make a list of the fifty things that you have always wanted to do but have not yet done.

2. Make a list of ten to twenty of your most prized accomplishments. Rank your list in order of most prized to least prized.

3. Make a list of your worst habits. Rank this list, too, from worst bad habit to least bad habit.

4. Shop in a store that does not necessarily appeal to you, and buy something there. Eat in a restaurant that serves food you have always claimed to dislike.

5. Ask people what they think of you. Ask if they think you are smart, if they like your clothes, or if they would choose you for a friend or relative if they had a choice.

6. Be honest for an entire day. Notice how you feel about that.

7. Go to church (any church will do). Or, if you do this already, go to church on a day you normally would not go.

8. Describe three people—real or fictional, current or historical— that you most admire. Describe them in detail, and indicate why you admire them.

9. If you had $10 million, what would you do next with your life?

10. If you could change anything about your childhood, what would you change?

11. What was the most important value you learned from your father as you were growing up? From your mother? From another significant relative or friend?

12. If you could live anywhere, where would you live, and in what kind of house?

13. If you could do your life over again, what would be the most significant change you would make?

14. Write down one thing you are so ashamed of you have never told anyone. If you are brave enough to share it with someone, do so. If you are not yet brave enough, seal the piece of paper in an envelope and hide it from others until you are ready.

15. After you are dead, what one thing would you most like to be remembered for?

## Evaluating Your Responses

If you have truly applied yourself to the questions and tasks above, you should have acquired a great deal of information about yourself. Now gather up your notes and begin sifting through them. Read them over and over several times until you begin to see patterns, both in your behavior and in your thoughts and beliefs. These patterns are the foundation of your new life plan. Share your notes with others to see what patterns they notice. You will be surprised how often someone tells you that he or she knew about this or that pattern all along.

Many of your life decisions have been made out of habit or because your parents told you to do something or because of a foolish consistency. Look past these patterns to the patterns that truly reflect the inner you. If $10 million would allow you to go back to school to study zoology, and you won several 4-H awards as a child, and you would live on a ranch in Wyoming if you could live anywhere, and you wear cowboy boots with your three-piece suits and donate liberally to the Humane Society, what are you doing living in an apartment in New York and running an advertising agency? What are the patterns here?

---

**SELF-ASSESSMENT EXERCISE 3 (CONT'D)**

After developing a list of patterns and priorities in your life, play with different possibilities for a while. Perhaps you can continue living in New York, running your ad agency, and wearing cowboy boots, but now you can also develop a plan to attract Wyoming clients. Or you can develop a specialty in advertising for nonprofits that support animal rights. And on holidays and vacations, you can head out to your ranch and ride your favorite horse.

## Summarizing Remark

Write one sentence or a brief paragraph summarizing what you learned from this exercise and what you want to change.

---

Not long ago a physician was so depressed about failing the medical board exam for his specialty in radiology that he sought me out for hypnosis. He was hoping that hypnosis would assist him in passing the test. After his third failure, however, he was finally ready to examine the real problem. He certainly was bright enough to pass the exam. The other physicians he worked with were ready to make him a partner when he passed it, so he was well liked and his work respected. However, when we dug deeper, he revealed that going to medical school was something his father had wanted him to do. In fact, it was so important to his father, and indeed the entire family, that the father had paid out of his own pocket for his son's medical education. However, all along what the doctor really wanted was to be in show business. He loved music especially. After doing the necessary planning to integrate all areas of life in his plan, this man sold his house, gave up a potential medical partnership, and moved to another town to take a position as a disc jockey with a radio station. From there his plans involved gradually introducing himself into music production.

Not everyone's story is this dramatic, of course. Nor is it always necessary to make such drastic changes. The following couples have made more modest, though still life-enhancing, changes in their lives by following their personal life plans.

Howard and Andrea turned Howard's interest in tinkering into a chain of hardware stores. Allison, a massage therapist, and Chris, a chiropractor, were drawn together when Allison came to work in Chris's office; they hit it off so well both personally and professionally that a romance bloomed. Ross and Nalani run a conglomerate of businesses that employs a number of family members, which meets their need to be close to family, as well as their need for variety in their work. Gisela has turned her secretarial skills into top-notch management tools for her business in public relations; her husband, Marty, who is an attorney, is her legal advisor.

## Plan for the Worst

No doubt in your brainstorming you discovered some personal flaws or some unfinished personal development work. Perhaps you have not been attending to your health lately and need to get back into a healthy program of nutrition and exercise. Or you may have emotional or psychological problems due to past traumas. These insecurities will hamper your success. Admit that you are not perfect, that you made mistakes in your life, or that others did. Get professional help to put you back on the path to a balanced and healthy life. Why should you continue to suffer over bad decisions from your past or the pasts of others? Why cling to old, outdated decisions that were made when you weren't as educated or experienced or brave as you are now?

After attending to the obvious flaws in your character, start developing contingency plans for other aspects of your life plan. Remember that planning for the worst eases your fears about the unknown. If you plan for the worst and it never happens, you can feel blessed. If you plan for the worst and it *does* happen, at least you are not taken by surprise.

Chris and Allison offer an example of planning ahead in all areas of their lives together—as individuals, as a couple, as a family and for the business. When they first married and combined their respective health care practices (hers as a massage therapist and his as a chiropractor), Chris and Allison were thrilled about their new life together as copreneurs. Each day they could work with the one they loved, doing work in which they took pride. Even when their baby came along, their clinic schedule could be designed to accommodate family needs and schedules. Working part-time for a while, Allison hired a receptionist/secretary to handle the other office responsibilities that she no longer had time for.

As the years went by, their clinic grew and the family could afford a number of luxuries, such as a new home, a vacation condo, and private school for their son.

They set up retirement accounts and a college fund. When the huge crisis hit, they were prepared for that also. Chris was injured in an automobile accident, creating nerve damage and causing him to be in chronic pain and no longer able to perform chiropractic adjustments on his patients. The couple had disability insurance that would take care of the loss of income. And because they had a successful practice, they sold the business to a young chiropractor just starting out. Of course, they had to handle the emotional loss, which you are never totally prepared for, but with the material concerns taken care of, Allison and Chris had a much better start on their next business venture: running a bed-and-breakfast in the San Juan Islands in northwestern Washington state.

Chris and Allison are not without problems, but because they had a life plan that met their needs in most areas and they worked the plan together, they are better able to handle life's inevitable setbacks and obstacles. Chris and Allison are the kind of people who take care of themselves. They attend church, seek out psychotherapy when they need it, attend to their physical health, read widely to keep current professionally because they love their work, and seek opportunities to grow as individuals. However, they are concerned about the transition to their new copreneurial venture. Allison wants to continue her work as a massage therapist, but Chris will be going through a major identity crisis as he leaves his professional role behind to run the bed-and-breakfast. Their son will also be making a major adjustment from city life to rural resort life. He may be lonely, especially since he is an only child. As this copreneurial couple negotiates the waters of life transition, they will need to remain flexible and open to new ideas, while at the same time retaining their personal integrity.

## Be Flexible

By incorporating all of the ground rules for successful life planning into the development of your personal life plan, you will automatically be using your flexibility. The combination of discussing your dreams with others, practicing your listening skills, brainstorming, remaining open to all possibilities, shooting for the moon, and planning for the worst, puts you in a position to really get to know yourself. Once this is accomplished, you are able to utilize this knowledge to shape your personal life plan.

Getting to know your real self and learning to develop a life plan that taps into your personal attributes and skills is incredibly hard work. As I said, most entrepreneurial couples just wing it. It is time- and energy-consuming to do this work, and most people are too impatient or lazy to dedicate themselves to the process. It may appear that Allison and Chris had it easy just because my brief annotation of their lives pointed out their successes. However, it was not an easy process for them to come to terms with who they are as individuals. For example, they did not marry until they were in their early thirties, and by then Chris had been married before. Chiropractic was not Chris' first career, nor was massage therapy Allison's. Allison experienced two miscarriages before the birth of her only son. It is a great disappointment and loss for both Chris and Allison that they can have no more children. And it remains to be seen how Chris will handle the transition to a radically different occupation at age forty-five.

The key to flexibility is trusting that there are *always options*, even if you do not yet know what they are. You really have infinite resources within yourself and those around you to brainstorm solutions to life's contradictions and dilemmas. As a member of an entrepreneurial couple, you will undoubtedly have many opportunities to challenge your personal life plan. Be brave enough to take these challenges as opportunities to compose a life.

## Your Relationship Life Plan

At the beginning of this chapter, I described Gail and Ron, a young couple who neglected to plan for their life as a committed couple, married or not. They fell in love, moved in together, and conceived a child. At that late date they had to make a decision about whether they wanted to stay together and if there was enough substance to the relationship to consider marriage. Certainly this is not a new story. Most young couples do not plan for success or contingencies. Rather, they live in the moment, trusting that life will deliver just what they need. Often, to their surprise, life delivers a needed lesson in the importance of planning.

Your relationship life plan is just as important as your personal life plan, your family life plan, and your business life plan, but the work is more than half done when you've completed your personal life plan. Knowing yourself well can guide you to choose a life partner who shares many of your goals and values. However, most of the readers of this book are already married and involved in an entrepreneurial relationship with their spouse, so you are already past choosing a mate. Nevertheless, your relationship life plan still needs some review. It may be that changes are in order to better fit your new view of yourself. It can be a frightening process to reevaluate a marriage, but following a foolish consistency may be interfering with your marital development. Transitioning to an entrepreneurial style of marriage can cause a number of forced adjustments for couples. It is better to face the changes required up front. There are also past decisions that you will have to face, decisions that may have cost you dearly. Now is the time to deal with them.

Jonathan and Brooke did not plan for their marriage even though both were in their thirties and both had been married previously. Brooke worked for Jonathan for several years in the advertising firm before they started dating. They knew it was risky to date within the company, but they fell in love and ignored the risk. They reasoned that there should be few problems because Jonathan was the boss and Brooke was well respected by her coworkers. Still, they felt it best to keep their personal involvement a secret for a while. When Brooke was approached by a coworker who suspected they were dating, Jonathan and Brooke knew the cat was out of the bag. They took a positive approach and announced to the company their intentions toward each other. In a year they were married.

Still there was little planning even though the situation was complicated by Brooke being Jonathan's employee, his wife, and also a shareholder in the company. Brooke is a talented employee and probably would have advanced into management and the executive team sooner or later, but now it appeared to some that her advancement was a result of being Jonathan's wife. No matter what her accomplishments, some employees resented her status. Brooke was hurt by this and angry at Jonathan for not supporting her more when employees complained. Aside from the complications this situation caused the business, Jonathan and Brooke did not plan for the stress to their marriage of the boss marrying an employee.

**Brainstorm Your Relationship Life Plan**

As you work through the questions and suggestions included in Self-Assessment Exercise 4, put yourself in a frame of mind to be open, to examine all possibilities, and to be fearless. As with working on your personal life plan, you need to follow the ground rules for successful life planning; that is, get feedback, practice communicating, brainstorm, be open, shoot for the moon, plan for the worst, and be flexible. You will probably find that you have chosen the right mate for you, but undoubtedly some changes are in order. Even for those of you who are experiencing serious marital stress, there are reasons to consider that this spouse is in your life for an important purpose. Look for the patterns and the deeper meaning.

I suggest that you do Self-Assessment Exercise 4 on your own first, then share the results with your spouse or partner. Ideally, your partner has also done both this and the Self-Assessment Exercise 3 (on personal life planning). In this way you

## Your Relationship Life Plan

Answer the following questions as honestly as you can. There are no right or wrong answers. The purpose of this exercise is to help you identify your values and goals for a primary relationship, so that you can build one that reflects them.

1. How did you and your partner meet? What attracted you to him or her?

2. Why did your partner choose you?

3. What did you learn about marriage from your parents?

4. What did your partner learn about marriage from his or her parents?

5. If you could do it all over again, would you choose this same partner? List your reasons.

6. What would you change in your partner to make the relationship better?

7. What do you need to change in yourself that would improve the relationship?

8. What are your partner's most deeply held beliefs? His or her most prized accomplishments? His or her most cherished dreams?

9. The people whom you dated before getting involved with your current partner—what were they like? Why did these relationships not work out?

10. The people whom your partner dated before getting involved with you—what were they like? Why did these relationships not work out?

## SELF-ASSESSMENT EXERCISE 4 (CONT'D)

11. What is your favorite recreational activity? Your partner's?

12. Name three important lessons you have learned from your partner.

13. Describe how you feel about sex with your partner.

14. Describe the ideal marriage. Describe your ideal mate.

15. Describe one important way you have disappointed your partner and one way she or he has disappointed you.

16. How do your children or other significant family members view your primary relationship?

## Evaluating Your Responses

You have come a long way if you have done these exercises honestly. You may have had some sleepless nights and long talks with your partner. Ideally, your partner is working on these exercises too. The goal here is to build and/or rewrite a life plan that encompasses the individual life plans for each of you as well as a relationship plan that you create together.

As with the exercise on your personal life plan, sift through the information you have gathered here. Look for patterns, themes, and foolish consistency. Begin to ask why and why not. Explore new forms of commitment with your partner. If there are areas in your relationship, such as intimacy and sex, that are no longer working, begin problem solving with your partner.

## Summarizing Remark

Write one sentence or a brief paragraph summarizing what you learned from this exercise and what you want to change.

will come to this point in composing a life plan where you can really do some serious analysis and reconstruction with your spouse or partner.

Marty and Gisela came to my office beleaguered by marital problems that had escalated to the point that Marty began having an affair with his secretary. Over the years the couple had been through many trials and tribulations together, such as losing jobs, moving across the country to reestablish themselves financially, and losing a child to drug addiction. They were determined to make it through this crisis, too, because they knew that they still loved each other.

In therapy they focused on their sexual incompatibility. Marty remembered how rewarding and passionate their love life had been when they first married and wondered where all that had gone. Gisela was dumbfounded that Marty would want sex now when she was overwhelmed by their personal problems. Over the years she had given in to his desire for sex when she really did not feel like it herself, only to discover that she wanted sex less and less. Now she felt like sex was a duty, and she resented Marty for constantly asking her to fulfill it.

A simple exercise turned things around for Marty and Gisela. I asked the couple to forgo all sexual intimacy for two weeks *unless* Gisela initiated it. When two weeks went by, Gisela had still not initiated sex because she did not feel like it, but something had changed in her. She recognized that her husband was generally interested in resolving their problems. Marty had not made any sexual advances toward her during that two-week period, respecting her need not to be pushed. And he was willing to agree to an indefinite time period of waiting until she was ready. Tentatively, Gisela began making sexual overtures toward her husband and was pleased to discover that he was willing to follow her lead.

The mistake that Gisela and Marty had made was to fail to discuss their problems, even their most intimate problems. Therefore, they did not learn that they had different approaches to expressing sexuality. Marty viewed sex as separate and distinct from other things in life. Even though he and Gisela were having financial problems or problems with the children, he always felt he could find release in sexual loving with his wife. Gisela, on the other hand, could not separate one aspect of her life from the others. If things were stressful at her public relations business, or if she and Marty had fought about something at home, she took that stress to bed with her. At these times her husband's desire for sex was repulsive to her because she thought he was being insensitive to her concerns and emotional state. Now, however, Marty and Gisela understand each other better. They still have slightly different views on sex, but they are respectful of the differences between them.

Do not just focus on problems. Discuss the ideal marriage. Do not limit yourself to the way it has been or the way others do it. Confront your perception of reality. Be willing to change and to ask your spouse to change. Consider how you and your partner can cocreate a fantastic marriage, even after all these years. Use those newfound communication skills to get to the heart of the relationship. Purge what is not working, and build a new structure based on respect, love, and creating miracles. Because Marty and Gisela would not settle for a loveless marriage, because they were willing to shoot for the moon, they turned a crisis into an opportunity to greatly enhance their relationship.

## Plan for the Worst

You may feel that you have already experienced the worst in your marriage. If you have weathered some of these hard times, you can weather anything. However, entrepreneuring with your spouse is tough on marriage. It presents challenges to your belief system that no other experience can. So it is wise to reexamine your relationship plan for weak spots.

In 1972 researchers Bernard and Gove discovered that marriage presents a health dilemma for men and women. Married men live longer and are healthier and happier than single men. Yet single women live longer and are healthier and happier than married women. One way to read this data is that marriage is healthy for men and unhealthy for women. However, this fact does not stop women from getting married. Apparently, women and men want the benefits of marriage even if they have yet to figure out how to solve the problems.

One way to solve the problems is to plan for them up front. For example, plan for the fact that your wife may not be as happy about change as you are. Tom and Karen had this problem. If you recall from Chapter One, Tom is a pioneering solo entrepreneur, and Karen his supportive spouse. Tom is an engineer who made millions fairly quickly with an innovative idea. In spite of the wealth, Karen became unhappy and seriously depressed. She clung to their sons for moral support. She refused to have a life outside of decorating their house. She complained bitterly that her husband was not the man she had married, that he was insensitive and inattentive.

Tom was bewildered because Karen had been so happy about their marriage and so supportive when he started his own business. He knew that Karen was lonely during those first three years of marriage and starting his company, but she had encouraged him to do it. Even when the first years of hard work were done, and Tom was actually able to be home more, Karen was still unhappy. She complained that he did not take out the garbage soon enough, or that he did not play properly with the children.

There were several problems that Tom and Karen did not plan for. First, though they love each other deeply, they have very different personalities. Tom is an aggressive, creative, risk-taking entrepreneur. His wife, on the other hand, is a conservative, reliable, hardworking farm girl. Speed and risk are not comfortable to her. Although Karen found Tom charming, he was nothing like herself or the family she grew up with. Therefore, Tom and Karen needed to plan for the contingency that their differences could erupt into quarrels. This couple needs to spend a great deal more time talking and learning about each other. If Tom wants Karen in his life, he may have to move much more slowly.

A second problem that Tom and Karen did not plan for is that their marriage would be disrupted by the development of a new business. The two of them did not get a honeymoon; they launched the business within days of getting married. There was no time to establish the relationship plan or routine. Perhaps this style works for Tom, but Karen cannot function without order and specific, well-thought-out plans.

A third problem is that when the couple became wealthy, Karen chose to quit her job. They did not need her income, and she thought she would enjoy the break. However, without work, Karen had no place to dedicate her adult energy, so she complained. She really did not want to return to work, but she did not want to be part of her husband's business either, even though he asked her often. The real problem is that because Karen had never before been in a position to be able to fulfill her wildest dreams, she did not know what they were.

Being the spouse of a pioneering solo entrepreneur is challenging. Karen has very simple values and they do not include instant wealth and power. She is struggling to become a member of the social circle that her husband has joined because of his prominence in the community. She will need to find an identity of her own in addition to being Tom's wife.

## Be Flexible

Gail and Nathan, Jonathan and Brooke, and Tom and Karen—indeed, all of the couples in this book—struggle with flexibility when it comes to their intimate partnerships. It is much easier to stay flexible within your own personal life plan, but the problems grow exponentially when you must include the developing progression of your partner in the plan.

As I have examined the lives of these couples and discussed their decisions, some of you have probably been rolling your eyes and wondering how they got themselves into these messes. Others of you can clearly see similar patterns in your own lives and are wondering how to get your act together. First, recognize that it is useless to brood over your mistakes. Life is complicated. On the positive side, your planning skills should improve after reading this chapter and working through the Self-Assessment Exercises, but not everything that life throws our way can be anticipated or accounted for. Flexibility is most needed when you have to seek new ways to resolve long-standing, seemingly impossible problems.

Second, do anything but what is not working any more. Start with some small change like rearranging the assignment of household chores. Take over the checkbook or open two separate checking accounts to see how that affects how the two of you deal with money. Make a date with your spouse once a week, just the two of you, to rediscover each other. Go golfing with your wife even though you hate to golf. Buy a new bed and make the bedroom off-limits to work discussions.

Jonathan and Brooke eventually realized that they had made a major mistake in getting involved. At least it was a mistake in terms of the havoc it caused at work. They were not mistaken about loving each other, nor about being a good match otherwise. But now they could no longer ignore the problems created when the boss marries an employee. So they got flexible. Jonathan essentially left the business. He turned the entire local operation over to Brooke to run. She no longer answered to Jonathan in any way. The advertising agency was now hers, and Jonathan devoted himself to special projects and international development. Without being in Jonathan's shadow, Brooke could prove herself the capable executive she really was.

In order to make such a big change, Jonathan and Brooke had to make a major shift in consciousness: They needed to stop seeing the business as Jonathan's. They needed to recognize that each of them is a strong, competitive pioneering type of entrepreneur who needs room to express himself or herself. They needed to recognize that marriage can be defined as they wish it for themselves. Jonathan married Brooke because she is a powerhouse and an achiever. Brooke married Jonathan because he is a visionary and she wanted to help him achieve his visions. Regardless of what others think about Brooke's rise to the top, the most important thing that Jonathan and Brooke learned is that if they work on the problem together, there is no stopping their success.

## Your Family Life Plan

"Shower, coffee, go!" That is how Mike describes his early-morning routine. Karla, Mike's copreneurial wife, on the other hand, describes a more complicated morning. She is up early and puts on the coffee before she goes to feed the baby and change his diapers. Once the baby is sleeping again, Karla wakes the preschooler to feed and dress him. While he is in front of the television set watching cartoons, Karla takes a shower and dresses for work. The nanny arrives in time for Karla to leave for preschool with her older boy in tow. Karla finally arrives at work an hour after her husband and begins making her rounds with managers and forepersons. She skips breakfast and settles for an orange at noon.

In my work as a consultant and even in my research, I often hear from adults who grew up in family-owned businesses that they would "never do that to *my* kids!" When pressed further, these grown children complain that there was never time for family activities, that the business consumed their parents. They report that their fathers especially were rarely home and that their mothers were dead tired trying to do double duty as business partner and homemaker. Regardless of the present age of these offspring, the feelings are the same. They believe that their parents cared more about the business than about them—which has caused a permanent strain in the relationship.

In this chapter you have reviewed and reevaluated your personal life plan and your relationship life plan. Soon you will assess your business life plan. As much as entrepreneurial couples seem to ignore planning in these areas of their lives, they consider even less the development of their children. It is as if providing food, shelter, and clothing is enough. Entrepreneurial couples can be so focused on achievement and the future that they spend little time nurturing their children. The children may have Nintendo, a big-screen television, piano lessons, and $150 Nikes, but do they have your attention?

Planning for the healthy growth and development of children requires education. The function of this chapter is planning; education about quality parenting is left to Chapter Seven. Therefore, this section on family life planning will be fairly brief. You will have a better idea on how to plan parenting when you really understand what is required. That is why I have dedicated an entire chapter to educating you as a parent. However, to get yourself started, ask yourself how much attention you have paid to each individual child. Parenting is about getting to know your children, not just providing for them. Evaluate what you really know about how to rear a child. Are you just winging it in that area, too?

The reality is that not just entrepreneurial couples but most couples wing it when it comes to parenting. It is as if children are like little tomato plants. You just plant them and wait for them to mature. However, children are highly sophisticated organisms even before they are born. Each child requires a great deal of specialized attention to grow into a healthy human being. Virginia Satir, a noted family therapist and author, has said that parents are in the role of "people making."

When you get to Chapter Seven, you will have an opportunity to brainstorm your family life plan (see Self-Assessment Exercise 12 on page 156). For now, you consider your personal life plan and your relationship life plan and how they interact with your business life plan. Consider also how your decisions are affecting the development of your children. Each move you make undoubtedly influences your children directly or indirectly. Compare the situation of Ross and Nalani to that of Larry and Dorothy. Ross and Nalani have a family enterprise of many levels with several family members employed, whereas Larry and Dorothy will probably have to sell their agriculture business because their son is not a capable heir and their daughter is estranged from the family.

To be sure, no two families are alike, and there are reasons other than parenting that affect whether a child will be successor material, but there is a clear difference in how these two couples related to their children. Larry's business was *his*, a reflection of his need for achievement, recognition, and power. On the other hand, Nalani and Ross built an empire out of a need to *provide* for their family. That is why they considered each other's needs and those of their children at each step in their journey. Not all of their children work in the family business, but each child feels loved, appreciated, and accepted.

From this brief introduction to parenting, you may already have some ideas that you want to discuss with your partner. Take the time to do that before moving ahead to the business life plan. Your life plan as a whole cannot be complete without consideration of the children, if you have them. Therefore, allow your life plan to evolve as you read the rest of the book. Remember the basic rules of composing a life: Discuss your thoughts with your partner and your children, practice communicating, brainstorm, be open to all ideas, shoot for the moon, plan for the worst, and at all times be flexible.

## Your Business Life Plan

In Chapter One and at the beginning of this chapter I discussed the planning mistakes of Stan and Rhonda. Rhonda thought that she and Stan were copreneurs. Stan, on the other hand, considered the business venture his creation as a solo entrepreneur, and Rhonda his supportive spouse. This major misunderstanding nearly cost them their marriage, as similar misunderstandings have cost many other entrepreneurial couples their marriages.

As you enter the phase of planning your life with regard to your business, it is vital to include your spouse or partner in the planning. This is not just to get feedback on your ideas, nor to practice communication skills. You must include your spouse so that you define your business venture according to the most appropriate style of couple entrepreneurship—(1) solo entrepreneur with a supportive spouse, (2) dual entrepreneurs, or (3) copreneurs—and whether you are or want to be a family firm. As you wrestle with defining your style, take note of the entrepreneurial personality of you and your partner and how each personality type is suited to the different forms of entrepreneurship and family business—(1) all-rounder, (2) organizer, (3) routineer, or (4) pioneer—Once your entrepreneurial style is defined, it is much easier to delegate authority and responsibilities and to plan for the development of the business.

## Brainstorm Your Business Life Plan

You may feel that of all the areas in your life plan, the business plan is the most clear. After all, you spend the bulk of your day at work. You may even have a thriving enterprise and see no need to revamp your plan for it. However, this time you will be brainstorming within the context of a *holistic plan*. We are not talking here about whether your business is competitive in the marketplace or whether it is time to expand into a new warehouse. We are talking about whether your business honestly reflects your life values and those of your spouse. We are talking about noticing psychological trouble spots such as the one that plagued Stan and Rhonda and the other couples I have described. We are talking about composing a life wherein your personal style, your relationship style, your parenting style, and your business style are fully integrated to reflect your most deeply held values and beliefs.

As with the previous exercises, take your time as you and your partner work through the questions and suggestions in Self-Assessment Exercise 5. You may of course adapt some of the questions to better reflect your individual situation. We will then attempt to pull together *all* your life plans in the final section of this chapter.

Frank and Louise, whom I first described in the Preface, started their electronics business as a flexible way for Frank to work within the limitations of a chronic illness. After Frank had recovered, however, his illness was no longer a defining or limiting factor, and he wanted to expand the business. He also wanted Louise to assume a more active role in it. He even considered other products to develop and market. Louise, however, was not really an entrepreneur, but simply a supportive spouse. She wanted children and to pursue career interests of her own.

# Your Business Life Plan

Answer the following questions as honestly as you can. There are no right or wrong answers. The purpose of this exercise is to help you identify your business/career values and goals so that you can pursue and develop a business or career that embodies them.

1. Describe why you and your partner chose to work together as an entrepreneurial couple.

2. Whose idea was it to start the business?

3. How did you pick the service or product to market?

4. Who is the boss? Why?

5. How did your parents make decisions, especially if they were an entrepreneurial couple?

6. If you had a million dollars, would you sell your business? Ten million? A hundred million?

7. Describe your business goals in terms of their meaning to you, your partner, and your family.

8. What plans have you made for your business when you retire?

9. Could your partner step in and run things if you were disabled or deceased?

10. In what ways have you prepared your children for participating in the business?

11. Describe one of your greatest business failures and what you learned from it.

12. What are you most proud of with regard to your business?

## SELF-ASSESSMENT EXERCISE 5 (CONT'D)

13. How are you and your partner viewed in the community as a business couple?

14. What image or reputation does your business have in the community? What image or reputation would you like it to have?

15. If you could start all over again, how would you design your business differently?

## Evaluating Your Responses

There are many more questions that I could ask you, but if you have been honest, you are off to a good start on brainstorming for your business life plan. Notice patterns and themes. Notice contradictions and inconsistencies. Marvel at and appreciate the ways in which you and your partner are "in sync." The questions and directives given here may spur you to many discussions. I hope so. Notice where you and your partner agree and disagree. You may be even more confused before you are finished. Do not be discouraged. Confusion often indicates that old, encrusted foolish consistencies have been knocked loose and are rattling around until you can find a new organization or framework for your life.

## Summarizing Remark

Write one sentence or a brief paragraph summarizing what you learned from this exercise and what you want to change.

As an all-rounder, Frank discovered that expansion was not all that he thought it would be. He became overwhelmed by employee problems. He could not seem to find workers or managers with the same commitment to the business that he had. When he found himself in the middle of a lawsuit, and his health was failing again, Frank realized that he needed help redesigning his life.

In consultation with his wife, Frank looked at his priorities and at those of Louise. First, the couple finally realized that Frank was a solo entrepreneur and Louise a supportive spouse. Second, they realized that whatever business direction they took needed to consider all of their life plans. With a new baby, Frank was keenly aware of his responsibilities to raise a healthy, independent child. Third, they realized that whatever life plan they develop today will probably need modification occasionally as life creates new challenges and possibilities.

Frank and Louise developed a strategy for making business decisions that would help them stay within the guidelines of a holistic life plan. Simply put, *all* business decisions had to meet three criteria. (1) The decision needed to be supportive of Frank's health. (2) It needed to contribute to the growth of meaningful relationships with his family. And (3) it needed to reflect his spiritual beliefs. If the business decision would cause problems in any of these three areas, then Frank and Louise would not go in that direction. They would continue to brainstorm until they came up with a solution that mirrored their values.

You have met many entrepreneurial couples in this book, and they have had a variety of reasons for starting their own businesses. Seldom has the reason been just to make money. However, there are some people who are driven to do so. Making money for them is fun, exhilarating even. In Chapter Eight, on wealth management, I will discuss the meaning of money more thoroughly. But for now consider that if you really think you are an entrepreneur because you love money, you might ask yourself just what you want the money for. Ask your spouse the same question. For Frank and Louise, the purpose of making money is to provide them with the opportunity to live well, but it is also to provide a quality of life that includes health, loving relationships, and contributing to a rewarding future for their children.

### Plan for the Worst

An interesting study by McKinley in 1984 shows that widows are unwilling to sell the family business, even though they may have no idea how to run it. Most of these widows were supportive spouses or copreneurial spouses, but they were not the leaders in the business so they were often unaware of the real demands of keeping the business going. Yet they were committed to taking over and leading the business after the deaths of their husbands because they found self-employment very rewarding.

Salganicoff, in a 1990 review of research, concluded that women in family firms are often "invisible" when it comes to management and decision making in the business. Male founders do not consider their wives as successors any more than they consider their daughters—not that they plan for succession much, anyway. The typical assumption is that a son will inherit the business if it is to be passed on to anyone.

Planning for the worst in your business plan should include the eventuality that you will die. There is no reason to retire if you are healthy, challenged, and having fun with your business, but who will take over when you die? You may think that it does not matter, but you will be leaving many people without any guidance for their futures if you do *not* have a succession plan. Consider those widows in McKinley's study. They had supported their husband's dreams and worked hard right beside him to build a family and a business. But they were never included in the planning for the business, so they had to rely on attorneys, bankers, and other advisors to guide them after their husband died.

If you think you and your spouse are different, I applaud you. However, as recently as 1991, the double standard was alive and well. In that year Wicker and Burley studied the decision making of copreneurial couples. Essentially, husbands wield the authority most of the time. Only in businesses that have a more feminine orientation, such as a nail salon, do the husbands listen to their wives, and even then the wives wield only fifty percent of the decision-making authority. Without developing leadership and decision-making skills, how can a wife or a child or another employee be ready to take over when the need arises?

There are other worst-case scenarios to plan for that you will uncover as you do your brainstorming. You may become disabled, as Chris did, and be forced to find another vehicle for your entrepreneurial or professional energies. You may become divorced, such as Jay and Celia, and go through the lengthy legal process of separating business assets. You may have to consider a successor from among your children's cousins or outside the family altogether because your own child is not suitable. You may be involved in a family enterprise for reasons that no longer suit you today. How do you change?

Be fearless. Examine all of the possible worst-case scenarios you can think of. Planning for contingencies puts you in a better position if and when the time comes. Even if something pops up that you did not plan for, you will probably have the confidence to face it because you have been willing to look at other problems. In the long run, if all of your planning proves to be just an exercise, you can be grateful that your life has gone so smoothly.

## Be Flexible

Things blew sky-high when Rhonda quit her job and went to work full-time with her husband, Stan. Rhonda had no idea that the man she loved could be so deceptive and ruthless. Rhonda thought she had authority and responsibility for a range of business decisions; however, not only were her decisions and orders countermanded by Stan, but he placed an employee in authority over Rhonda. Rhonda felt shamed and refused to come to the store; Stan took her defiance to mean it was time to quit the marriage.

Stan and Rhonda were in a major crisis when I met them, and it seemed that there was no turning back the tidal wave. They both felt betrayed by the other. As we learned earlier, each had a very different notion of the role of their partner in the business. It required incredible flexibility to listen to each other and to reorient their business plan. Stan had not realized how covetous of the business he was. The business represented an important developmental milestone for him as a person, and he wanted to continue to build and run it alone. When he and Rhonda understood the purpose of the business, Rhonda was not upset about bowing out. She could find another way to develop herself. If a copreneurial venture were in her future, she would discuss the situation in more detail with her spouse next time to be sure of his real motives.

# Bringing the Whole Plan Together

This chapter has probably created more work for you than you ever imagined. If you have done it thoroughly, you have examined and begun to revamp many areas of your life—personally, as a spouse, as a business partner and as a parent. Even if you are still confused, you have the blueprint for completing the work. If you follow the basic ground rules for successful life planning and remember that your plan must be holistic, you will eventually make the necessary transitions.

The final step, after drawing up preliminary life plans in the major areas of your life, is to integrate them into one interdependent composition. You might even sit down and write a contract with your partner regarding all that you have decided. When you took your marriage vows you entered into a contract (i.e., "for better and for worse"). Why then should you not have a contract as a business partner and parent? Include in your contract your personal goals as well and how you will assist your partner in accomplishing his or hers. The contract can be flexible. It can be modified from time to time as the need requires. Include plans for how to modify the contract. Perhaps review the contract annually to see if you are still on track.

Your final plan for life will also require the advice of professionals. How your personal life affects the business and how the business affects your personal life have ramifications legally and financially. Do not be afraid to ask your life partner to meet with you and a professional. The contract may not be formally recorded at the courthouse, but it can still include the wisdom of your attorney and accountant. As well, you may also want to have more formal agreements such as pre- or postnuptial agreements, partnership agreements, trusts, and so on. All of this will be determined by what you have discovered about yourself and your spouse as you developed your life plan.

Ultimately, most entrepreneurial couples discover at least one basic value that has guided them throughout life and continues to guide them in their marriage and business venture. With this planning work completed, you may be more aware of what that guiding principle is for you. For Frank and Louise, it took the form of health, loving relationships, and spiritual growth *first*. For Don and Marla it was the awareness that "whatever I do is for the benefit of the family as a whole." For Marty and Gisela, it was to never settle for second-best. For Jonathan and Brooke, it was to preserve independence while still operating as a team.

Look for that basic value or guiding principle among the plans you have developed. Make it your *mission statement* for your entrepreneurial business. Frame it and hang it over your desk at work or over the mantle at home. Try it on for a few weeks and see how it fits. If it needs some modification, modify it until you get it just right. If you find that your mission has been to win at all costs, to make money but not have fun, to cooperate and avoid conflict, or some other compromising attitude, these are not healthy basic values. These are mistakes you have made by living unconsciously. Now that you are more conscious of who you and your partner really are, live your life as if you have been given a second chance—and do it right this time!

# Equality or Equity: How to Find Fairness in Your Partnership

Trish and Kurt are an example of an *egalitarian* couple. They each have a career that they are committed to, and decisions regarding work and family are made jointly. They consider themselves equal partners in everything. Ted and Charlene, on the other hand, are a more *traditional* couple. Even though Charlene actually started their very successful real estate sales and investment business, she defers to her husband's judgment on most major business decisions. These are only two of many possible relationship styles. Just as we learned in Chapter One that there are many permutations of entrepreneurial styles among couples, there are also many permutations along *the continuum from traditional to egalitarian entrepreneurial couples.*

This continuum is defined by research with entrepreneurial couples that explores marital satisfaction, role conflict, stress, work/home boundaries, and sex-role orientation. *Sex-role orientation* refers to your perception of yourself in relation to your gender. We tend to see sex-role orientation played out in the way couples divide household and work responsibilities or in how they adjust to having the boundaries of work and home intersect.

In this chapter, I will interweave a discussion of my own and others' research on these topics with case examples. You will discover just where you and your spouse fall on the continuum from traditional to egalitarian relationships. You will be able to compare yourselves to other couples along that continuum and learn from their trials and triumphs. I will discuss some of the differences between men and women as popularized lately in the literature. But it is important not to make too much of these differences. It is more important to be sure you are paired well with your partner. For example, it would be difficult for an egalitarian wife such as Trish to quit her career altogether, just as it would be a strain for Charlene to assume shared leadership in her marriage of fifty years and begin making decisions jointly with her husband.

Much of this chapter is taken from my own research comparing dual-career couples to copreneurial couples. Bear with me as I review my research data. The changes you and your spouse are considering that drew you to this book may require more theoretical foundation than most self-help books. While practicing a few simple techniques may improve some marital communication, understanding your nature on a deeper level separates *superficial* from *meaningful change.* By reading this chapter carefully, you will gain a better understanding of your place on the continuum from traditional to egalitarian entrepreneurial couples.

I should clarify that in my study I compared *dual-career couples who did not work together full-time* (which included self-employed dual entrepreneurs, solo entrepreneurs with a supportive spouse who was employed full-time at a career, and dual-career couples who were not self-employed) *with copreneurial couples* (i.e., those couples who share ownership, commitment, and responsibility for an enterprise). Furthermore, all of the study participants were working full-time, so I have no data on supportive spouses who are homemakers or part-time employees. In other words, the major distinction between the two groups in my study is whether the members of the couple worked *together* full-time, as with the copreneurs, or separately full-time, as with dual entrepreneurs, solo entrepreneurs, and employed dual-career couples.

As a result of separating out only copreneurial couples, the results of my study do give a distinctive picture of copreneurs. However, because the other entrepreneurial couples are grouped together and included with dual-career couples who are not self-employed, it is difficult to draw conclusions from my study for each entrepreneurial couple subgroup specifically. This process is characteristic of the scientific method in that it allows the researcher to study one small piece at a time. Future research will separate out the different styles of entrepreneurial couples to see how they compare with each other.

Furthermore, because I was the first to begin this line of research, my results need to be interpreted carefully. The conclusions I present in this chapter are specific to copreneurs first. Some generalizations can be drawn to the other entrepreneurial couple subgroups, but these generalizations are also based on my professional experience with individual participants in the study. I will try to be clear from where I am drawing the facts to support my conclusions.

## Identity Crisis, Identity Transformation

In Chapter Two, I discussed dialectical psychology, the system of psychology underpinning this book. Klaus Riegel, the founder of *dialectical psychology,* proposes that the only way to understand a human being is to see him or her as a "changing individual in a changing world." For example, who has not heard of the "midlife crisis"? If you have not been there yet yourself, you certainly know of people who seemed to change right before your eyes. The crisis or transformation that is occurring during this stage of life involves reevaluating one's life and mission. Those pursuits or accomplishments that seemed so important in one's twenties and thirties are no longer challenging or appealing. The forty-year-old asks himself or herself, "Is this all there is?" People at forty are looking for new ways to make or find meaning in their lives because they want to make the most of the second half of their life.

The forties transition or midlife crisis is an example of developing progressions interacting to produce conflict, confusion, change, reorganization, and growth. Some of the developing progressions that can touch one person include his or her own developmental timetable, the development of his or her spouse or partner and children, and the development of an entrepreneurial enterprise. As these developing progressions interact, the dialogue changes everyone involved. And as the world of developing progressions changes, the forty-year-old must change also.

Entrepreneurial couples are in the position of trying to develop a couple identity that includes the developing progressions of two individuals as well as the developing progressions of their marriage, family, and business(es). In order to accomplish this tremendous task, entrepreneurial couples look to the models they grew up with, such as their parents' style of marriage, religious precepts, the examples of teachers and friends, even lessons learned from television. However, since most Americans are socialized to hold beliefs, meanings, and values about marriage and work that are more consistent with the traditional marriage (i.e., the nuclear family, where the father works outside the home and the mother nurtures the family), attempting an entrepreneurial couple style automatically puts such couples into an incongruous situation. To further complicate things, there is a two-level hierarchy between the entrepreneurial couple and society, which suggests that no matter what unique shared beliefs, values, and meanings a particular couple evolves, they will still be subordinate to the beliefs, values, and meanings of the larger society.

Ted and Charlene, for example, are unwilling to challenge the larger society. In spite of the fact that Charlene is the company founder and has the expertise in real estate (as well as the entrepreneurial spirit), she sees Ted as the leader. Trish and Kurt, however, chose to challenge the status quo when Trish refused to follow Kurt to his last promotion. This refusal took a huge psychological toll on the couple as they spent months renegotiating the terms of their marriage and eventual business partnership. There were times when Trish and Kurt thought divorce would have been easier than resisting the pressure of family and friends. Kurt feared that he looked weak to others for giving in to Trish's needs, while Trish feared that she appeared too aggressive for a woman in insisting that her needs be met. In other words, Trish and Kurt had little outside support for their decision to evolve an egalitarian style.

Much is being written these days about gender differences. One best-selling author, John Gray, suggests that men and women are just different, plain and simple. He contends that if we would honor those differences, there would be much less conflict. Certainly, this latter proposition makes a great deal of sense, but I would put a new spin on it. That is, *individuals* are different. Therefore, it is important to notice differences in light of the uniqueness of each individual. If you pigeonhole a person because of gender you may miss qualities that do not fit with the stereotype, but that could be very useful in enhancing the marriage and the business. While it is true that we are strongly influenced by our culture, there are some couples out there who are challenging the system and winning. Although they are in the minority, perhaps they are creating new cultural models for future generations to follow.

In sum, our identities (e.g., individual and marital) are formed by a combination of innate tendencies, culture, parenting, and other environmental influences. However, these identities are not stable—times change, people change, marriages change, and the marketplace changes—because development is constant. The conflicts that ensue from these changes and interacting developing progressions are what propel us from an identity *crisis* to our next identity *transformation*. Ted and Charlene have no need to change from their traditional style of marriage, but should they experience a crisis such as that faced by Kurt and Trish, they may find themselves questioning whether their current relationship and partnership identities still work.

## Sex-Role Orientation

As a result of identity crisis and identity transformation, we each develop a sense of self that we tend to live with for a while, and that can actually be measured on psychological instruments. In my 1994 study I used the *Personal Attributes Questionnaire*, developed in 1978 by Spence and Helmreich, to measure sex-role orientation, and the *Work-Home Identity Scale*, developed by Friedlander in 1990, to measure a person's self-concept at work as compared to his or her self-concept at home. I wanted to see the influence of culture on entrepreneurial couples. And I wanted to see if those couples who were challenging the traditional style of marriage and business partnership had a different sex-role orientation and sense of self from those couples who were adhering to the status quo.

The *Personal Attributes Questionnaire*, or *PAQ*, measures sex-role orientation. This instrument provides independent assessments of masculinity and femininity in terms of an individual's self-perceived possession of personality traits stereotypically believed to differentiate the sexes but considered socially desirable in both sexes. It also provides an assessment of masculinity versus femininity in terms of the individual's self-perceived possession of personality traits stereotypically believed to differentiate the sexes but considered more socially desirable for one sex than for the other. Another attribute of the PAQ is that it is a two-dimensional test of masculinity and femininity, thus supporting the notion that, to some degree, men and women each possess *both* masculine and feminine traits. Finally, the traits measured are not *global* masculinity or femininity but, rather, self-assertive/instrumental traits and interpersonal/expressive traits, which are more relevant to how husbands and wives live and work together. Self-Assessment Exercise 6 is a simplified version of the PAQ I used in my study.

I discovered clear differences between the two groups in my study, copreneurs and dual-career couples (i.e., all other full-time self-employed entrepreneurial couples, and dual-career employed couples). Copreneurial wives adhere to a very traditional *feminine sex-role orientation,* while their husbands demonstrate a more traditional *masculine sex-role orientation.* The dual-career couples, however, are more evenly matched in terms of sex-role orientation. That is, instead of scoring at the extremes of masculine or feminine traits, husbands and wives in dual-career couples score highly on *both* masculine and feminine traits. This style is known as an *androgynous sex-role orientation.* (*Androgynous* sounds as if it might mean *asexual* but really has nothing to do with sex. Rather, it means that an individual has developed traits from both sides of the masculinity/femininity personality continuum. Among career-minded couples in which both husband and wife are committed to meaningful careers, it is not surprising that they both score highly androgynous.)

In terms of the qualities that distinguish sex-role orientation, the copreneurial wives demonstrate more of the interpersonal/expressive traits stereotypically attributed to females, such as emotionality, submissiveness, excitability in a crisis, ability to devote oneself to others, gentleness, helpfulness, kindness, home orientation, needing others' approval, having easily hurt feelings, being aware of others' feelings, crying easily, understanding others, warmth, and having a strong need for security. The copreneurial husbands score the opposite of their wives on the PAQ,

## Your Sex-Role Orientation

From the following three columns of words, check the ones that best describe your personality. Check only those words that describe you *most* of the time, not the words that describe you only sometimes. For example, if you are cool in a crisis most of the time, but once in a while excitable in a crisis, check only the first description. However, if the words or terms from the first two columns really do apply equally, check "Both."

| | | |
|---|---|---|
| Aggressive ____ | Passive ____ | Both ____ |
| Independent ____ | Dependent ____ | Both ____ |
| Unemotional ____ | Emotional ____ | Both ____ |
| Dominant ____ | Submissive ____ | Both ____ |
| Cool in a crisis ____ | Excitable in a crisis ____ | Both ____ |
| Active ____ | Kind ____ | Both ____ |
| Rough ____ | Gentle ____ | Both ____ |
| Competitive ____ | Noncompetitive ____ | Both ____ |
| Worldly ____ | Home oriented ____ | Both ____ |
| Decision maker ____ | Helpful ____ | Both ____ |
| Tenacious ____ | Understanding ____ | Both ____ |
| Stoic ____ | Strong need for security ____ | Both ____ |
| Self-confident ____ | Need approval ____ | Both ____ |
| Superior ____ | Inferior ____ | Both ____ |

## SELF-ASSESSMENT EXERCISE 6 (CONT'D)

| | | | | | |
|---|---|---|---|---|---|
| Reserved | _____ | Warm | _____ | Both | _____ |
| Stress-resistant | _____ | Low stress tolerance | _____ | Both | _____ |
| Selfish | _____ | Selfless | _____ | Both | _____ |
| Feelings seldom hurt | _____ | Feelings easily hurt | _____ | Both | _____ |
| Totals: | _____ | | _____ | | _____ |

## Evaluating Your Responses

Although this exercise is not scientific, it is loosely based on the instrument I used in my study and asks about the traits or qualities stereotypically associated with masculinity and femininity. Tally your responses from each column. The more qualities you have from column one, the more masculine your orientation. The more qualities you have from column two, the more feminine your orientation. The more qualities you have from column three, the more androgynous is your sex-role orientation.

## Summarizing Remark

Note whether you are predominantly masculine, feminine, or androgynous in your orientation. What is your partner?

with such self-assertive/instrumental traits as aggressiveness, dominance, not at all excitable in a major crisis, worldliness, indifference to others' approval, not having easily hurt feelings, crying rarely, and having very little need for security.

The husbands and wives in dual-career couples, by comparison, fall somewhere in between the extremes of the feminine copreneurial wives and the masculine copreneurial husbands. They rate themselves highly (wives slightly higher than their husbands) on desirable feminine traits such as being emotional, gentle, helpful, aware of others' feelings, and so on. And they rate themselves highly (husbands slightly higher than their wives) on desirable masculine traits such as independence, activeness, competitiveness, making decisions easily, self-confidence, and so on. On those polar attributes that are stereotypically believed to differentiate the sexes and considered more socially desirable for one sex than for the other, such as submissiveness/dominance, never cries easily/cries easily, needs security/has little need for security, or home-orientation/worldliness, wives and husbands in dual career couples fall somewhere in the middle. Therefore, in this sample husbands in dual-career couples are androgynous with a tendency toward the masculine stereotype, while wives in dual-career couples are androgynous with a tendency toward the feminine stereotype.

How these results on sex-role orientation play themselves out in real life can be seen in the couples I describe in this book. Copreneurs Howard and Andrea, for example, represent the traditional orientation. With two generations now working in their chain of hardware stores, Andrea and her daughter assume classic feminine roles. They are helpful and supportive of Howard's leadership, but they themselves play minor roles in the business so that, as Andrea puts it, "I can showcase my husband's talent." In other words, she has no desire for an androgynous, egalitarian role. Rick and Chris, on the other hand, are an androgynous couple who have great respect for each others' business sense and share active leadership of their restaurant chain. As the third generation in their family-held business, perhaps they have expanded on the models of Rick's father and grandfather to evolve a more egalitarian style than either grew up with. Even though they are copreneurs, Rick and Chris more resemble the sex-role orientations demonstrated by dual-career couples.

## Work/Home Self-Concept

Self-concept is another useful way to distinguish entrepreneurial couples along the continuum from traditional to egalitarian. Self-concept is not limited to sex-role orientation but includes attributes that can be true of anyone, male or female. Just as with sex-role orientation, I was interested in my own research in discerning whether self-concept at work and at home is related to cultural norms or lifestyle choices, and if these relationships could accurately identify or predict entrepreneurial styles.

In my study I used Friedlander's *Work-Home Identity Scale*, or *WHIS*, to measure self-concept. The WHIS provides a rating of participants' self-concept when they are at work and when they are at home. The scale consists of a list of bipolar adjective pairs addressing concepts of energy level (e.g., relaxed/focused), sociability (e.g., leader/follower), and activity level (e.g., active/passive). The self-administered instrument is taken twice, once to describe the participant's self-concept at work, and the second time to describe his or her self-concept at home. Thus, this scale measures the participant's psychological *transition* from the work domain to the home domain. Self-Assessment Exercise 7 is a simplified version of the WHIS I used in my study.

My analysis of self-concepts and how they change when participants move from the domain of work to the domain of home reveals different patterns for copreneurs and dual-career couples. Whereas copreneurial husbands and both husbands and wives in dual-career couples move into a *leadership* self-concept at work, copreneurial wives do not change much on this factor. Rather than experiencing themselves as leaders at work, copreneurial wives perceive that they *share responsibilities* with their husbands. At home, copreneurial husbands retain some of their leadership role, while their wives assume full responsibility for the home front. Husbands and wives in dual-career couples, on the other hand, have similar self-concepts to each other and similar shifts in self-concept from home to work. While at work they are both leaders; when they return home, they relinquish some leadership and see themselves as *social partners,* each shouldering an equal amount of responsibility for the home front.

As you can see, self-concept is linked with certain entrepreneurial styles. In addition to administering the WHIS, I also interviewed many of my study participants and had them fill out a lengthy questionnaire, the results of which also support the findings of the WHIS. For example, when asked what was their formal title in the business, copreneurial husbands would state "owner," "president," even "co-owner." Their wives, on the other hand, would state their title as "secretary," "bookkeeper," or "treasurer." (I was particularly curious about the responses I would get from Charlene and Ted, since Charlene founded their business of real estate sales, investments, and property management. True to their traditional roots, Ted announced that he was "vice president" and Charlene stated her position as "sales associate," again deferring to her husband's authority, even though she is the true president and founder of the company.)

Furthermore, among the dual-career couples in my sample who do not work together, many exclaimed that working with their spouse would be the last thing they would want to do, fearing that their competitive spirits would destroy the marriage. Even though in my study I have combined self-employed and employed dual-career couples and compared them to copreneurs, it seems that the basic fact

## Your Work/Home Self-Concept

Get two pens, one with red ink and the other with black ink. From the following list of word pairs, circle the words that most describe you *at work* in black, and then those that most describe you *at home* in red. It is okay to circle the same word with both black and red ink if that is your self-concept both at work and at home. Remember to circle the word that *most* describes you, not the word that describes you only sometimes. It is highly unlikely that anyone is *always* formal at work or *always* ineffective at home, for example, but if these are your tendencies, circle those words.

| | |
|---|---|
| **Formal/Informal** | **Participative/Autocratic** |
| **Active/Passive** | **Producing/Developing** |
| **Leader/Follower** | **Demanding/Allowing** |
| **Powerful/Powerless** | **Directive/Nondirective** |
| **Contribute/Receive** | **Unemotional/Emotional** |
| **Impatient/Patient** | **Extrovert/Introvert** |
| **Task-oriented/Person-oriented** | **Confrontive/Supportive** |
| **Relaxed/Tense** | **Advising/Directing** |
| **Covert/Overt** | **Relaxed/Focused** |
| **Collegial/Hierarchical** | **Unilateral/Bilateral*** |
| **Serious/Fun** | |

*Bilateral* means that you share duties and responsibilities with your partner, whereas *unilateral* means that you handle the duties and responsibilities yourself.

## SELF-ASSESSMENT EXERCISE 7 (CONT'D)

Next, list the word pairs where you *changed* from work to home. That is, if you circled "Focused" in black ink but "Relaxed" in red ink, then list that word pair below.

Finally, compare the word pairs where you changed with those of the participants in my study.

1. If you changed from black to red on the following word pairs (the first term in each pair being black), you more resemble the *copreneurial husbands* in my study:

   Formal / Informal               Active / Passive

   Producing / Developing          Leader / Follower

   Demanding / Allowing            Powerful / Powerless

   Contribute / Receive            Impatient / Patient

   Directive / Nondirective        Tense / Relaxed

   Extrovert / Introvert           Serious / Fun

   Focused / Relaxed

2. If you changed from black to red on the following word pairs (the first term in each pair being black), you more resemble the *copreneurial wives* in my study:

   Formal / Informal               Tense / Relaxed

   Advising / Directing            Focused / Relaxed

   Bilateral / Unilateral          Serious / Fun

103

3. If you changed from black to red on the following word pairs (the first term in each pair being black), you more resemble the *husbands* in *dual-career couples* in my study:

| | |
|---|---|
| Formal/Informal | Active/Passive |
| Leader/Follower | Contribute/Receive |
| Unemotional/Emotional | Task-oriented/Person-oriented |
| Extrovert/Introvert | Tense/Relaxed |
| Focused/Relaxed | Serious/Fun |

4. If you changed from black to red on the following word pairs (the first term in each pair being black), you more resemble the *wives* in *dual-career couples* in my study:

| | |
|---|---|
| Formal/Informal | Active /Passive |
| Leader/Follower | Powerful/Powerless |
| Tense/Relaxed | Focused/Relaxed |
| Unilateral/Bilateral | Serious/Fun |

## Evaluating Your Responses

Again, this exercise is not scientific, but the variables it asks about are similar to those used in my study. Of course, you may not resemble any of the four types in my study. Remember, these are statistical averages, so you may be one of the exceptions to the rule that got swallowed up in the averaging process. For example you may look like a leader at work but more like a copreneurial wife at home. Or perhaps you do not consider yourself a leader at all because your company consists of only you, but you do

### Evaluating Your Responses (cont'd)

not resemble a copreneurial wife at work either. Nevertheless, even if you do not score identically to one of the four types, you probably look similar to one of them. Look for a pattern or dominant theme.

### Summarizing Remark

In a nutshell, how would you say your self-concept changes from work to home?

of working together full-time distinguishes copreneurs from other entrepreneurial couples with regard to work/home self-concept. In other words, work/home self-concept is a powerful factor in defining our identities within an entrepreneurial relationship.

## Role Conflict

By now perhaps you are getting a feel for where you and your spouse fit on the continuum from traditional to egalitarian entrepreneurial relationships. However, as interesting as classification systems are, they are somewhat simple and restrictive. The truth is that we are changing individuals in a changing world. No one pattern will be right for you throughout your lifetime. Anton and Carrie are a case in point.

Anton and Carrie came into their marriage each having experienced successful entrepreneurship. Only Carrie, however, had experience being a supportive spouse to a solo entrepreneur. Even though she had loved her first husband dearly and was happy being his supportive spouse, she had changed. In her marriage to Anton, she more resembled the androgynous wife in a dual-career couple than the traditional feminine wife she had been in her first marriage. She brought a successful business into the partnership and expected to share leadership with Anton of their joint venture. However, this caused great stress and confusion for Anton, who wanted to continue operating as a solo entrepreneur with a supportive spouse.

While Anton assumed the dominant cultural male role—a masculine sex-role orientation and a leadership self-concept—Carrie had moved away from the dominant cultural female role to embrace a more androgynous sex-role orientation and a leadership self-concept of her own. The conflict ensued when this couple was faced with accepting each other's style. Anton struggled with crossing traditional sex-role boundaries. While he could appreciate his new wife's determination to continue her leadership role, he was frightened of the changes this would require in him. Researchers Rapoport and Rapoport refer to this resistance to crossing the boundaries of culturally sanctioned sex-role attitudes, behaviors, and expectations as the *identity tension line*. If Anton wants to share business partnership and marriage with Carrie in a more egalitarian style, he must go against his social conditioning and cross that identity tension line.

Carol found herself in a different predicament with regard to the identity tension line. She did not recognize herself as the entrepreneurial spirit in her marriage even though she had founded the nursery and garden supply center. She included her husband, Bob, in all planning and decision making. However, when Bob began to avoid business responsibilities and spend most of his day on the golf course, Carol had to examine the situation in more depth. What she realized is that the business was a result of *her* vision and leadership, not his—and not even theirs. She did not have to deny her feminine spirit to also acknowledge her leadership abilities. But the major conflict for Carol was acknowledging that Bob did not fit the dominant cultural role for a man. He was *not* a leader, and he was more than content to support his wife in her entrepreneurial venture. Carol found that she had married not a strong, fearless, aggressive husband who would protect her, but a sweet, gentle, supportive soul who would follow her anywhere. For Bob and Carol, crossing the identity tension line meant accepting a role reversal from the traditional norms.

These kinds of *role conflicts* are common for entrepreneurial couples, as many of you already know. You have struggled with redefining your roles—some of you successfully, while others are still in the process. Rather than be distraught over these conflicts, view them as part of the requirement for successful evolution as a person, a spouse, and a business partner. For example, my research shows that wives in dual-career couples who are not involved in a copreneurial venture lead the pack when it comes to androgyny. Though their husbands scored androgynous as well, these wives scored significantly higher. And their androgynous nature is undoubtedly rocking the boat in their intimate relationships.

Furthermore, widows, such as Carrie, who had been a supportive spouse before the death of their husband, prefer to take over the business as a solo entrepreneur rather than sell it or turn it over to other family members. Therefore, it appears that sex-role orientation *may change as circumstances change*, and the developing progression appears to be *toward androgyny*. This conclusion is supported by dialectical psychology, in which Riegel predicted that as there evolves more synchrony between the developing progressions of men and women, there will also evolve more equality.

# Putting Sex-Role Orientation and Self-Concept into Action

Another way to look at sex-role orientation and self-concept is to see them as the *beliefs* we have about ourselves. And these beliefs are not hardwired but are mutable programs. That is why we see transformation in individuals and couples such as the ones described in this book. Human beings demonstrate their beliefs about themselves by behaving in certain ways (i.e., their chosen lifestyle), such as unique dress, choice of profession, choice of marriage partner, style of house they live in, and so on. Among the participants in my study, I was interested in exploring how they demonstrated their beliefs (i.e., sex-role orientation and self-concept) by their decisions on how to assign *household responsibilities* and *work responsibilities.* Therefore, I asked them to fill out questionnaires identifying which spouse handled which household or work task. See Self-Assessment Exercises 8 and 9.

True to their beliefs about themselves, my study participants divided household and work responsibilities in alignment with their self-concept and sex-role orientation. The division of household responsibilities is fairly traditional among copreneurs, as their traditional sex-role orientation would suggest. Copreneurial husbands are responsible for small repairs and car maintenance, while copreneurial wives are responsible for washing dishes, shopping for food, doing laundry, cooking or preparing lunch and dinner, and general housekeeping. Although washing dishes and cooking or preparing breakfast are primarily the responsibility of the copreneurial wife, about one-third of the copreneurs reported that husbands are

# How You Divide Household Responsibilities

Complete the following questionnaire to determine if your division of household responsibilities more resembles that of dual-career couples or copreneurs. Circle the appropriate answer. Remember to circle the answer that most resembles your situation. For example, if the husband usually washes the dishes, circle "Husband." However, if you typically share the task, circle "Both."

| | | | |
|---|---|---|---|
| Who washes the dishes? | Husband | Wife | Both |
| Who shops for food? | Husband | Wife | Both |
| Who does the laundry? | Husband | Wife | Both |
| Who cooks or prepares breakfast? | Husband | Wife | Both |
| Who cooks or prepares lunch? | Husband | Wife | Both |
| Who cooks or prepares dinner? | Husband | Wife | Both |
| Who does the yard work? | Husband | Wife | Both |
| Who makes small household repairs? | Husband | Wife | Both |
| Who does the general housework? | Husband | Wife | Both |
| Who handles car maintenance? | Husband | Wife | Both |
| Who chauffeurs the children? | Husband | Wife | Both |
| Who supervises the children's homework? | Husband | Wife | Both |
| Who plays with the children? | Husband | Wife | Both |

## Evaluating Your Responses

Are household responsibilities fairly evenly distributed, as for most dual-career couples? Or are they assumed mostly by the wife, as for most copreneurial couples?

## Summarizing Remark

Note how it is and what you want to change.

# How You Divide Work-Related Responsibilities

Complete the following questionnaire to determine if your division of work-related responsibilities more resembles that of dual-career couples or copreneurs. Circle the answer that most closely resembles your situation. For example, if the husband usually handles customer service, circle "Husband." If you typically share the task, circle "Both."

| | | | |
|---|---|---|---|
| Who is responsible for bookkeeping, billing and collection, and payroll? | Husband | Wife | Both |
| Who is responsible for front office and secretarial functions? | Husband | Wife | Both |
| Who is responsible for budget planning? | Husband | Wife | Both |
| Who is responsible for business and market planning? | Husband | Wife | Both |
| Who handles customer service? | Husband | Wife | Both |
| Who handles sales? | Husband | Wife | Both |
| Who supervises employees? | Husband | Wife | Both |
| Who is responsible for quality control? | Husband | Wife | Both |
| Who makes major purchasing decisions? | Husband | Wife | Both |
| Who is responsible for building maintenance? | Husband | Wife | Both |
| Who handles stocking and shipping? | Husband | Wife | Both |
| Who maintains equipment? | Husband | Wife | Both |
| Who is responsible for product development? | Husband | Wife | Both |
| Who handles contract negotiation? | Husband | Wife | Both |
| Who manages paraprofessional services? | Husband | Wife | Both |
| Who manages professional services? | Husband | Wife | Both |

## Evaluating Your Responses

Are work-related responsibilities divided along traditional gender lines as for most copreneurial couples? Or are they distributed between husband and wife according to who is best suited to the task?

## Summarizing Remark

Note how it is and what you want to change.

sharing responsibility for these tasks. Yard work is as often shared as it is a husband's or a wife's task, indicating that this responsibility may be assigned according to preference or ability, or it is shared equally.

Among dual-career couples (including those entrepreneurial couples who do not work together full-time) there is a tendency to follow traditional sex roles, but the bulk of the household tasks are shared. Husbands still handle small repairs and car maintenance, while wives do the laundry and cook dinner. However, while there are still more wives than husbands in dual-career couples who handle shopping for food, cooking or preparing lunch, and general housekeeping, there are more dual-career couples who *share* responsibility for these tasks. Yard work is a task handled either by the husbands in dual-career couples or by both. Washing dishes and cooking or preparing breakfast are tasks equally likely to be handled by the husband, the wife, or both. Therefore, more household responsibilities for dual-career couples are either shared or assigned according to preference or ability than is the case among copreneurial couples.

With regard to work responsibilities, I have data only on the division of tasks *among copreneurs* since they were the only group in my study who work together full-time. One cannot draw any conclusions about how the division of tasks would be accomplished for the other dual-career couples should they decide to work together full-time. Nevertheless, it is not surprising that among copreneurs the division

110

of work responsibilities is decided along traditional sex-role and self-concept lines, just as the home responsibilities were. The copreneurial husbands are primarily responsible for building maintenance, equipment maintenance, and contract negotiations. The copreneurial wives are primarily responsible for bookkeeping, accounting, secretarial, payroll, and billing and collections. There are some tasks that, while still primarily the responsibility of the husbands, are beginning to shift to being shared by husbands and wives: budget planning, business planning, sales, marketing, employee supervision, and professional services. However, there are *no* responsibilities that are shifting from the responsibility of the wives to being shared by both husbands and wives. Finally, in the last category are those responsibilities that are either shared by husbands and wives or are assigned according to preference or ability: customer service, quality control, computers, and purchasing.

These data indicate that copreneurs tend to adhere to traditional sex-role orientations and self-concepts in both belief and action. The dual-career entrepreneurial couples, however, are shifting to a more egalitarian style. So, what is there about working together (i.e., being copreneurs) that slows the developing progression of synchrony between the sexes, such that household responsibilities and work responsibilities are divided along traditional gender lines instead of being shared equally or assigned according to skill and talent? The answer to this question lies in the *stress of crossing* both the identity tension line and the boundaries between love and work.

## Transition Stress

*Transition stress* refers to the physical and psychological stress incurred by a person as a result of transitioning from home to work and back again. We all experience the stress of adjusting our minds and bodies to the workplace and then readjusting them to our home environments at the end of the day. Indeed, sometimes these adjustments come hourly as we take personal phone calls at work and work phone calls at home. And we have all had trying days when we could not keep our minds on our work because we had a pressing personal problem. We all know what it feels like to have thoughts of work intrude on Sunday evening as we mentally prepare for the next day. Likewise, there is not one parent among you who hasn't been interrupted in a meeting by a call from the baby-sitter or school nurse.

For entrepreneurial couples, this transition stress interacts with the stress of crossing the identity tension line, especially among copreneurs. In my study I was curious about the level of stress entrepreneurial couples experience at different transition times of the day, such as in the morning before leaving for work, at midday, as the workday closed, or on the commute home. Interestingly, my sample reported very little stress from these transition times. However, two groups of people do report high stress in the morning before leaving for work, and they report stress significantly greater than their spouses. These two groups of people are copreneurial wives and husbands in dual-career couples. In both cases, the explanation seems to be *the interaction* of transition stress and crossing the identity tension line.

If you recall, copreneurial wives are busy handling all of the household responsibilities in the morning as they prepare to leave for work. Their husbands are out the door and off to work with a cup of coffee in hand. While Mike's morning routine was "Shower, coffee, go!" Karla's morning involved not only making the coffee but caring for the children and arranging the household affairs before she could leave for the office at the couple's manufacturing plant. So for Karla, as for most copreneurial wives, there is considerable transition stress in the morning as she prepares for work, whereas her husband reports little or no stress at this time.

Another stress for copreneurial wives is the stress of crossing the identity tension line. As wives with a feminine sex-role orientation and a traditional female self-concept, copreneurial wives probably find it hard to leave the environment they prefer, the home, to venture out into the business world. They are willing to do so because part of their self-concept is care and support of the family, but working full-time is not their preferred mode. Remember that Andrea's goal in copreneuring is to "showcase" her husband's talents, not necessarily to develop a thriving enterprise for her own benefit.

The copreneurial husbands are feeling little or no transition stress as a result of crossing the identity tension line, since in fact they are not crossing that line. For the copreneurial husband work is life. In my study, these husbands worked an average of sixty hours a week, as compared to their wives who worked an average of forty-nine hours a week. This sixty hours was significantly higher than the number of hours worked by any other group in my study (husbands in dual-career couples worked an average of forty-seven hours a week, and their wives worked an average of forty-four hours a week). In other words, to avoid the stress of crossing the identity tension line, and to avoid the stress of transitioning between work and home, copreneurial husbands *overwork*.

Husbands in dual-career couples (including dual entrepreneurs and solo entrepreneurs) experience as much stress in the morning as do copreneurial wives, which is a surprising finding to some. Yet the explanation becomes clear when comparing these husbands to their wives. As androgynous men, they are committed to equality in their relationships with their wives, which means that *they* may be making the coffee in the morning. However, their wives are significantly more androgynous than they are, which means that these men are still experiencing the stress of crossing the identity tension line to help their wives with household routines. Furthermore, the morning routine is probably hectic and demanding, requiring the skills of an experienced homemaker or *housewife*, something most adult males in our culture received little or no training in when they were boys. So it is likely that these husbands in dual-career couples are experiencing the stress of having work on their minds but being unable to leave for work until the household is in order.

The wives in dual-career couples, just like the copreneurial husbands, report little stress at this time of the morning. Considering their highly androgynous sex-role orientation, it is likely that they are comfortable with their multiple roles as partner, leader, homemaker, and career woman. They are not experiencing stress as a result of crossing the identity tension line, since they probably crossed that line years ago when they went to college or started their entrepreneurial venture. And they are not experiencing transition stress because they have a partner who shares in the maintenance of the household, so they are more able to strike a balance between the demands of work and the demands of home. Unlike the copreneurial husbands, who *increase* their stereotypically male behavior by working more hours to avoid these transition stresses, the wives in dual-career couples who are not copreneurs seem to have *transcended* stress by renegotiating the traditional roles.

## Which Is Better, Egalitarian or Traditional?

Looking at relationships, whether personal or professional, in a black-and-white manner is not very useful. There is not one right style for everyone, nor one right style for a lifetime. Because development is constant, change is constant. While I do believe that the egalitarian style is the result of a natural evolution of developing progressions between men and women, it may also be that we revisit a more traditional style from time to time as we mature. For example, couples with young children may relinquish the egalitarian style in order to accommodate the needs of the children for a full-time stay-at-home mom (or dad). Conversely, retired couples may try an egalitarian style for the first time when they start a home business, because they are no longer hemmed in by corporate demands (such as work schedules and out-of-state transfers). Adult development is not like early childhood development, when six-year molars predictably grow in at the age of six or seven.

Adult development is more holistic and less predictable. There are certain stages we must pass through, but when and how often is up to the individual in synchrony with the developing progressions of significant others.

Still, I was curious about whether the entrepreneurial couples in my study were *satisfied* with their current lifestyle, whether it was traditional or egalitarian. With copreneurs I assessed their satisfaction with their partnership in both the home domain and the work domain since they share these arenas full-time with their spouse. For the other entrepreneurial couples, I looked only at marital satisfaction. (As with most research, there are limitations. In order to reduce confounding variables and to make the results easier to interpret, I used only long-term married couples in my study. However, if you are not married to your partner, the results may still apply.)

While the division of household and child-care responsibilities is a measure of which spouse actually *handles* certain responsibilities, *marital equity* is a measure of how *satisfied* each spouse is with the division of responsibilities. The marital equity measure was determined by having all participants rate themselves on the *actual* amount of responsibility they have versus the *ideal* amount of responsibility they would like in seven specific areas: (1) control in decision making, (2) household money management, (3) personal investment management, (4) housekeeping responsibilities, (5) child-care responsibilities, (6) arrangements for leisure activities, and (7) balance of household responsibilities. Self-Assessment Exercise 10 is a simplified version of my study questionnaire on this topic. The findings reveal that for all couples in my study there is a great deal of satisfaction with the division of household and child-care responsibilities, even though the actual division of household responsibilities is quite disparate for copreneurs. That is, even among copreneurs where the division of household responsibilities is *not* equal, the participants consider it to be fair and reasonable.

I used a similar method for measuring how satisfied copreneurs were with their current division of work responsibilities. While the division of work responsibilities is a measure of which spouse actually *handles* certain responsibilities, *business partnership equity* is a measure of how *satisfied* each spouse is with the division of responsibilities. The business partnership equity measure was determined by having all participants rate themselves on the *actual* amount of responsibility they have versus the *ideal* amount of responsibility they would like in seven specific areas: (1) control in decision making, (2) day-to-day operations, (3) financial management, (4) investment management, (5) product/service development, (6) personnel management, and (7) balance of work responsibilities. Self-Assessment Exercise 11 is a simplified version of my study questionnaire on this topic.

## SELF-ASSESSMENT EXERCISE 10

# Your Satisfaction with the Division of Household Responsibilities in Your Marriage/Personal Relationship

The following is a list of responsibilities that are common in running a household. For each area of responsibility, circle whether you are "Satisfied" or "Dissatisfied" with the arrangement you and your spouse have made with regard to who is responsible for each item.

| | | |
|---|---|---|
| 1. Control in decision making | Satisfied | Dissatisfied |
| 2. Household money management | Satisfied | Dissatisfied |
| 3. Personal investment management | Satisfied | Dissatisfied |
| 4. Housekeeping responsibilities | Satisfied | Dissatisfied |
| 5. Child-care responsibilities | Satisfied | Dissatisfied |
| 6. Arrangements for leisure activities | Satisfied | Dissatisfied |
| 7. Balance of household responsibilities | Satisfied | Dissatisfied |

## Evaluating Your Responses

Notice where you are satisfied and dissatisfied. In my study all categories of couples (copreneurs, dual-career employed couples, dual entrepreneurs, and solo entrepreneurs with a supportive spouse who is employed full-time) were satisfied with the division of household responsibilities even if the division was inequitable. How do you compare? Obviously, if there is some dissatisfaction it may be useful to discuss your feelings with your spouse so that you can avoid unresolved power struggles.

## Summarizing Remark

Write one sentence or a brief paragraph summarizing what you learned from this exercise and what you want to change.

# Your Satisfaction with the Division of Work Responsibilities in Your Business Relationship

The following is a list of tasks and responsibilities that are common in running a business. Even if you are not involved in running a business with your spouse, you may find the questionnaire helpful in assessing your satisfaction within your entrepreneurial venture or in a business partnership with someone else. For each area of responsibility, circle whether you are "Satisfied" or "Dissatisfied" with the arrangement you and your spouse (or other business partner) have made with regard to who actually handles each item.

| | | |
|---|---|---|
| 1. Control in decision making | Satisfied | Dissatisfied |
| 2. Day-to-day operations | Satisfied | Dissatisfied |
| 3. Financial management | Satisfied | Dissatisfied |
| 4. Investment management | Satisfied | Dissatisfied |
| 5. Product/service development | Satisfied | Dissatisfied |
| 6. Personnel Management | Satisfied | Dissatisfied |
| 7. Balance of work responsibilities | Satisfied | Dissatisfied |

## Evaluating Your Responses

Notice where you are satisfied and dissatisfied. In my study all copreneurs were satisfied with the division of work responsibilities even if the division was inequitable. How do you compare? Obviously, if there is some dissatisfaction it may be useful to discuss your feelings with your spouse or other business partner so that you can avoid unresolved power struggles.

## Summarizing Remark

Write one sentence or a brief paragraph summarizing what you learned from this exercise and what you want to change.

Once again the copreneurs reported that regardless of the nature or equality of the division of business responsibilities, they are highly satisfied with the division. That is, copreneurs have a division of business responsibilities that is fair and reasonable to them.

These results are fascinating and prompt many people to ask the chicken-and-egg question. That is, are copreneurs traditional in their marriage and business partnership because they work together, or are they drawn into this lifestyle because they have a traditional orientation in the first place? Likewise, are egalitarian dual-career entrepreneurial couples a product of their environment, or did they create the egalitarian entrepreneurial venture? The answers to these questions do not reside in the marital and business partnership equity data. All we know for certain is that at this moment in time, the people in my study were satisfied with the design of their partnership, which is not a bad place to be. In terms of personal, relationship, family, and business development, it works well to enjoy where you are now and to develop that system to its full potential before moving on to the next stage.

## The Boundaries of Equity and Equality

If you have read this far, you are well on your way to understanding your place on the partnership continuum from traditional to egalitarian. However, if you are still reeling under the weight of my research findings, please read this section, wherein I will summarize what we have learned in this chapter.

Results from the PAQ demonstrate that copreneurs are quite traditional in their sex-role orientations, while dual-career couples are more androgynous. (Remember that my dual-career couples sample included dual entrepreneurs, solo entrepreneurs with a supportive spouse who works full-time at a career, and dual-career couples who are not self-employed.) Specifically, 80 percent of the copreneurial husbands espouse a stereotypical masculine sex-role orientation, and 76 percent of the copreneurial wives espouse a stereotypical feminine sex-role orientation. Dual-career couples, on the other hand, espouse sex-role values that are less stereotypic, and more equally embrace both the desirable masculine and the desirable feminine traits, thus contributing to their androgyny.

The differences in these two orientations are demonstrated in the division of household and work responsibilities. Among copreneurial couples, wives handle the bulk of the household responsibilities, leaving only car maintenance and small repairs to the copreneurial husbands; while among dual-career couples, these tasks

**117**

are more equally shared. At work, copreneurial wives handle traditional "women's" work, such as secretarial and bookkeeping functions, while their husbands handle traditional "men's" work, such as equipment maintenance and decision making (i.e., contract negotiations). There is evidence that copreneurial wives are taking on more of the tasks and responsibilities formerly handled only by their husbands, such as sales, business planning, and professional services, probably because they are becoming better trained in these areas. Yet the converse is *not* true: Husbands are not assuming some of their wives' tasks and responsibilities. Instead of crossing the identity tension line and helping their wives with home and work responsibilities, copreneurial husbands work significantly more hours than any other group. In other words, copreneurial husbands *increase* their role behavior in order to maintain traditional sex-role boundaries.

Regardless of the division of labor, both copreneurs and dual-career couples are in agreement that they are satisfied as marital partners and business partners, which indicates that the distribution of work is considered fair or equitable, if not exactly equal. Moreover, this finding has been consistently supported in the literature on dual-career couples where there has been no distinction between copreneurs and other styles of couple entrepreneurship.

Dual-career couples certainly appear much more egalitarian than their copreneurial counterparts. While there is still a tendency for wives in dual-career couples to handle more household responsibilities than their husbands, the gap is narrowing. The predominant mode in these households is to share tasks fairly equally. Again, this trend of growing equality between husbands and wives in dual-career couples has been noted by other authors as well. The popular press has suggested that copreneurs, too, are establishing a new model of egalitarian marriage. However, this seems to be far from true. While these couples feel that the division of tasks at both home and work is equitable, it is not equal. On the contrary, it is quite disparate. And while these couples say that the business is equally owned, wives seldom identify themselves as the owner or president of the company, even when it is clear that they are.

Copreneurs strongly identify with the traditional style of partnership. Responses to the WHIS indicate that the husband is the leader and decision maker at work and at home, while the wife is consistently the support person. Copreneurial husbands work more hours, leaving management of the household to their copreneurial wives.

The findings of my 1994 study demonstrate that copreneurs create identity *boundaries* based on sex-role orientation. That is, rather than relying on a conceptual boundary between work and home, copreneurs rely on a conceptual boundary

**118**

based on gender differences to define their roles within the overlapping domains of love and work. However, sex-role orientation is not a factor in defining the boundaries of love and work for dual-career couples since their orientations are similarly androgynous. Rather, it is their self-concept that changes between domains for the members of these dual-career couples.

The members of dual-career couples who participated in my study are leaders at work. They are focused, formal, task-oriented, active, extroverted, and serious. At home they move from the unilateral leader role of work to a more bilateral sharing of power with their spouse. They are more relaxed, informal, person-oriented, introverted, and fun. Therefore, while copreneurs rely on a conceptual boundary defined by sex-role orientation, career-minded couples who do not work together satisfy the competing demands of love and work by shifting their self-concepts from a work persona to a home persona.

Copreneurs, on the other hand, demonstrate that self-concept is not as great a factor in defining the boundaries of love and work. While copreneurial husbands do change self-concept from home to work similarly to the husbands and wives in dual-career couples, their wives change very little. In both the domain of work and the domain of love, copreneurial wives are following, allowing, passive, introverted, and less powerful. Copreneurial wives do sense a shift from a more bilateral self-concept at work to a unilateral self-concept at home, which can be explained by the fact that they are responsible for nearly *all* aspects of the household while they do share in business management. But in neither domain is the copreneurial wife the leader.

Now that I have drawn generalizations from the research data, I want to reiterate that the average includes extremes at both ends. There are copreneurs who espouse an egalitarian style, though they are in the minority for their group, and there are dual-career entrepreneurial couples who espouse a traditional style. Rick and Chris as copreneurs of their restaurant business operate as equal partners in decision making and the division of responsibilities. When a sales representative comes to their office and requests the owner, the receptionist is just as likely to refer the caller to Chris as to Rick. On the other hand, Frank and Louise are a dual-career couple who espouse a traditional orientation. Frank is a solo entrepreneur, and Louise a physical therapist. Even though now with the birth of their baby Louise has become a full-time stay-at-home mom and no longer works outside the home, this couple has always adhered to traditional standards.

Changes over time are also possible. When Tom and Karen were first married, they represented the typical egalitarian dual-career couple, each a leader in their respective fields. However, with the rapid growth and success of Tom's business, the couple found themselves becoming more traditional, which contributed to a number of conflicts. In their case, their androgynous natures conflicted with the traditional design of their lifestyle, where Tom earned the money and Karen managed the household. Conversely, Sharon and David started out traditional, with David the solo entrepreneur and Sharon his supportive spouse. Yet when Sharon tasted the excitement of entrepreneurship as a self-employed real estate broker, their relationship changed to a more egalitarian style (although not without some hard work).

Wherever you find yourself on this continuum from traditional to egalitarian, recognize that your relationship is changing even now as you read this chapter. Conflict, chaos, reorganization, and growth are the natural order of things. If you are comfortable with your current style, do not change it. But if your style is getting a little tight, be brave enough to rewrite your life script. Be willing to detach yourself from tried-and-true methods when they no longer work. If necessary, confront your partner and ask to renegotiate the terms of the relationship and business partnership. And be willing to accept your partner's confrontation. Finally, always try to work toward a solution that satisfies *both* of you.

# Women Entrepreneurs:
# Are They Different from Men?

Much is being made these days of the innate differences between men and women. John Gray has captivated Americans with his books (e.g., *Men Are from Mars, Women Are from Venus*), wherein he depicts the communication, relationship, and problem-solving style differences between men and women. However, are these differences really gender specific? And are they really innate?

Even among identical twins, two individuals who develop from the same ovum and have identical DNA, the concordance rate for I.Q. is only .85 for twins who were raised together, and drops to .67 among identical twins raised apart. This means that intelligence is a function of environmental influences as well as heredity. In 1969 Jensen defined this relationship for I.Q. as the *heritability index*, which is the ratio of the variance in intelligence attributable to heredity to the variance attributable to heredity plus environment. The heritability index for I.Q.s is .80. That is, 80 percent of an individual's I.Q. is due to heredity, and 20 percent is due to heredity plus environment. Some scholars question Jensen's research and in particular the percentage of intelligence attributable to heredity. Nevertheless, most agree that intelligence is a function of both heredity and environmental influences.

If environmental factors play a part in the development of I.Q., even among identical twins, then certainly gender-defined traits may be similarly influenced. Although it is valuable to notice the differences between men and women, and to honor those differences, it is just as valuable to notice the similarities. Not every difference nor similarity can be explained by gender or heredity. Also, as we learned in Chapter Two, we humans know ourselves in relation to others by comparing our uniqueness and similarities.

In 1983, author Harry Levinson wrote, "There are few highly successful women entrepreneurs, because entrepreneurship requires a tremendous and highly focused aggressive drive. Men have a head start, being biologically more aggressive than women." Despite this pronouncement, women are starting businesses at an ever-increasing rate, three to five times that of men. These figures certainly contradict Levinson's notion of biology and destiny. There appears to be a transformation toward self-employment occurring in our society, and women may be leading this transformation.

In this chapter, I will discuss more than mere statistics. There are differences between men and women in terms of how they run their businesses, but the entrepreneurial desire is just as strong for women today as it is for men, perhaps stronger. The common problems that plague women entrepreneurs are how to deal with the differences between themselves and their husbands, and how to balance home life and work life.

For example, Sarah came up to me after a presentation I had made on entrepreneurial couples, and she complained that her marriage and business had been suffering since her husband, Buck, quit his job and came to work for her. Sarah started her business in her home as a way to supplement the family income. She made gourmet popcorn. As demand for her popcorn increased, she branched out and started selling other gourmet treats (gift baskets of nuts, popcorn, and chocolates, cookie bouquets, and so on). Soon the business required her efforts full-time. She hired staff and rented a professional kitchen, warehouse, and office space.

Although Sarah did not ask her husband to join her, he quit his job in order to do so. She gladly accepted his help at first, but all too soon the trouble started. Buck continued to think of Sarah's business as a part-time endeavor. He worked short hours, leaving most afternoons to go fishing with his friends. In spite of his lack of commitment, he would make major decisions for the business without consulting Sarah.

It was clear that Buck had been unhappy in his career in agricultural sales and saw Sarah's business as a way out. He wasn't really committed to the business, although he supported his wife emotionally. Instead, he saw the business as a way to support his own early semi-retirement. When Sarah realized that Buck was not really an entrepreneur, she needed to make a decision about how to take the business back and still save her marriage.

Maggie had a different concern when I first met her and her husband, Paul. Maggie, who is an organizing solo entrepreneur, is a veterinarian who has developed a successful feline specialty practice. She loves her work, is hardworking, and has a loyal clientele. In fact, she has been asked to take over another clinic on the other side of town because so many of her customers travel a long distance just for her competent animal care. Maggie's husband, Paul, is ten years older than Maggie and well established in his own career as a deputy district attorney. He has no interest in going into private practice himself, although he helps his wife around the clinic. Instead, he has his eye on the political arena: One day, after he has moved up the public service ladder a bit more, he would like to run for public office at the state or local level.

The concern that brought this couple into my office is children, or the lack thereof. Maggie and Paul had been married for five years, and at the age of twenty-eight, Maggie was getting anxious about wanting to have a baby. Paul, on the other hand, has two children from a previous marriage, and felt that he needed to pre-serve his energy to parent those two, who are now teenagers. As the noncustodial parent, he felt an obligation to be even more attentive to his children, and he wor-ried that a new baby would interfere in his relationships with the teenagers.

Neither Paul nor Maggie was concerned about a child interfering in their careers, or even in Maggie's business expansion. Neither were they worried that a child would disrupt their marital life, although most parents-to-be underestimate this factor. The real problem was Paul's concern about being a good parent. So we set out to develop a plan for parenting that would meet both Paul's and Maggie's needs. At this point, six years later, the couple has two more children and a house in the coun-try for their many animal friends, and Maggie has two thriving veterinary clinics.

Sarah and Maggie represent only two styles of entrepreneurship for women and only two ways that women entrepreneurs are affecting the ones they love. If the predictions are true about the phenomenal growth of women-owned busi-nesses, then the marketplace is changing dramatically. The influence of women solo entrepreneurs, women in dual entrepreneur relationships, and women in copreneurial relationships cannot be ignored. If you are one of these women entre-preneurs or the partner of one, this chapter will be enlightening. I have already reported on the qualities of male entrepreneuers in Chapter One. In this chapter I will take you beyond simple gender differences to an understanding of how women and the world of work interact.

# Women and the World of Work

To be sure, the phenomenon of women working is nothing new. Women have always made an important economic contribution to the family. In nineteenth-century America, women contributed to the family economy through many activi-ties, such as farming, migrant labor, and sewing. Prior to the industrial revolution, the traditional norm was family work, not individual work. In our postindustrial society, women are now taking on work outside the home, but this is just a varia-tion on the theme of contributing financially to the family.

In the 1970s sociologists predicted that the dual-career marriage was the most likely model to replace the male-breadwinner/female-homemaker paradigm. The female labor force in the United States is both larger and more demographically diverse today than it was just a few decades ago. Not only do women make up 50 percent of the total labor force, but they are also more likely than they were in the past to be in administrative and professional occupations, to be married, and to have children under the age of six. Women who represent the conjunction of these data—that is, married professionals with young children—are growing in number as well. In 1975 about 720,000 married women with children less than six years old were employed in professional and technical occupations; by 1988 that number had increased by half, according to the U.S. Bureau of Labor Statistics, formerly the U.S. Department of Labor.

By sheer numbers, women entering the workforce are making an impact on the way America does business. And for women entrepreneurs, this is even more true. Female entrepreneurial ventures are on the rise. According to the U.S. Census Bureau, in the United States between 1977 and 1982, the number of female nonfarm sole proprietorships grew at an annual rate of 6.9 percent, whereas all nonfarm sole proprietorships grew at an annual rate of 3.7 percent. By 1984 there were 3 million female-owned nonfarm sole proprietorships in the United States. Based on 1972 census information, fewer than 5 percent of U.S. businesses were owned by women, but by 1982 this number had increased to 28 percent.

The census data identified only those women-owned businesses that were sole proprietorships. The National Association of Women Business Owners (NAWBO) report, however, that only one-third of women-owned businesses are sole proprietorships (see Knocke, 1988). In addition to sole proprietorships, NAWBO's study showed that 37 percent of women business owners owned corporations, 23 percent owned S corporations, and 6 percent owned partnerships. Moreover, women are starting businesses at a rate *five times faster* than men. If this trend keeps up, women could own half of all U.S. businesses by the year 2000.

Looking at the ownership data in another way reveals that there are even more entrepreneurial women to add to the totals just mentioned. Typical of the copreneurs described in this book, there are increasing numbers of women working with their husbands in jointly owned sole proprietorships. And according to the Small Business Administration, the number of nonfarm jointly owned sole proprietorships is increasing at 5 percent a year.

The growing phenomenon of dual-career couples, female entrepreneurs, and copreneurs indicate that women are committed to career and motivated by achievement, just as men are. This is true in spite of the fact that the dual-career couple and entrepreneurial couple lifestyles create multiple role demands and increased stress for these women. Twenty-five years ago, when the dual-career couple phenomenon was still fairly new, researchers discovered that marriage was more stressful for women than for men. For example, in 1972 researchers such as Bernard and Gove found that married women have more illnesses than single women, while married men are more healthy than single men. With the current demands of work and home life in the late 1990s, entrepreneurial women must have even more to adjust to than their counterparts of twenty-five years ago, but the evidence suggests that these career women consider the rewards of work to outweigh the costs.

# A Psychology of Women and Work

According to Simone de Beauvoir, "One is not born, but rather becomes a woman. No biological, psychological, or economic fate determines the figure that the human female presents in society; it is civilization as a whole that produces this creature" (1952, p. 301). In other words, growing up female is a complex process of weaving together several influences or developing progressions.

The standard for women in our society is to become submissive, passive, docile, dependent, and lacking in initiative and generally to be pleasing to the dominant group (i.e., men). However, those women who eventually choose entrepreneurship have taken a path that is uncharacteristic for women and that requires the courage to take risks. According to the theories of noted psychiatrist Alfred Adler, entrepreneurial women have rejected the cultural norm for women and moved in a *masculine* direction, but the price they pay may be economic hardship, social ostracism, and psychological isolation.

For Sarah the risk—and the potential price she might have to pay—was losing her husband, her business, or both. She just did not know how to gracefully remove her husband from the business. Sarah's dilemma is a common one for entrepreneurial women. The pull to be loyal and to nurture the family as wife and mother is quite strong because of cultural imperatives. Yet women have also been exposed to our culture's notion of success as the achievements that can be measured by grades and dollars. Women who want both a family and a business venture must develop an alternative way of viewing what it means to be a woman in our culture.

Although men are bound by the same holistic principles of dialectical psychology as women are, women are keenly aware of their identity in relation to others. They are caregivers, wives, and employers. While men strive for autonomy first

125

and learn about relationships second, women develop their sense of self first in connection with others, even in connection with the world. Therefore, a woman's sense of worth is highly dependent on the consequences of relationships.

Even though Sarah, all on her own, had achieved financial success with her business, her real sense of success came with how her husband would adjust to the developing enterprise. Sarah was facing the classic struggle that most entrepreneurial women must grapple with at one time or another, that of choosing to take care of her own needs or the needs of others. If Sarah's definition of self-worth is based on her ability to care for others, then she will fail as a woman if she chooses her business over her husband, Buck.

Career women struggle with societal values and their own internalized beliefs about what is required of the *competent professional* versus the *good wife and mother*. In order to ease the struggle to define themselves, women can opt for the traditional homemaker role and not work outside the home. However, as I have already noted, work proves to be powerfully alluring to women. Therefore, career women and entrepreneurs among them have chosen other methods to resolve this struggle.

Most commonly, working women *overwork*. Instead of asking for changes from their husbands, changes in the workplace, or even changes in society, career women increase the time spent in nurturing relationships as they increase their commitment to work. For example, researchers Biernat and Wortman reported in 1991 that among couples who are both university professors, the professor wife not only provides more child care than her professor husband, but her level of child care increases with her level of income.

Recognizing that women perceive the world in relational or interpersonal terms explains why many women downplay their occupational achievements. This is particularly evident with the women in family firms. The copreneurial wives in my study are a case in point. They are reluctant to acknowledge their role as co-owners of their businesses. They adhere to traditional definitions of femininity. They manage their households entirely without the help of their husbands. And they assume no leadership of the family either at work or at home. They do, however, work as many hours at the business as the other wives in dual-career and entrepreneurial couples, only to go home and work full-time managing their children and households as well.

In our culture, both men and women apply *masculine* criteria to achievement. In other words, a man who achieves in his field is considered successful, but a woman must be married and have children to be considered successful. If a woman only achieves success in business, she runs the risk of being considered a failure as a woman. For example, Sheila has already run up against criticism of her desire to pursue entrepreneurship. Because she is currently childless, people assume that she will drop her enterprising ideas when the children come along. Carol, on the other hand, has been criticized for wanting children. Because she is a solo entrepreneur with a thriving garden center and is in her mid-thirties, people have been so bold as to advise her that she would not make a very good mother. Her business, they assume, would compete in an unhealthy way with parenting. It is unlikely, however, that men face similar criticisms.

With all of these pressures on women, it is a wonder that the number of women entrepreneurs is on the rise. Further, it is somewhat surprising that entrepreneurial wives report satisfaction with their careers and their marriages when it is such a struggle to define oneself as a woman in a man's world. Apparently, these women are committed to discovering a way to integrate love and work into their developing sense of self. For example, I found in my research that the most satisfied women were the wives in entrepreneurial and dual-career couples who did *not* work with their husbands. Contradicting Adler's theory, these women seem to have both a highly developed masculine side and a highly developed feminine side, which allows them to feel successful both as autonomous executives and as nurturing wives and mothers.

Maggie appears to have achieved this balance. Maggie is not in the position of choosing between her career and her husband, or between her career and her children. Instead, she has a partner who encourages her entrepreneurial spirit and assists her in balancing both home and work responsibilities. Paul has no compunction about doing child care or housework. In fact, he believes strongly in the importance of being an attentive father to his children. His androgynous style has also served him well as a prosecuting attorney because he can be firm yet diplomatic. Most important Paul married Maggie because he wanted a spirited partner to share the family leadership with him.

# What Do Women Entrepreneurs Want?

Although there are conflicting reports, most of the research on female entrepreneurs shows them to be very much like their male counterparts. That is, like male entrepreneurs, women are motivated by the challenge of being one's own boss and the opportunity to make more money or achieve personal goals. In fact, some experts believe that there is a *second generation* of female entrepreneurship developing. The first generation consisted of women who, due to a variety of personal crises, were *forced* to initiate business ventures. These women went into business without much experience or training. However, today's female entrepreneur is almost indistinguishable from the average male entrepreneur, because they have the same training, skills, and experience. They also have the same motivation—very strong needs for achievement, independence, and control.

Unlike men, women are also motivated to develop their own businesses by problems unique to women in our culture. For example, the "glass ceiling" phenomenon puts pressure on women with highly developed management skills to seek self-employment as a way to further their career advancement. Furthermore, female entrepreneurs also cite parenting and child-care responsibilities as reasons for pursuing self-employment. They want the flexibility to be part of their children's lives and to develop a thriving enterprise. On the other hand, there has yet to be a study in which male entrepreneurs indicate parenting as a motivator for their pursuing self-employment.

Women entrepreneurs are usually married, which defies the stereotype of the masculine woman who cannot achieve success in marriage and career. They are also just as well educated as their male counterparts—and frequently better educated, according to the 1986 work of Stevenson. The liberal arts education of the typical entrepreneurial woman, however, leaves her less prepared to start and manage a business, which may be the reason she typically chooses to operate in a service industry rather than in a technical industry.

All entrepreneurs face barriers to achievement; in fact, this is probably a major defining characteristic of entrepreneurs. Entrepreneurs by their very nature thrive in a challenging, even inhospitable environment. Still, the challenges faced by entrepreneurial women are different from those faced by men, and further shape their destinies. For example, a male entrepreneur often has not only the emotional support of his wife but her unpaid help in the business as well. A female entrepreneur, on the other hand, does not have the benefit of her husband's unpaid help. Typically, the husband is emotionally supportive, but it is up to the wife to manage her business as well as her child-care and household duties, while he works outside the business. Debbie Fields of "Mrs. Fields' Cookies" fame had such a marriage. Although her husband was remarkably supportive of his wife's enterprise for many years, he acknowledged that he would withdraw his support if she failed to meet her obligations as a wife and mother.

Another barrier for women entrepreneurs is the lack of formal education that would prepare them for business ventures. While boys are encouraged to study subjects related to business, our society steers girls toward the liberal arts, which are considered more feminine. As a result, many young women do not develop the business skills necessary to realize their entrepreneurial ambitions. As they stumble along without these skills, banks turn them down for loans and customers view them as less competent than their male counterparts. As they fall farther and farther behind in terms of basic business skills, it becomes increasingly difficult for women entrepreneurs to compete with men who not only have advanced business skills but also a well-developed network of influential contacts.

In spite of these barriers and lack of skills, women entrepreneurs are starting businesses at ever-increasing rates—and are succeeding, too. But they are using unconventional methods of business management. For example, women entrepreneurs rarely have formal operational policies, formal planning processes, or formal job descriptions. These relaxed standards may be a result of their lack of formal business management education; however, they are not interfering with their success. Women entrepreneurs are making an impact on the American economy. For example, in one year (1987) 30 percent of the businesses in the United States were owned by women, with receipts of $280 billion, or approximately 14 percent of the United States' total gross receipts, according to the U.S. Commerce Department.

The relaxed style of management can also be seen in how women entrepreneurs treat their employees, suppliers, and customers. They seem to prefer a more *people-oriented* style. According to Putnam's 1993 study of entrepreneurial women in Oregon, women entrepreneurs *blend* their personal and their business identities. They base their management of the business on relationships rather than on the development of business plans. Employees are considered friends. Family and spouse support are elements without which the woman would not consider an entrepreneurial venture. Rather than network within traditional business organizations, entrepreneurial women rely on strong personal relationships with their customers and vendors. These findings led Putnam to describe the business orientation of entrepreneurial women as a "web of interconnected relationships."

# Women in Family Firms

If the web of interconnected relationships is characteristic of women entrepreneurs, it is even more characteristic of women in family-owned businesses, where the boundaries of home and work overlap for men as well as women. In fact, this web is the defining characteristic of these businesses in general. While some may say that wives of entrepreneurs are not really entrepreneurs, and while it is true that copreneurial wives are different from other entrepreneurial wives, learning about how women in family firms balance the competing demands of love and work will round out our picture of entrepreneurial women.

In spite of the fact that family firms make up roughly half of the businesses in the United States, they have not been well researched. It's as if the reality is so close to home, so much a part of how we live, that scientists have never thought to examine family firms. Male entrepreneurs have been well researched, and the research on female entrepreneurs is catching up, yet research on the *family system* (including those traditional wives who support their entrepreneurial husbands) *that creates a family-owned business,* is still in its infancy.

Furthermore, as Salganicoff has pointed out, "If the literature about family business is in its infancy, then literature on women in family business is still gestating." Salganicoff goes on to describe women in family firms as *invisible.* This invisibility is probably due to the culture of family businesses in general, which tend to foster stereotypical gender differences. Family businesses are *closed systems.* That is, the family firm operates according to its own rules with very little influence from the outside. (If you doubt this phenomenon, just ask anyone who has worked for a family firm but is not a member of the family. They will report how difficult it is to break into the family system and change anything.) Because of this closed system, the roles women play in the family are reinforced in the workplace, regardless of their job title. Women who work in family businesses are wives, mothers, and daughters *first;* employees, managers and executives *second.*

Also, there are developmental differences between men and women that contribute to the invisibility of women in the family business. Men move toward individuation and autonomy in early adulthood, whereas women move toward intimacy and affiliation. Thus women have a strong need to maintain the family, even at the expense of their own professional development. In a family business setting, where family values take precedence over the needs of the business, women are more inclined to preserve the family than pursue independent goals that could risk family cohesion. Interestingly, as men and women reach midlife, the developmental imperative shifts in the opposite direction. Women begin seeking autonomy and individuation, while men are moving toward intimacy and affiliation. However, by this stage in life, with careers and families well established, it is more difficult for women to change the course of their lives, especially if they work in a family firm.

On the other hand, there are numerous benefits for women working in family-owned businesses. The careers that women can pursue in family businesses are often more lucrative and nontraditional than what they could find on their own. Mothers have more flexibility to arrange their hours around child-care needs. Wives and daughters are guaranteed job security, even if they leave for an extended period, such as to give birth and raise children. As I mentioned earlier, among the widows in McKinley's study, the option of selling their husband's business was not considered because the rewards of self-employment were so great.

The studies of women in family businesses, though limited in number, demonstrate that there are other developing progressions interacting with the family and the business besides that of the male decision maker. Women, the invisible partners, are the caretakers of the family and the family values. They contribute to the family business in the same way that they nurture the family and protect generational continuity. Unfortunately, their role has been invisible because it is overshadowed by the more obvious task orientation and market competitiveness of the business.

Research with copreneurs, another type of family-owned business, is just as limited as research with the women in family businesses in general. However, I find it fascinating that my research study of copreneurs upholds the findings of similar studies that are twenty years old. For example, in 1971 Epstein examined copreneurs who were law partners and found a very traditional division of labor. Not only that but the law partner wives saw themselves as wives and mothers first and as professionals second. My study participants reported similar perceptions. Karla's long morning routine is evidence that she sees herself as a wife and mother first, and a business partner second. And Andrea's selfless devotion to Howard and their hardware stores also supports the conclusion that copreneurial wives take responsibility for nurturing the family and leave business development to their husbands.

Another twenty-year-old study demonstrates the inequity in stress level for copreneurs. In 1976 copreneurial psychologists R. and J. Bryson and M. and B. Licht reported a study of psychologists married to psychologists where the two members of the couple worked together, primarily in academic settings, and compared them to a group of psychologists in dual-career couples who were *not* married to psychologists and did not work with their spouses. (Although those in the first sample group are not technically copreneurs because they do not own their own business, the fact that they work together presents a similar situation to the copreneurs I describe in this book.)

Consistent with my own research results, the Brysons and the Lichts found an unequal division of household labor and child care among these quasi-copreneurial psychologist couples. Most striking is that they found that the psychologist wives were the most stressed by the arrangement of working with their husbands, while their husbands were the least stressed. In fact, the psychologist husbands were more satisfied with both their marriages and their work than any other group in the study. Like the copreneurial husbands in my study, these psychologist husbands are not in conflict over their role as a traditional male, nor do they have excessive transition stress since their wives work full-time *and* do all of the housework and child care.

You may recall from the previous chapter that in spite of this unequal division of household labor and the gender-driven division of business tasks, the copreneurial wives in my study reported satisfaction with their marriages and business partnerships. In other words, they thought the bargain was equitable, which is to say fair and reasonable, if not exactly equal. Other more recent studies confirm these findings. The 1991 study of Wicker and Burley and the 1993 study of Ponthieu and Caudill demonstrate that copreneurs are exceedingly happy with their work/home arrangements, even if the decision making and division of responsibilities are unequal. Furthermore, copreneurial wives in these studies report that working together has enhanced their marriage. For example, not only does Andrea (a copreneur) support Howard selflessly, but she exclaims, "I wish more wives could discover how rewarding it is to work with your husband!"

# Achievement Through an Interconnected Web of Relationships

One day in my office, Carrie could not contain her frustration. She was trying to explain to her husband, Anton, why it was important for her to attend to her duties as president of their local trade association. Although Anton had never shown any interest in the organization, Carrie was an active participant and was proud of her election as president. Anton, on the other hand, could focus only on the fact that her "socializing" took her out of the office and away from her business duties. He resented that she had all this "free time" while he worked hard running their joint venture.

Carrie and Anton were both solo entrepreneurs before they married and combined their homes and businesses. So both have strong needs for achievement and for control over their respective destinies. They frequently find themselves in battles because of these needs, but this particular battle is a result of one of the differences between male and female entrepreneurs. As we have learned in this chapter, Carrie, as a woman, runs her business so as to establish and maintain *a web of interconnected relationships.* To her, participating in the trade association and developing close friendships with other members is just as vital to running the business as is providing the actual business product or service. Close relationships not only bring in new business, but they also help Carrie define who she is. In other words, Carrie defines her *achievements through a web of interconnected relationships.* Anton, on the other hand, can appreciate that networking is good for business, but as a more traditional man, he defines himself by producing a quality product, not by whether he is liked.

If Carrie and Anton are to resolve this conflict, they will need to appreciate the differences between them. Quality work is a sure way to develop a good reputation in the community and is likely to keep business coming in. However, customers often buy your product or service because they like you and nothing more. Among husband-and-wife teams, the feedback I get from their customers is that in spite of the hard work and dedication to quality that the husband demonstrates, the customer prefers to talk to the wife because she cares about them personally.

## The Impact of Entrepreneurial Women

In this chapter we have learned that the numbers of entrepreneurial women are increasing rapidly, at a rate three to five times that of entrepreneurial men. We have also learned that because women are socialized differently than men, they tend to organize and run their businesses differently, though they are no less a force on the American economy. Some estimates are that by the year 2000, women will own half of all American businesses. With this type of influence, we will certainly witness not only a change in the way America does business, but a change in the way Americans do marriage and family as well.

Paul and Maggie long ago accepted Maggie's entrepreneurial style, and with children of their own found a new way to integrate intimacy, family, and meaningful work within their egalitarian marriage. Sheila and Robert do not yet have children, but it is likely that Robert will have to assume significant child-care responsibilities if he is to continue his support of Sheila's entrepreneurial aspirations. Now that Carol has recognized that she is the solo entrepreneur, she and her husband, Bob, need to reassess how to integrate Bob's more laid-back style with Carol's drive to achieve. Sharon and David have struck a nice balance in their dual-entrepreneurial relationship, but that might change as Sharon's income begins to rival David's. And Sarah needs to evaluate the level of resentment she will feel if she gives up her business to rescue her marriage with Buck.

# How Do You Achieve Balance as an Entrepreneurial Wife?

As women gain in confidence, as they encounter career barriers such as the glass ceiling in corporate life, and as their husbands adopt a more egalitarian attitude and approach in the marriage, we are seeing more and more women embarking on entrepreneurial careers either as solo entrepreneurs, as dual entrepreneurs, or as copreneurs. Regardless of entrepreneurial style, these women are reporting that they are highly satisfied with their lives and wouldn't arrange them any other way. In other words, working from a web of interconnected relationships, entrepreneurial women want personal achievement just as entrepreneurial men do. Given these trends, it is hard to imagine that just fifteen short years ago, Harry Levinson suggested that women were not biologically destined for entrepreneurship.

Although this chapter is not the definitive work on women entrepreneurs, there should be enough here to challenge you and your partner to reevaluate the arrangements you have made, as well as the assumptions underlying those arrangements. Think about what you have learned about entrepreneurial women compared to how you and your spouse relate to your work and your home life. How do you compare? If you are a woman, are you cut out for the entrepreneurial life and all the struggles that women entrepreneurs face? If you are a man, are you prepared for the changes you must make to support your entrepreneurial wife? Now that you know more about the differences and similarities between men and women, male and female entrepreneurs, how can you reorganize your relationship, your business, and your personal life to create an arrangement that works better for *both* of you?

# Parenting and Family Life: Rounding Out Your Life Plan

In the course of my work, I meet people who have grown up with copreneurial parents or have worked as teenagers in the family business. Often these grown children remark that they would never inflict an entrepreneurial lifestyle on their own children. They feel that their childhood was handicapped by unavailable parents, that the family business took priority over the children and family life. And in fact, my research shows that entrepreneurial couples are willing to spend time at work *at the expense of* family life and personal life. For example, these couples are willing to go to work early and leave for home late three to five times a week. They are willing to leave work early, perhaps on a Friday, only once a month. And they are *never* willing to leave late for work. Copreneurial husbands are even more willing to sacrifice home life for work. They work an average of sixty hours a week in the business, while their copreneurial wives work an average of forty-nine. Other research supports these findings. While managers and executives report that the most important aspect of their lives is their families, they get the most rewards from work.

With all of the demands of entrepreneurial life, it may seem impossible to reconcile intimacy, family life, and work. As I have repeatedly noted in this book, finding a way to balance both home and work effectively is a challenge for all entrepreneurial couples. Parenting especially is an awesome responsibility. Many couples do not plan this aspect of their lives any better than they plan marriage and career. But with some education about healthy parenting and a plan on how to implement or achieve it, it is possible to integrate the competing demands of love and work.

In this chapter I will discuss how to plan for children and how to parent them throughout their growing years. I will not attempt to replace more in-depth books on parenting: I recommend you read those books too. On the other hand, I know of no books on parenting specifically written for entrepreneurial couples, so this

## The Seven Basic Principles of Good Parenting

**1.** Be a strong, authoritative leader.
**2.** Get to know your children by assisting them in discovering themselves.
**3.** Be an educated parent.
**4.** Build resilience in your children by helping them through troubled times.
**5.** Move slowly with change, especially in creating a blended family.
**6.** Create independent, not obedient, children.
**7.** Leave your children with fond memories.

chapter will put parenting into perspective for those special families where Mom and Dad are an entrepreneurial couple. Parenting advice is usually the last thing for which a businessperson consults a professional, yet for those entrepreneurial couples striving to balance intimacy, family life, and meaningful work, integrating a parenting plan with a business, personal, and relationship plan is vital. Like Chapter Three, on communication, this chapter does not offer specific parenting techniques but rather gives you *seven basic principles* to guide you in your parenting decisions.

For those of you who have children at home, as well as those of you contemplating having children, this chapter is obviously important. But for those of you whose children are grown, I would still suggest reading the chapter. Children are never too old for parents. As you review the decisions you made with your children and compare them to the recommendations in this chapter, those of you who are parents of adult children may find some strategies to resolve long-standing problems with your children. Finally, for those of you who have no children and do not intend to have any, this chapter may not be as meaningful to you. However, you may want to read it anyway to get a better handle on your own childhood lessons. How your parents parented you has affected your decision in some way to participate in the entrepreneurial life. It may be helpful to discover what those connections are and how they continue to shape you.

The single most important element in successful parenting is *getting to know each individual and unique child.* Changing diapers is a snap in comparison to the delicate job of building self-esteem. Parenting by the numbers won't work either. Each child requires something different from each parent. Consequently, a life/career plan that doesn't consider the successful development of the children will ultimately fail.

Frank and Louise had a hard time at first putting their parenting responsibilities into perspective. They thought that having a child would be a breeze. Frank had a thriving electronics business in which Louise occasionally helped. Louise was transitioning from her career in physical therapy to something more creative when she and Frank decided it was time to have a baby. The crisis hit when Frank found himself envying Louise's role as the mother. He felt that his only contribution to the family was monetary, and he desperately wanted to parent more.

Dual entrepreneurs Earl and Crystal were at a very different stage of the parenting cycle. They had grown children and grandchildren but needed help reconciling the family. The children had become alienated after leaving home, and Earl and Crystal did not know why. As we explored their plight in psychotherapy, we discovered a great many parenting mistakes that they had made. Crystal, Earl, and their children are a *blended family;* each of the parents came into the relationship from a divorce and had children from those previous marriages. Rather than taking the time to help all of the children adjust to this blending, Earl and Crystal just went back to work, each developing his or her own enterprise. Over the years Earl's and Crystal's businesses thrived, but the children suffered. Not only had the children lost their nuclear family through divorce, but now they were expected to raise themselves while their parents put all of their energies into their respective businesses. As adults, none of the four children has chosen to follow his or her parents into entrepreneurship, none has gone to college, all have struggled with failed marriages, and all lack meaningful careers.

Both of these couples needed planning. They also need education about parenting and how to integrate family life with work life. Frank and Louise still have time to get to know their child, to develop a healthy relationship with him, to build his positive self-esteem. Earl and Crystal, however, may have lost their chance. The regrets that fill their hearts now are a huge price to pay for lack of preparation and planning for the entrepreneurial life.

# Be a Strong, Authoritative Leader

Recently copreneurs Rick and Chris were profiled in a local business paper as the hardworking family behind their restaurant business. New on the scene is their sixteen-month-old daughter, who is shown with her smiling parents in a picture at the top of the article. Once again Rick and Chris are demonstrating their understanding of how to balance home and work. From the very beginning of their relationship, the two of them have worked together to develop a healthy home life and a successful business. They operate the business as egalitarian partners. They preserve the sanctity of home life by discussing business only at the office. Now they are introducing their young daughter to family/business life by including her photo in the business news. Chris has a crib and playpen at the office so that she can be close to the baby. And Rick has the flexibility to take his daughter with him on business errands. With their new parenting responsibilities and raised consciousness, the couple is considering offering a child-care plan to employees too.

Things will undoubtedly change as their daughter gets older and requires more supervision and stimulation. But Chris and Rick will probably be up to the challenge because they take the responsibility of creating healthy family relationships seriously. Rick learned from a three-generation family business not only to plan but to keep his priorities straight. One of those priorities is to *put family first.* And in order to do that, as parents you must be *strong leaders.*

The challenges and assaults on family life are tremendous these days, especially for entrepreneurial couples. Just as a successful business requires strong, decisive, innovative leadership, so does the family. Unfortunately, most parents view parenting as an afterthought. Busy with the demands of career, community commitments, and the ordinary problems of daily living, entrepreneurial couples often leave their children to raise themselves emotionally. Children may develop some self-sufficiency this way, but more often they develop low self-esteem, a legacy that would shock and shame most entrepreneurial couples.

The qualities of a strong leader include high self-esteem, vision, and fearlessness. Strong leaders are willing to take on tough issues when others wilt. They admit their mistakes and are willing to educate themselves in areas where they are ignorant. They take a responsible attitude about their decisions; they do not pass the buck. They view change as opportunity and in fact seek out change constantly. A strong leader deals immediately and resoundingly with saboteurs and negativity in the system—any system, be it business or family. Finally, a strong leader determines whether an institution such as a family or a business survives crises.

Rick has moved from sweeping the floor in his grandfather's restaurant as a child to now co-owning a chain of restaurants with his wife. He has witnessed leadership and developed leadership himself by weathering many transitions. Likewise, Chris has leadership qualities, which is why the couple have an egalitarian relationship instead of a more traditional copreneurial style. Her leadership is not only demonstrated in the business but in the community, where she contributes liberally of her time to various social causes.

Strong parents are neither *permissive* nor *authoritarian*. Permissive parents are those who provide their children with few controls or demands and display moderate levels of warmth. Children of permissive parents are usually impulsive, aggressive, self-centered, and low in achievement and independence. This is because they are left alone a lot and begin to assume that they are not much cared about. Authoritarian parents, on the other hand, impose absolute standards of conduct, stress obedience, and are willing to use physical punishment to gain compliance. Their children are often irritable, dependent, and submissive and have a limited sense of responsibility and lower levels of academic achievement. Although these children receive a lot of attention, it is often of the negative kind, which reinforces feelings of inadequacy.

Many children rise above the standards proscribed by permissive or authoritarian parents, but the majority develop emotional problems that follow them into adult life. Authoritarian parents may secure obedience from their children, but at the price of fear. Children of permissive parents do not learn teamwork. As adults these children run the risk of having imbalance in their marriages and their work lives. Certainly, children with low self-esteem are not likely to make good successors for leadership of the family business when their parents retire.

The ideal, however, is to be an *authoritative* parent who combines warmth with moderate levels of control. Authoritative parents are rational, receptive, and flexible. They encourage independence in their children, but give them only as much responsibility as they can handle. Instead of demanding blind obedience, they set clear rules and are willing to explain those rules to their children. Children of authoritative parents are independent, assertive, self-confident, and socially responsible and tend to do well academically.

The authoritative parent is a strong leader. The child knows where he or she stands with the parent and believes that he or she is loved. Because the parent is a leader and not an authoritarian, the child admires the mother or father and looks to her or him for guidance instead of obeying out of fear. Because authoritative parents allow the child to try things out for him- or herself, under their supervision, the child develops a sense of mastery of the environment, which leads to positive self-esteem. Children raised in this type of environment develop a strong sense of self. They are aware of their strengths and their weaknesses and are prepared to work on both. Whether they come to work in the family business or make their mark in some other unique way, children of authoritative parents have a much better chance of maintaining a healthy balance between love and work.

# Get to Know Your Children

Even though children are dependent on their parents and quite impressionable, especially when they are young, a child comes into this world with a lot of traits already "hardwired." Any parent who has more than one child will tell you that each baby was different almost from the moment of conception. Even when brothers and sisters have the same parents, grow up together in the same house with their siblings, and inhabit roughly the same sociocultural milieu as the rest of the family, they turn out differently. The reason, as Jensen pointed out, is that each individual on the planet is a product of both heredity and environmental influences.

But the development of a child is still more complex than heredity plus environment. The reason that twins not only don't have the same fingerprints but don't even have the same I.Q. score is that as individuals they have *free will*. In other words, each child uses his or her innate resources (heredity) to *perceive* and then *interpret* the experiences (environment) he or she is exposed to. One person may interpret that tingly feeling in the spine as fear, while another person perceives the same feeling as thrilling. As your child interprets or makes sense of the environment over time, he or she acquires a number of *beliefs* about the world. These beliefs develop into a larger structure within which your child builds a life. Perception after perception, interpretation after interpretation, belief after belief evolve and shape the individual into a one-of-a-kind human being.

As parents you are in a wonderful position to be part of this unfolding of your child. However, it is important that you understand that your job is not to mold and shape your child as if he or she were a little lump of clay. Your child is a dynamic being who is *discovering* himself or herself while growing up. Your job is to *assist in that discovery*, to guide and protect, and to provide opportunities for even more discovery; but your job is definitely not to dictate your child's life.

Another way to look at parenting is that your job is to *get to know your child*. I learned this lesson with my older daughter. This child has always been quite talented artistically. Even as a preschooler, she drew a Nativity scene for her Christmas card to Mommy and Daddy, when the other children struggled to draw a snowman or a triangle-shaped Christmas tree. Perhaps other children at the age of four are capable of drawing a Nativity scene, but there were two things that distinguished my daughter's drawing and made it unique to her. First, the teacher had asked the children to draw a picture representative of Christmas. My daughter felt that the actual birth of Jesus was the most important thing about this holiday. Second, her drawings of Mary, Joseph, and baby Jesus were anatomically correct!

I learned a great deal from this incident. I learned that my daughter has qualities that I do not possess. I learned that she is delightful to get to know. And I learned that I can learn from her, too; that she is part of the environment that I am constantly interpreting even as I am a part of hers. Human development is never ending. Just as you are assisting your child in the unfolding of his or her identity, he or she is assisting you in the same way. Riegel calls this interacting of the developing progressions of two individuals a *dialogue*. Thus the name *dialectical psychology*, which is the system of psychology that provides the theoretical foundation for this book.

Some of you are in the stage of parenting and in the stage of your business when you have not yet begun to think of retirement or whether any of your children will join you in the family business. However, the research on children in family-owned firms is quite revealing about what does and doesn't work when it comes to parenting a healthy child. By far the greatest consideration for a child who works with his or her parent is whether the relationship is a good one. If the child feels loved by his or her parent, respected and valued for his or her unique contributions, then the salary or task assignment is much less important.

If you as the parent are a strong leader, and if you realize that your job is to get to know your child while at the same time getting to know yourself, your child will develop normally and with positive self-esteem. And with positive self-esteem, your child will be prepared to handle most anything that comes his or her way. Knowing and liking who he or she is makes it easier for the child to ask questions, take risks, and correct mistakes. If you show your child that he or she is a valuable person by demonstrating your interest, your child will feel comfortable about going out into the world to discover how to best use his or her talents, whether or not he or she comes to work for the family business.

## Be an Educated Parent

Having the right attitude about parenting is an important first step. Being a strong leader with a commitment to getting to know your child puts you in the enviable position of being able to learn something new and exciting—how to raise a son or daughter. There are few people out there who already have the necessary skills to parent before they embark on this important venture. Some people think there should be formal educational requirements, testing, and a government-issued license before you're allowed to have a child. Without going to that extreme, there are some things you can do to better prepare yourself for parenting, even if you are in the middle of the process or have grown children.

Read everything you can get your hands on. Browse the bookstore and library for books that jump out at you with titles that speak to your special situation. Ask friends and family to recommend books they have found particularly helpful. And don't be afraid to ask the experts for advice. Take a parenting class. Make an appointment with a psychologist or a marriage and family therapist. You don't have to be sick or have a problem to ask for guidance.

Reread Chapter Two of this book to refresh your understanding of life cycle theory. It is important that you really comprehend how people evolve. We are a product of heredity plus environment, but in a dynamic interaction of multiple developing progressions both within ourselves and in relation to the developing progressions of others. For example, two researchers, John Davis and Renato Taguiri, in 1989 studied family firms to discover the influence of life stages on the work relationship of fathers and sons. Interestingly, they found that both the age and the stage of life of both the father and the son have a powerful impact on the relationship and on the son's transition from adolescence to adulthood. Let me walk you through the stages in the relationship of a father and son who work together to give you a clearer picture of just how interactive human development really is.

When a father is in his forties and his son is between seventeen and twenty-two, the relationship is relatively problematic. A man in his forties realizes that there is an end to life and begins to question his accomplishments. There is an urgency to make changes, to correct one's mistakes before time runs out, to prepare a legacy to leave behind (i.e., the family business). In other words, men in their early forties are facing the midlife crisis and generally pour themselves into their work. They are very controlling of their destinies at this stage and don't take kindly to suggestions from a youngster who is either still in or just out of college.

The son, on the other hand, is in the stage of life where he is still in the process of separating from the family. This separation is a necessary component of growing up. Without it, the growing son cannot learn who he is apart from his parents. Conflicts with his father are common and emotionally charged at this time. Going to work for one's father at this stage of life is like extending a young man's childhood, which he can hardly tolerate.

However, as the father moves into his fifties and the son is between twenty-three and thirty-three, the working relationship becomes harmonious. In fact, fathers and sons both report that the best working relationship during the entire period of working together occurs when the father is between fifty-one and sixty and the son is between twenty-three and thirty-three. This time for the father is a period of tranquillity. He has weathered both his own midlife crisis and his son's coming-of-age turmoil. Now his goal is to use reason instead of control to run the company and his life. He may still want to maintain the "old" ways of doing things but is much more willing to negotiate. Men at this stage have proven themselves and are now less competitive and less critical of others, need fewer possessions, and are more attentive to relationships, including their sons' developmental needs.

Sons between twenty-three and thirty-three are not particularly emotionally stable. However, this is a good time for father and son because the son needs a mentor. The son is experimenting with life, work, and relationships in an effort to find his true calling. An older man who can guide him in the process is welcomed because the son feels extreme pressure to grow up, now. Since his father is no longer so competitive and is even inclined to encourage his son's development, the son can feel free to nurture his dreams and develop mastery in an area. By the age of thirty to thirty-three, the son has typically made a commitment to marriage and a career. It is during this stage of development that a father is finally able to give his son recognition for his accomplishments.

A shift away from harmony and toward problems occurs as the father enters his sixties and the son is in his forties. Men in their sixties are facing retirement even if they own their own firm and expect to work until their death. At this age men are aware of their decline and the eventual loss of meaningful activity. Many fathers at this stage are unwilling to turn over the family business to their sons because of this fear of death. They still have a strong need to demonstrate their skills and authority during this period. At the same time that fathers are facing aging and decline, their sons are now facing their own midlife crisis. The sons have a strong need to reevaluate their relationships. They no longer want a mentor. Rather, they want recognition, advancement, and security. They resent having to report to their father. They feel held back by their father and annoyed by his old-fashioned ideas. As the son feels more confident in his role as a competent adult and authority figure, he may challenge his father more, causing considerable strife in the workplace.

An equally revealing study by Collette Dumas in 1988 examined the relationships between daughters and fathers within family firms. Because female development is different from male development, the interaction of a father's and a daughter's developing progressions creates a contrast to that seen between a father and a son. Although daughters also have challenges that they must face in order to grow up, they are not in competition with their fathers. A daughter's identity is strongly allied with nurturing the family and assisting her father in accomplishing his dreams. Therefore, a daughter is often well suited to work side by side with Dad

**143**

throughout the development of the business and through the crises of identity that propel both of them toward maturity. Oddly enough, however, fathers frequently overlook their loyal daughters when it comes to picking a successor to take over the family business. Yet a preponderance of entrepreneurial women have entrepreneurial fathers.

There is much more I could say about the fascinating subject of human development and the interaction of developing progressions. In fact, there are dozens of books on the subject, so I encourage you to read more. If you educate yourself about normal human development and add to this your knowledge of the unique qualities of your children, your spouse, the other adult children in your family, and yourself, you are in a much better position to help your child grow into an independent and creative adult.

# Build Resilience in Your Children

Parents can feel overwhelmed with the responsibility of helping a child through a traumatic time. I remember how sick I felt when my daughter experienced her first major loss, a baby-sitter who was moving out of the country. She cried for a long time, huge, heaving sobs of grief as she realized that she would never again see this person she loved. It broke my heart, and my first reaction was to try to take her pain away. But I caught myself before I went too far, and remembered that grief is *healing*. Grief is a *normal* human reaction to an extreme event. If my job is to be a strong leader, and to assist my child in her own unfolding, then I need to help her grieve. I need to teach her that grief is normal and healthy. I need to teach her that *she* is normal and healthy to be grieving. So on the day she realized that she would never see her baby-sitter again, I held her little sobbing body and cried with her.

Parents are models of how to do life. Although your child is an autonomous being entrusted to your safekeeping for a short time, he or she also imitates your every move. Your child is interpreting his or her world by trying on models, one of which is yours. It is not so much *what* trauma your child experiences that will shape him or her, but *how* your child handles it. Divorce, for example, is a trauma for every member of the family, even extended kin and friends, because it means major changes in lifestyle. However, if you as parents, even divorced parents, handle the parting amicably and respectfully, children can retain their self-esteem.

Children need help understanding *how* to cope with these things. I remember one nine-year-old girl named Susan who was throwing tantrums right and left when her divorced mother was planning to remarry. She had always been such a happy child and a good student, but now was causing major commotion at home and at school. Even during her parents' divorce she had not exhibited such serious tantrums, because her parents had been tolerant and respectful of each other during the separation and legal proceedings.

When I talked with Susan privately, she assured me that she liked her Mommy's boyfriend and did not even mind that they were getting married. What concerned her, however, was *how* to have two Daddies. This problem was pretty easy to clean up. First, I explained to Susan that she had one Daddy and one Ron (her soon-to-be stepfather). Second, I assured her that there was enough love to go around for everyone. In other words, she did not have to choose between two men, and she did not have to stop loving her Daddy just because she had a growing affection for Ron. With this explanation, Susan had a new way to interpret her situation that gave her room to be just who she is in her unique family system.

There is a great deal being written these days about how children handle their parents' divorce, or how healthy it is for them to grow up in single-parent homes, or the effects of extended day care on their psychosocial development. If you read the research you will discover that the results are mixed and confusing. Some children handle these psychological traumas poorly; some coast on by without a scratch; others have problems at home but not at school. The bottom line is that "it all depends."

What it depends on is *how* the trauma is handled by the child and his or her parents and significant others. Once again, as the child's primary role model, you can *reframe* the trauma into a learning experience. Your child will experience many difficult times while growing up, and adult life is certainly not problem-free either. By working with your child to resolve his or her feelings of fear, anger, and grief, and by also working through your own, you are helping your child learn how to handle the stresses and strains of human life.

Too many Americans, especially, feel that they are entitled to "life, liberty, and happiness," when the reality is that the Declaration of Independence states that we are entitled to "life, liberty, and the *pursuit of* happiness." That word, *pursuit*, makes a very important distinction. No one can guarantee happiness to you, not even the American government. Because we Americans often get confused about this distinction, we can become angry when life deals us a blow, and as parents we may feel that our children should never have to suffer.

However, another way to look at suffering is that it is an *opportunity to grow*, to become stronger, more resilient. Crises are challenges that put us to the test, but they also offer us a chance to learn things that we otherwise might not have had a chance to learn. As parents, do not deprive your children of experiencing the

**145**

hardships that face the family. Do not hide dissension between you and your spouse. A fair fight between Mom and Dad that results in a fair and appropriate resolution gives your child a chance to see *how* conflicts get resolved. If you shelter your children from the hard times, they may not know that hard times exist ahead for them, and they may not learn *how* to cope when they do come.

Another problem with sheltering your children from life's hardships is that they then have nowhere to go with their feelings. I have had too many parents tell me that their children do not really know of the hardship the parent is facing. The reality is that the child knows something. Just like the animal who can smell danger, your child can feel the tension in the house, even if he or she cannot describe in words what is wrong. If your child does not get your help in understanding the family problem, he or she can only imagine what's going on—and usually imagines the worst.

I have had four-year-olds tell me of their parents' pending divorce, when not even the respective spouses knew, but it eventually proved to be true. I have had ten-year-olds tell me the extent of Dad's alcohol problem, down to where he hides his bottles, when Mom was still in denial about her husband's alcoholism. I have had teenagers tell me of a parent's extramarital affair because they were afraid to tell this "secret" to anyone else.

I have also known grown children who are still dealing with or covering for some family problem, even though it was long ago resolved by their parents. In one situation, the parents had long ago forgiven each other for a time of great stress when the father threatened to kill the mother and even brandished a revolver in front of the two-year-old. Thinking that their son was too young to remember this event, the parents never spoke to him about it, yet as an adult of thirty, the grown child still felt he needed to protect his mother from his father. That bit of carelessness on the part of these parents wreaked havoc in the family system, perhaps causing long-lasting damage in the relationship between the father and son. (The situation is further complicated in that the parents are copreneurs and the son works for them in the family business.)

Obviously, you do not want to expose your child to harm, nor use the sink-or-swim method of parenting. Yet as you act in your role as family leader, and as you get to know your child, you can *assist* him or her in *discovering* every aspect of life, the good as well as the bad. You can encourage your child to use his or her psychological and physical resources to resolve new problems, thus building your child's confidence that he or she can handle tough things. You can demonstrate through facing and overcoming your own obstacles that even though life is no cakewalk, if you are open to learning new things, you can resolve most of the dilemmas that life dishes out. With those problems that cannot be solved, such as death, you can teach your child that there is room for loss and acceptance, even as we embark on a new adventure in life.

## Move Slowly with Change

As we saw with Earl and Crystal, *blending* a family of "his" children and "her" children is a complex process. It can be compounded further by adding "our" children to the mix. I have reserved a whole section in this chapter to discuss divorce and remarriage because being part of a blended family presents parenting challenges that are very different from those faced by intact families. Also, since divorce and remarriage are a very common part of American life, children are exposed to the problems of blended families every day even if they themselves live within intact families.

It is very confusing for children to be told by their parents that the norm is an intact nuclear family, when in fact the norm for them is quite different. As I review the entrepreneurial couples discussed so far in this book, fully 40 percent are remarriages. Of those 40 percent, 92 percent resulted in blending families of children. These statistics are fairly consistent with what we are now seeing in our culture.

Therefore, if you are to be strong leaders as parents, getting to know your children, educating yourself about child development, assisting your child in his or her unfolding and helping him or her to attend to and learn from crises, it is important that you be honest with your child or children about the family system of which they are a part. It is important for you to talk with them about how their family came into being. And it is important that you model for them healthy ways of being in this unique family. It is important that you help them adjust to the changes that come from blending a family.

This last point cannot be stressed enough. There is a saying in my profession that a system can move ahead only as quickly as the slowest moving member. If you remember that a family is a mix of multiple developing progressions in interaction with each other and that this dialogue of progressions defines the evolution of everyone in the system, then each individual's development as a person depends on the growth of each member in the system. And that growth can happen in a healthy way only as quickly as each child can move toward a resolution of family conflict.

Think about it for a minute. Did you really know what it would be like to be a parent before your first child came into your life? Do you now understand better why your father or mother said, "Just wait until you're a father; then you'll under-stand"? Have you had to alter your parenting strategies with each child depending on their unique needs because what worked with one doesn't work with the other? Did you once think that since parenting one child was so easy, parenting two shouldn't be difficult, only to discover that two feels like ten? Your growth as a par-ent depends not only on having children, but in learning from them about how to be a parent to each unique child. No matter how you slice it, your development as a person is inextricably intertwined with your child's development from the moment of conception until the day you die.

Your development is also intertwined with each and every member of the fam-ily system, even a former spouse you have divorced. Once you and your partner create a child together, you will forever be tied to a system that is larger than each individual. You will furtively eye your ex-spouse across the soccer field as he intro-duces his date to your son. You will exchange a few uncomfortable words with your ex-spouse as you meet at your son's high school graduation. Which mother, Mom or step-Mom, will sit in the front pew at his wedding, or will you both sit there? How will you orchestrate holidays and summer vacation visits? How will you feel when your son spends Christmas day with your ex-husband and Christmas Eve with his in-laws, not visiting you until the day after Christmas?

As a young child, your son or daughter counts on you to help him or her make sense of major changes in his or her life. When marital problems can be resolved only through divorce, or when a child is expected to accept a new family configura-tion through blending, you must take the time to help him or her understand and adjust. The guiding principle here is to *slow down*. You may be lonely, or feel you are ready to start a new relationship, but is your child ready for that? Talk to your child or children about what is happening. Answer their questions. As with Susan, if you notice a peculiar behavior, get professional help. Research shows that following a divorce, children get less attention from their mothers than before the divorce, but more from their fathers. This change is neither good nor bad, but it is a change that children must adjust to. Help them with it.

With entrepreneurial couples, the mix of problems from divorce and blending is further compounded by the likely dissolution of the business partnership. For example, Lynne and her husband, Sid, divorced after several years of marriage, dur-ing which they established a successful restaurant and brought two children into the world. In the divorce settlement Lynne was awarded custody of the children because she had been the primary child-care provider. Lynne was also awarded pri-mary ownership of the restaurant because it was her money that got the business going. However, Sid was the chef and responsible for the reputation the restaurant had for fine Asian food. So Lynne and Sid continued to work together with Lynne as the owner and Sid a valuable employee.

Years later this divorced couple still works together as an ex-wife/owner and an ex-husband/employee. They parent together, too. While Lynne remains single, Sid has remarried and is the father of another young daughter. However, if you ask the older children to describe the family system, they are hard-pressed to come up with an answer. Even as teenagers they avoid the subject as if it is some kind of secret that their parents are divorced. The problem is that Lynne and Sid have not discussed this complicated family and work situation with the children. While the parents seem to get along well enough and have created a restaurant that continues to prosper in spite of the divorce, the children are painfully aware that they have a different family system than many of their friends. Without help from their parents, the children have no way to resolve their grief about the loss of their first family and no way to structure a definition of the new family created from divorce and remarriage.

It is not a sin to make mistakes. Life is about learning something new every day. Sometimes the lessons cause injuries, sometimes permanent scars. But if you really listen to your child and get to know him or her, you can assist your child in learning how to survive divorce and the subsequent blending of families. If your child is confident and has positive self-esteem, and if you are honest with him or her, your child can forgive you your mistakes even if he or she does not like the divorce and is still grieving the loss of the first family.

One mistake you *cannot* afford to make is to deprive your child of the other parent. Even if you remarry, even if your ex-spouse is a derelict, children need access to that parent. They will always be attached to their parents in profound and inexplicable ways. No stepparent can take the place of Daddy or Mommy. Stepparents need to understand this and not get their feelings hurt. As a stepmother or stepfather you can become the child's *friend*. You can be one of the role models your stepchild may imitate. Your stepchild may even prefer your company to that of her Dad or Mom, but in her heart her first parents come first. After all, it is through her first parents, all those years ago, that she had her first experience with discovering herself. That was a memorable period even if only in terms of feelings. Psychologists call this process *bonding*, and it is something that cannot be learned later in life.

It is important to honor this bond even if the child seldom has a chance to see the noncustodial parent. Being willing to talk about the absent parent, sharing photographs of happier times, and helping the child to learn the story of his or her earlier life keep the continuity of life going for the child. Your children need to know that they have a whole life that is unique to them, that has helped to shape them, that may be slightly different from yours. And they need to know that all they have been through is helping them to grow stronger and more beautiful each day—even extreme hardship. They are not bad because bad things have happened to them; and you can prove this by being willing to experience life *with* them.

## Create Independent, Not Obedient, Children

The healthiest children seem to grow up having both a mother and a father to learn from. Each parent has different qualities to provide children. For example, it is not the mother's career but the father's that will determine what career path a daughter will take. Also, a number of researchers have demonstrated that a significant factor in the drive for a woman to become an entrepreneur is that she had a self-employed father. The simple explanation for all of this is that mothers provide nurturing for children and teach them about relationships, while fathers teach their children about the world around them, including the world of work.

When my daughter was five, she put on an apron, stepped into a pair of my cast-off high heels, put her dolly in a stroller, picked up her Crayola case, and headed for the back door. She looked over her shoulder and announced, "Bye-bye, Mommy; I am going to a meeting." On another occasion I overheard her telling a friend what her mother does for a living. She said, "A psychologist is a Mommy who sees clients in the basement." Both of these incidents demonstrate that for my daughter I am a Mommy *first* (or someone she has a relationship with) and a professional *second*.

On the other hand, children are quite clear about their father's career identity. He may be a daddy, but he is an attorney *first*—or an engineer, or a video store owner, or someone who does things "out there." They are often very proud of Dad's accomplishments in the work arena and somehow come to identify with those accomplishments. It's as if they know that if Dad can do it, so can they someday. This is a very important lesson. In fact, *both* lessons are important to healthy child development. That is, children need to know that they are loved and can develop loving relationships, as they have discovered with their mother. And they need to know that they can accomplish tasks and work their way up a worldly hierarchy, as they have discovered emulating their father.

This doesn't mean that the mother's career development is irrelevant to a child, nor that the father's love isn't as important as the mother's. It is more like the concept of yin and yang from Chinese cosmology: Both masculine and feminine energies exist in each individual, with one energy or the other in the forefront at any one time. Until the child has mastered a delicate balancing act, he or she tends to need the lines more clearly demarcated. But as children mature, we see girls who earn straight A's becoming prom queen *and* captain of the track team; and we see boys on the football team, studying madly for their SATs, *and* donating mentoring time to the Special Olympics. These adolescents are demonstrating that they can combine feminine and masculine traits into one unique identity whether they are male or female.

In the 1950s and 1960s, parents emphasized *obedience* in their children. From the 1970s to the present, parents have increasingly emphasized *independence* as the primary prized trait of their children. Even for those parents who still consider obedience of primary importance, you must come to recognize that the rest of society is affirming independence as the goal, and your children are feeling this influence. This is one reason that the prom queen can also be a track star and the football hero can nurture a disabled child. Children and adolescents are seeing more and more models of a more androgynous style, the kind of adult who is high in both masculine and feminine traits. Even though Mom is still the primary model for loving relationships and Dad is the still the primary model for pursuing a career, independent children are learning to define themselves as individuals, not along gender lines.

Independence does not negate the value of obedience. There is a place for obedience, too, and loyalty and respectfulness. The child with positive self-esteem has confidence that he or she can handle life and still work within our society. Such a child can value the lessons learned from his or her family and also move beyond what the parents have accomplished. After all, each succeeding generation has the job of improving the world that they inherited from their parents.

Entrepreneurs sometimes have trouble with this concept. If their child is not suited to the family business or desires to try his or her wings elsewhere, entrepreneurial parents can feel betrayed. If you have been fostering positive self-esteem in your children, then it is logical to assume they will reach a place someday when they want to test out the adult world. They will want to try out their talents to see if they can fly without the aid of their parents. If you do not give them this room, how can you be sure they'll have the maturity to fill your shoes when you eventually retire?

I firmly believe that children need to leave home if they are ever to return as full-fledged adults. For those of you considering a business succession plan involving one or more of your children, be watchful of the huge shadow you cast. How can your child or children ever hope to compete with you unless they carve out

**151**

their own niche in the world? For example, forty-year-old Cathy has worked in her family's restaurant business for twenty-five years. Her older brother, Charles, has done the same. Both have matured with the family business and have seen it grow from one restaurant to five. Cathy's parents, the founders, are nearing retirement and want the business to carry on under the care of their children. Cathy and Charles are ready and well trained (both on the job and with appropriate college degrees) for succession. They also work well as a team, so there is no competition for leadership.

The problem is their younger sibling, Brian. At thirty-five, Brian has never worked in the family firm, preferring to try his hand at other ventures. Unfortunately, everything Brian has tried has failed. Always there to help, his parents have bailed him out of one jam after another. Now as they face retirement, the parents want Cathy and Charles to hire Brian and to share with him ownership and management of the family business. Needless to say, Cathy and Charles are beside themselves with anxiety. They don't want to offend their parents. After all, without their parents neither Cathy nor Charles would be in the fortunate position of owning a thriving business. However, Brian's inexperience, lack of maturity, and questionable work ethic may cause considerable problems in the business. And neither Cathy nor Charles relishes the idea of taking care of their brother indefinitely, as their parents have done.

This type of problem is all too common in family-owned firms. Being a parent is the single most important job in anyone's life. Most of us cherish this responsibility and are very reluctant to give it up when the children leave home. In family firms where children may *never* leave home, the parenting role may continue indefinitely. In Brian's case, this appears to be true. A parent's job is to nurture, protect, and guide children so that they can grow up healthy and capable of independent adult life, but parents don't teach independence directly. Independence is a state of mind that children must conquer for themselves. In order to acquire that state of mind, a child must prove himself or herself in the adult world. This proof often comes by *leaving* the parental home and facing one's fears about being out on one's own.

Some children can acquire maturity while working for their parents, perhaps by going off to college. But most children will have a very difficult time developing the strength of character necessary to run a business if they have not themselves attended the "School of Hard Knocks." If this sounds cruel, think for a moment about where your greatest lessons in life came from. Chances are you grew the most and gained the greatest confidence from facing and overcoming the obstacles that no one else could remove for you. Most entrepreneurs have faced hair-raising challenges in getting their businesses off the ground, so you have had ample opportunity to prove yourself in the adult world. But what of your children, who have never had to look for a job, or feel financial pressure, or rise from the ashes of defeat?

There are a variety of strategies for ensuring that the second- and third-generation members in family firms really grow up. The strategy that will work best for your business and your child depends on the business, the parents' skills, and the personalities of the children. Rick, for example, went off to college and tried his hand at working elsewhere before returning to the family business. When he did return, he wasn't handed the business on a silver platter; he and his wife, Chris, had to buy it! This negotiation not only required adult skills but insured Rick's and Chris' total commitment to the restaurant business.

Whatever strategy you evolve to assist your child in developing independence, the child needs an environment in which he or she can prove himself or herself capable of leadership in the family business. For some this means leaving the business for a while and working elsewhere. For others it means earning a graduate degree before returning to work in the family business. Still others may benefit by working their way up from the mailroom with no preferential treatment from their parents. Finally, some children will be better family members and more capable adults if they never return to the family business.

## Leave Your Children with Fond Memories

One of your most valuable legacies as a parent is to leave your children with fond memories of their childhood. If you have been a strong leader, really took time to get to know your children, assisted them in discovering themselves, helped them through troubling times, and fostered independence, there is no doubt that your relationships will be strong and meaningful. Your children will not only remember the good times but will appreciate how you were there for them during the bad times, too.

Developing fond memories is not just about good times, but they are important. As the saying goes, "Take time to smell the roses." Read bedtime stories to your children. Teach them how to fish. Take them on vacation. Discuss politics at the dinner table, and really listen to their opinions. Include your children in your work. Even a seven-year-old can sweep up the shop or carry out the garbage. Older kids can, for example, set up a computer program to monitor rent and expenses on a real estate investment.

Parenting never ends, even if you have grown children, grandchildren, and great-grandchildren. Parenting is a multigenerational process. Even as you baby-sit your grandchildren, you are providing them with an opportunity to learn more about their history. You have lessons to pass on to them that even your own children never learned. As a grandparent and great-grandparent, you are giving children a sense of belonging and continuity, which is a vital part of anyone's identity.

Ultimately, you will be a model to your children and grandchildren of how to age gracefully. You may not be around to witness your children aging, but you will be their model nevertheless. Be aware of the developmental imperatives of midlife for your children, and be prepared to pass on the leadership of the family business to them. There is more to pass on than just the leadership of the business, however. There is also the responsibility of caring for the family and planning for the welfare of future generations. Teaching your grown children about being good caretakers of the future is an important aspect of parenting, too. It often takes until the third generation of a family firm before the family is in a position to give back to the community. If you have given your children fond memories, they will have grown into loving people who will want to continue to create fond memories for others.

## Your Family Life Plan

In Chapter Four you worked hard and drew up some plans for your personal life, your relationship life, and your business life. In this chapter I have reviewed the *seven basic principles of good parenting*. Now that you have a basic understanding of what is involved in good parenting (although you will of course want to keep educating yourself), you can draw up a family life plan. The questions and directions in Self-Assessment Exercise 12 are a good place to start. Be honest with yourself and your spouse when appraising your parenting skills. Review the seven basics of sound parenting, and evaluate your skills and understanding of these precepts. Be brave enough to change what you are doing as a parent if it's not working. Though it is time-consuming and hard work to really plan your parenting, it will pay off in the long run where it counts the most—in healthy, independent, creative offspring who can carry on the family legacy.

I won't take the time here to review everything from Chapter Four, but I'll remind you of the seven ground rules for successful life planning. Applying these ground rules to your family and parenting plan will bring all of your plans to the same level so that they can be integrated into one holistic, ever-evolving master plan.

1. *Plan with your spouse and others who are significant in your life, including your children.* Getting others' feedback is imperative. It keeps you aware that you are not in this life alone. Even when you are planning a life goal that seems so personal that it could not possibly be relevant to anyone but yourself, ask others for their opinions. Many of your personal goals can be thwarted by the unexpected demands of other areas of your life.

2. *Develop the communication attitudes and skills discussed in Chapter Three.* Becoming an excellent communicator will assist you in communicating with yourself as well as others. As important as these skills are in learning about the ones you love and work with, learning to listen to yourself (i.e., to trust your intuition) will move you toward the most powerful decisions in your life.

3. *Brainstorm.* Be open to new understandings about the interdependence of love and work. Look at different models than what you are used to. Brainstorm as many options as you can think of for redefining your relationship, yourself, your family life, and your business structure.

4. *Be open.* Let go of all the reasons you should not or cannot do something. Do not turn away any option while you are brainstorming. Later, as you develop a plan to integrate these new notions, you can discard the unworkable ones. But remember, even the unworkable option today may prove workable sometime in the future.

5. *Shoot for the moon.* Allow yourself and your significant others to dream. Plan for the optimum in all areas of your life. A common mistake is settling for the average when with a little extra effort you could produce something extraordinary. You may not get to the moon in all cases, but you are certain to fail if you never try.

6. *Plan for the worst.* This sounds a little pessimistic, but the value is in planning. If you have contingency plans, you feel less threatened by the unknown. However, it is important to not be guided by your thoughts of the worst possibilities. Then your plans take on the shape of fear and failure.

7. *Be flexible.* Ultimately, the life plan you develop will encompass as many areas of your life as you are aware of, but no plan is perfect or permanent. Life is full of surprises. Be prepared to change the plan with the evolution of yourself as an individual, as a marital partner, as a parent, and as a business owner or partner.

## Your Family Life Plan

Answer the following questions as honestly as you can. There are no right or wrong answers. The purpose of this exercise is to help you identify your parenting and family values and goals, so that you can plan for yourself, your partner, and your children a life that is consistent with those values.

1. Make a list of the people who were most significant to you as a child and indicate what you learned from them or how they influenced you.

2. Make two lists for each of your parents. In the first column, list those parenting qualities you most admire about that parent. In the second column, indicate those parenting qualities you least admire. Which parent are you most like and least like? Which of their parenting qualities do you possess? What would you like to change?

3. Repeat step 2 with grandparents, teachers, and other significant adults from your childhood.

4. What are your fondest memories from childhood? Why?

5. What do you think your children would recount as their fondest memories? Ask them.

6. How would your children describe you if asked about you as a parent and as a person?

7. What do your really know about your children? What do they like? What makes them laugh? Do they have opinions about anything? Who are their heroes?

8. Sit down and have a meaningful conversation with each child and let her or him take the lead.

9. Have a family meeting with all family members and discuss how the family might reorganize itself and raise everyone's consciousness about healthy family relations.

10. What are the qualities you believe are responsible for your successes in life? Are you teaching those qualities to your children?

11. Do you and your partner share the same parenting philosophy? If not, what is your plan to get on the same track?

12. Pick up a good book on parenting and begin educating yourself. With your partner, read and discuss one chapter each week. Then apply what you are learning.

## Evaluating Your Responses

By now you are probably getting pretty good at sifting through your responses and those of your partner. You have been evaluating and reevaluating other aspects of your life plan. Now it is time to reorganize your parenting priorities too. Look for the patterns in your answers. Really listen to what your children and your partner are telling you. Notice where the discrepancies are between your good intentions and your actual behaviors. How can you bring them together? If you are continuing in an unhealthy pattern, now is the time to change it. Notice, too, what you are doing right, and build on those successes.

Taking into account all that you have learned from this exercise and from each other, including the children, what will it take for you to become an authoritative parent who takes time to get to know your children, who takes seriously the responsibility to foster resilience and independence in your children, who understands that children need time to make changes, and who wants your children to remember their childhood fondly?

## Summarizing Remark

Write one sentence or a brief paragraph summarizing what you learned from this exercise and what you want to change.

# 8

# Wealth Management: How to Balance Health and Wealth

Money is a powerful thing for most people, yet we seldom examine our attitudes about it or have a plan for its wise management. Most of the entrepreneurial couples who read this book have acquired wealth or soon will. Many of them, however, are no better prepared to handle money and its consequences than are individuals of more modest means.

Not everyone can afford to fly home on weekends to resolve their marital problems, as Kurt did when he was living apart from Trish. Not everyone can give up a steady job and open a retail business, as Stan and Rhonda did. Not everyone can afford a nanny, as Mike and Karla can. These couples have worked hard and used their creativity to earn money—a lot of money. But many of these couples do not feel wealthy, in spite of the size of their bank accounts. And for many of them *money is a trap*, causing strain in the relationship and dysfunction in the family.

In this chapter we will explore the meaning of money. Like everything else in an entrepreneurial relationship, money needs to be discussed and planned for. Becoming aware of your own biases and skewed perceptions about money will help you break through unnecessary roadblocks to handling wealth. Developing a solid plan for the management of your wealth requires a thoughtful dialogue with your partner, or your dreams may be foiled.

Jonathan and Brooke had a prenuptial agreement to protect the assets that Jonathan had acquired before the marriage. Years later, after Brooke had assisted Jonathan in revitalizing the advertising agency and expanding its success into the international arena, the prenuptial agreement had been forgotten. At least, Brooke *thought* it had been forgotten—until Jonathan said he wanted to revise it. Brooke was crushed that her husband did not trust her and that he was unwilling to give her credit for her contribution to their success. He maintained that their success was due to his financial investment even though he acknowledged Brooke's contributions in other areas.

Connie and Ray had known each other since they were teenagers. On the surface, they are the epitome of the American success story. Never having even finished high school, the young couple got married and launched a successful wholesale health food business. However, in their early thirties now, with three children and a multimillion-dollar business that employs several family members, Connie and Ray have a serious problem with drug addiction. They had never had a model for handling wealth, and they foolishly indulged in drug use and now find that their lives are out of control.

Amy and Evan are a quiet couple who met in college, got married after graduation, and settled in the suburbs. With two young children of school age, Amy has returned to full-time teaching. Evan has been developing his career as a freelance technical writer and is quite successful. This couple is earning more income than their parents did at the same age and will likely outstrip the lifetime earnings of their working-class parents as well. Also lacking any models for handling wealth, Amy is constantly worrying that there will not be enough money. She questions Evan about every penny he spends, especially when he spends money to promote his business. Having never been self-employed herself, and having never seen her parents with any money, Amy is unclear about what level of business expenditure is appropriate.

All three of these couples need to bust some of the myths that they have about money. They need to reexamine what money means to them and what they want it to mean. They need to plan a strategy for acquiring wealth and what it really takes to create wealth. Some people expect to create wealth by working at careers they enjoy; this isn't necessarily true. Others expect wealth to come to them only through some magical means. Still others never plan for wealth at all, and when it arrives are so overwhelmed by it that they become emotionally distraught.

This chapter will primarily look at earned wealth, rather than inherited wealth. However, in family-owned businesses, the business owners need to plan for the succession of the business to their offspring, who have not earned the wealth and who may have different beliefs about money than their parents did. Even entrepreneurial couples who do not plan to pass the business on to their children need to have plans and strategies for managing wealth that also include passing their wealth on to the next generation. Seldom do family business owners have such a plan, which is why so few family firms make it to the second generation and why many offspring of entrepreneurs are a disappointment to their parents when it comes to handling money.

# The Meaning of Money

The following phrases and bits of wisdom are based on beliefs about money rooted in our cultural history. As you read through these phrases and statements, check out your feelings, your gut reactions to each. Do some seem more true than others? Does one comment or another make you feel uneasy? Which phrase or aphorism rings the truest for you? Which one delights you? And what other bits of wisdom about money can you think of?

► Money can't buy love.

► You can't take it with you.

► Dirty money.

► Filthy rich.

► Cold, hard cash.

► As phony as a three-dollar bill.

► A penny saved is a penny earned.

► Buy low, sell high.

► Two for the price of one.

► A fool and his money are soon parted.

► It's as easy to marry a rich man as a poor one.

► It is easier for a camel to go through the eye of a needle than for a rich man to enter the kingdom of God.

► Penny wise and pound foolish.

► Money talks.

► Love of money is the root of all evil.

This chapter will not provide a thorough analysis of money in our culture, nor even an analysis of the role of money in marriage or business partnership. It will not give you a brief course in economics or money management. Rather, this chapter is a guide to uncovering your beliefs about money and how they have affected your most intimate relationships. By coming to terms with your beliefs about money, you have an opportunity to challenge those beliefs if they are not healthy or productive. You have an opportunity to reorganize your priorities and to strive to achieve balance between love and work, between personal relationship and business partnership.

What brings most couples to psychotherapy are arguments about money, sex, or children. I have discussed children and parenting in the previous chapter, and while sex may be intriguing, I will leave that topic for other experts and other books. In this chapter, I am going to focus on money—specifically, the meaning we as human beings attach to it and how that meaning affects our loved ones.

Money is always on our minds. No matter how much money you have, you always have money problems. Financial problems are really just the tip of the iceberg for couples, concealing deeper, hidden issues between family members. Those entrepreneurial couples who have faced divorce discover that money is the tie that binds. It is often easier to give up a spouse than it is to give up one's money. Yet in spite of the power of money to entangle our personal relationships, few couples seek out psychotherapy when they have a financial crisis. Instead, couples continue to use money in a power struggle with their loved ones. Money is given, then taken away. Money is used to reward and punish. Money is a promise, a bribe, a threat. Rarely is money given as a gift with no strings attached.

In my experience, most entrepreneurial couples, who invariably have money as one cornerstone of their relationship, tend to ignore that cornerstone. They engage in a covert power struggle with each other in which money takes on the meaning of every important value in their lives. In other words, they place a price tag on each other, their respective accomplishments, the children, the business, their time together, and their time apart.

If you are to truly free yourself of the money trap, such as the various traps that have snared Jonathan and Brooke, Connie and Ray, and Amy and Evan, then you will need to assess your *money beliefs*, and to be honest about your biases and manipulations with regard to money. You need to acknowledge just how important money is to you. Just as you evaluated your values and goals for your personal life plan, your relationship life plan, your business life plan, and your parenting life plan, you will need to evaluate your financial values and goals and make sure that they are ethical and compassionate when it comes to your marriage and family.

In the following pages, I will introduce you to some of the specific money traps that have snared entrepreneurial couples I have known, in order to give you a better idea of your own biases and traps. Out of this knowledge about the *meaning of money* and the traps that these meanings can build, you will also learn how to short-circuit the traps and reorganize your lives so as to achieve a better balance between love and work.

# Desire Creates Desire

Tom and Karen struggled for several years to rebalance their lives after Tom's engineering business took off. Tom is a pioneering solo entrepreneur and Karen his supportive spouse. Because of their very different personalities, Karen was not really ready for the wealth that came so rapidly into her life. Neither she nor Tom had had wealth in the past, but Tom was more open to the lifestyle changes that wealth allowed. He took great pride in the dollars he was creating. He became involved in his community, serving on charity boards and donating his time to various civic functions. He also used his newfound money to create more money through additional projects and new business partners. He bought a big new house for his family, a vacation condo, new cars, and expensive vacations.

Karen, on the other hand, languished at home, barely able to take care of her two sons and decorate their new home. She complained constantly that Tom was unavailable to her, but she herself did not seek out new challenges. She essentially wanted her old life back. So it was surprising to Tom when one day she had a bounce in her step and a twinkle in her eye. When he inquired about the change, she told him that she had found the perfect bed for the master bedroom. Her entire perspective on life had changed because of a bed. She was consumed with thoughts of the bed—how to decorate it and arrange other furniture around it, what draperies would be complementary.

Although Tom was a bit confused that a bed could have such power over his wife, he was not opposed to her newfound project—until he learned that the bed frame alone cost $5,000! Of course they argued. Tom thought Karen foolish and superficial. Karen thought Tom insensitive and stingy. If a bed would make her happy, why was he so opposed to it?

It seems to be true among human beings that when basic needs are satisfied, new ones appear. Because Karen's basic needs were satisfied, she had nowhere to put her energy. She was no longer working because the family did not need her income. She could afford a housekeeper, a gardener, and a private school for her sons. She had wealth and a *desire* to use it but no guidelines on *how* to use it. So she fell into the trap of *spending* it. Tom was concerned, though, that if Karen thought the bed would make her happy, what would happen when the charm wore off the new purchase?

Economist John Kenneth Galbraith writes in *The Affluent Society*, "It is the process of satisfying wants that creates the wants." A characteristic that defines our modern society and makes us much different now than at any other time in history, is our ability to satisfy our wants. According to Galbraith, however, production to *satisfy* our wants only *creates* the wants. He says, "Production only fills the void that it has itself created." In Karen's case, a void was created by the wealth that Tom produced. And both she and Tom set out to fill that void. While Tom found socially acceptable wants (i.e., community and charity work), Karen struggled with her beliefs about money, until she finally hit upon the solution of buying extravagant *things*.

When I first met them, Barb and Kevin were much farther along the path toward accumulating their desires than Tom and Karen were. In fact, they were on the brink of divorce. As an entrepreneurial couple (Barb a solo entrepreneur and Kevin a well-paid sales executive), they had the ability to create considerable wealth, but they were always at the point of financial ruin. Instead of planning for wealth, instead of examining their beliefs about money, instead of working out a life plan together, Barb and Kevin just *spent* their money. They bought a huge house in the country for their four children, which required long commutes for everyone. They bought expensive cars. They bought a horse for their oldest daughter and paid for private riding lessons. They bought minibikes for their sons. And they recently sold one boat only to buy themselves a bigger one.

When Barb and Kevin sought my help, divorce was a foregone conclusion. Their debts were so large that they could not afford to cut back at work. In fact, they had to work longer hours to make ends meet. Therefore, they had no time for each other and to nurture the marital relationship. They also had no time for their children, who were now reacting to the lack of parental attention and supervision. The older children started turning in failing grades at school, and one son was regularly being suspended for fighting. The younger children were quiet and frightened; never knowing if their parents were going to fight, they hid in their rooms a lot.

Barb and Kevin thought that making money meant spending it. As they fulfilled one desire, another arose to take is place. As they made more money to pay for their increasing desires, they needed more. They lost track of why they had married in the first place. They lost track of what was exciting and appealing about their careers; their careers became just a way to feed their ever-increasing desires. They tried to handle the enormous responsibility of rearing four children by buying them things, expensive things, and sending them to fancy summer camps.

There is nothing inherently wrong with making money, nor with spending it. However, like everything else in life, if money matters outweigh everything else, there are likely to be unhealthy repercussions. It may seem contrary to common sense that satisfying a desire creates yet another desire, but this is a basic principle of human nature. If you want the Rolex watch and you have the money for it, go ahead and buy it. But before you buy the watch, ask yourself, *Why?* Is the watch merely a watch, or is it a status symbol, a reward for hard work, or a move for power? Whatever the reason, be clear about it and be prepared to handle the consequences. If Karen buys the bed she wants, she may be filling a void, but also creating a new one. After all, a $5,000 bed frame requires a comparable mattress, linens, and complementary furnishings, doesn't it?

# Poverty Consciousness
# Versus Prosperity Consciousness

In this chapter I have alluded to some of the beliefs Americans have about money, most of them negative. We want money, but we do not like to admit that we do. As a result, our secret desires are often expressed in unhealthy ways. We hoard money. We hide it from our loved ones. At one extreme we may deprive ourselves of the benefits of a large income, and at the other extreme lavish ourselves with expensive purchases we can barely afford. All the while we are confusing money with the values we want to live by.

Although Evan and Amy are a middle-income couple, they are wealthy by the standards of their extended family. And in the future, if Evan's business takes off as he has planned, the couple could move into a comfortable upper-middle-class status. At this level, they could afford almost anything they desired and certainly more than their extended family can afford. Therefore, Evan and Amy need to begin planning how to handle their new financial status.

The major problem facing this couple is *poverty consciousness,* which is a state of mind that affects how we perceive money and our access to money. Amy had grown up watching her parents struggle financially, which prompted her to go to college and get a teaching degree. She wanted a solid career so that she would never have to worry about paying her bills. She did not think about following a dream, but rather chose a career that was culturally acceptable for a woman and that would enable her to earn a satisfactory income. Amy has never examined her ability to make a lot of money. Rather, her only concern has been to *avoid* poverty.

Evan, on the other hand, has never concerned himself with how much money he made. He grew up in a family with an entrepreneurial father, so he learned first-hand of the excitement and problems inherent in that lifestyle. Although his parents never made much money, they lived a comfortable life in a middle-class neighborhood. As Evan grew up, his father encouraged him to follow his dreams, whether they be pitching for his Little League team or pursuing a career as a writer. Evan would really like to write a novel some day, but for the time being he is building a successful business as a freelance technical writer and occasionally contributes a creative piece to a magazine.

Evan is confused by Amy's negativity about his freelance business. Together their joint incomes produce more than the couple spends. They have bought a nice house in a pleasant neighborhood with good schools nearby. They have a tidy savings account, and both have retirement accounts as well as college funds started for each child. Yet whenever Evan expands his business, requiring an expenditure of capital, Amy is distressed. For his part, Evan believes in himself. He knows that the investment will pay off one way or the other. Even if there is not an *immediate* payoff in terms of increased income, he is confident that the increased exposure or the development of a new skill will produce benefits in the long run. This philosophy is known as *prosperity consciousness*. That is, Evan believes in *abundance,* that there is enough to go around. He believes that following his dreams will lead him to where he should be, and that there will be a payoff eventually.

With Frank and Louise the poverty/prosperity consciousness dilemma has taken on a slightly different twist. Frank is angry a lot that Louise does not want to work outside the home. He believes it is unfair that he has to earn all of the money, yet he does earn plenty of money now. Frank envies Louise's position as the primary child-care provider. He would like the freedom to stay home once in a while and play with the children. But he feels compelled to work because his wife does not.

The reality is that Frank works and, indeed, is a workaholic not because his wife produces no income but because he is afraid not to. His poverty consciousness drives him to work harder and longer, acquiring more and more wealth. He is afraid that if he does not work so hard, he will lose everything. Frank came from an impoverished childhood and began working as a young boy. His parents divorced when he was a child, leaving Frank to help parent the younger children. Dad disappeared for a few years, and he and Frank were reconciled only after Frank grew up. This is the classic story of an entrepreneur driven to financial success by the loss of a father and an impoverished upbringing.

While poverty and abandonment are powerful motivators toward acquiring wealth, it is difficult to let go of poverty consciousness once you have arrived in the world financially. It has become such a way of life, such a driving force that entrepreneurs with this style are afraid to use any other method. They often laugh at the idea that they could earn more money by working less. They rationalize that they love what they do, but their families know the other side, the dark side of their personality.

To break this pattern is difficult at this stage, so it is better to analyze your money beliefs early on and compare them to your spouse's. If you are operating under the principle of prosperity consciousness, but you have a spouse driven to avoid poverty, you are going in opposite directions. The ultimate outcome for an entrepreneurial couple with this poverty/prosperity consciousness dichotomy is often divorce.

People with a poverty consciousness are often not having any fun. If you think this may be true for you or your spouse, use this simple test: If you are waiting to have fun until you have made *enough* money, you are probably motivated by poverty consciousness. To break the pattern, do something fun today. Evaluate your life plan and look for ways to follow your dreams, instead of doing what's best, or most practical, or least scary. Notice your successes instead of only focusing on what you have yet to accomplish. Most important, get into psychotherapy. Poverty consciousness is usually the result of deep-seated emotional problems stemming from your childhood, such as is the case with Amy and Frank. A therapist will help you rethink the lessons from childhood and revise your money beliefs to include the possibility that you actually *deserve* prosperity. With this new belief, you might be able to start enjoying your wealth with your spouse and your other loved ones.

## How Much Is Enough?

It is unlikely that an entrepreneur motivated by poverty consciousness will ever become a spendthrift, so learning to have fun is not really a threat. Once you have learned to appreciate the value of hard work, you do not really forget that value as you relax a few standards and learn to enjoy your wealth. It is fascinating, however, to what extreme some entrepreneurs have to go to before they feel they have acquired *enough*.

Recently I read about Charles Feeney, a New Jersey billionaire who had secretly given away $600 million to a variety of charities and colleges. For fifteen years he gave away money in total anonymity, but with the sale of his business, an accounting would reveal his generosity, so he decided to go public. Typical of many entrepreneurs, Feeney had not grown up rich; he made his fortune owning duty-free shops in airports. At the time Feeney revealed his secret, he owned neither a house nor a car, and wore a $15 watch. Apparently finally free of the poverty consciousness that drove him to earn and accumulate $4 billion, Feeney answered the question of why he gave away so much: "I simply decided I had enough money."

Four billion dollars seems like more than enough to me, but everyone has their own measure of what feels right. David was having a difficult time deciding how much was enough for him. He and his wife, Sharon, are dual entrepreneurs. They have acquired enormous wealth between them, but David is loathe to spend it. David has the typical poverty consciousness that drove him to build a fortune through several business interests. Sharon, on the other hand, moved into entrepreneurial activity after her husband had achieved wealth, making it possible for her to start her own real estate sales business.

During a low point in their marriage, Sharon decided she could no longer live with David as long as spending money was so difficult. He questioned her every purchase, seeming to need to have complete control of their joint finances. He interrogated the children about how they spent their own money, even when they earned it at outside jobs. When questioned about how much money he needed to have in the bank in order to feel *safe*, David could not come up with a figure. No matter how much was in the bank, David felt that it was too early to spend it. Living under this kind of tyranny was too great a burden for Sharon, so she moved out into her own apartment.

This situation continued for several months. David was quite ruthless about the separation. He changed the locks on the doors and would not even allow his children to visit since they had moved out with their mother. He would not allow Sharon to take anything from the house to set up her new apartment, not even bath towels from the guest bath. David acted as if he had to fight for his life, a state that is characteristic of *extreme* poverty consciousness.

Then one day I got a call from David. I was surprised to hear from him since he had refused to return to marital therapy for several months. Sharon had been willing to continue our sessions even during the separation because she believed that there had to be answers to their problems and she still loved her husband, but she was not willing to live with him until he changed. Something in David's voice told me he *had* changed. When I met with him later that week, he told me the story.

When Sharon left, David felt that everything he had worked for was being taken from him. He was desperate, and out of desperation he withdrew from everyone. He tried to preserve what was left, his money and his things. He went to work with a vengeance and developed even more ways to make money. Then something profound happened. David said, "I was sitting in my living room, all alone, and as I looked around at my possessions I wouldn't have minded holding a match to them all. If I can't have my wife and family, what's the point of all these *things?*"

David finally had his answer as to how much was enough. He had also broken the money trap of poverty consciousness. From this point forward he worked on building a new attitude based on prosperity consciousness. After reconciling, he and Sharon attended seminars on personal and spiritual development as well as seminars on investment strategies. They combined the lessons from both types of seminars to create a life plan that included the best of love and work. Most important, David learned to have fun. And in doing so, he got his wife and family back.

# Competition or Collaboration?

In the early stage of marriage, many couples are in *competition* with each other. This is neither good nor bad but simply a common developmental stage. As the young couple is learning about living together, they must make adjustments to each other to develop their own couple style. Like children learning to share with a sibling or friend, young marrieds are learning to share their respective lifestyles and goals, and sometimes they will clash. To resolve the disagreement, newly marrieds often think that there must always be a winner and a loser. As I have discussed in previous chapters, there are other more creative and healthy ways to resolve conflicts, but at first this is all that most people know.

Entrepreneurial couples tend to remain at this competitive stage longer than other couples. As my research has shown, copreneurs especially are often trapped by a gender-based division of responsibilities and authority. The competition problem is settled by the husband assuming total leadership and the wife acquiescing to his benevolent authority. While this solution works for some, others chafe at the style, but have no other model for resolving the competition. Brooke and Jonathan represent this latter type of copreneurial couple.

Brooke and Jonathan have achieved tremendous success with the evolution of their advertising agency into the international arena. They have more than enough money—even if not by Charles Feeney's standards. Brooke recently bought herself a brand new Jaguar and paid cash. The couple is active in a number of community endeavors from politics to charities. Their oldest child is graduating from a top college, and the younger children are attended to by a devoted nanny. Jonathan has been written up in *Forbes* as one of America's up-and-coming young entrepreneurs.

Yet even with all of this success, competition between the two is still evident. When Jonathan resurrected the long-forgotten prenuptial agreement, Brooke was floored. They had tackled the competition problem many times in the past, and each time had worked it through to a mutually agreeable solution. The most notable time this happened, Jonathan decided to turn over the reins of the local business to Brooke, while he assumed full leadership in the international arena. This solution allowed the couple to stop competing with each other in the business. They began operating more as dual entrepreneurs than copreneurs, each with the freedom to develop their respective businesses along the lines of their own vision. With all of this success behind them, why then was Jonathan competing with Brooke again?

Jonathan readily admitted that the success of their enterprises was a joint effort. He acknowledged that Brooke was a talented executive and needed room to express her talents; thus he backed away from his role as president of the local business. Yet, still having a bit of poverty consciousness, Jonathan feared that if he did not protect his interests, he would lose everything. He viewed every step in the career process as a forum for competition and could not seem to escape this style even with his wife, his most trusted partner. Even when his attorneys told Jonathan that his and Brooke's fortune was so intertwined that a postnuptial agreement was pointless, Jonathan could not let go of the idea. He needed to have the upper hand.

Eventually Brooke agreed to a postnuptial contract, which was essentially not worth the paper it was printed on. Brooke felt that his interests were protected psychologically, but the price he paid was to keep the competitive spirit alive between himself and his wife. They had still not mastered the art of *collaboration*.

Collaboration is the quality seen in entrepreneurial couples who operate as social partners at home, each shouldering equal responsibilities for running the household and caring for the children. Collaboration involves appreciating each partner's contribution to the relationship, whether that contribution is financial or in some other form. Collaboration is possible when entrepreneurial couples have conquered desire and poverty consciousness. Collaboration is a result of embracing prosperity consciousness and finally realizing that you have *always* had more than enough to satisfy all your needs and wants.

After months of hard work in psychotherapy, Rhonda and Stan survived their competitive stage of marital development. Stan's ruthless competition with Rhonda was quelled when Rhonda chose to return to her former career and leave Stan to run the business. However, once Stan proved that he could be successful in business, he no longer needed to be better at something than his wife. He could allow her suggestions and even an occasional decision. He even went so far as to express

**170**

gratitude for the years Rhonda had worked outside the business producing income so that he could start his dream venture. Once again they became a team in spirit, though Stan still operated as a solo entrepreneur and Rhonda kept her corporate job.

Don and Marla are having a more difficult time moving out of the competition stage because of their traditional style of marriage. As a homemaker, Marla has never competed with Don in the business arena. She and Don divided responsibilities along traditional gender lines and, as so often happens with this style, grew apart. Each managing their own territory not only kept the competition between them intact, but it also made them totally independent of each other. There is no camaraderie, no sharing of each other's goals, no awareness even of the other's life. They essentially live *separate* lives, Don making the money and Marla raising the children.

When Marla suggested that she wanted to go to work part-time, not just handle the bookkeeping for Don, Don was supportive to a point. Although two children were in college and one about to graduate from high school, Don wanted assurances from Marla that her household duties would not be neglected or dumped on him. When Marla's independence of Don grew further by her involvement outside the home, Don got even more controlling. Marla became aware of how financially dependent on her husband she had become. She knew none of the details of their financial situation, so she approached Don with questions about investments, college funds, and retirement accounts. Because Don had managed all of this without keeping Marla informed for all these years, he somehow assumed that he controlled the money. He resented her questions and got even more secretive about money matters, even going so far as to secretly transfer funds to new banks. He was afraid that Marla would mismanage the money, an especially extreme reaction considering that Marla had been a bank manager prior to her marriage to Don.

Even with a traditional, gender-based division of responsibilities, it is a mistake for a couple to not share equally in the decision making that affects both their lives. One person may be the bookkeeper, for example, but both partners are responsible for how the money is earned and spent—just as one person may be the primary child-care provider, but both parents must be actively involved in parenting for children to grow up with a balanced view of marriage and family life. Competition interferes with the natural process of collaboration. To move beyond competition, find another arena in which to express your competitive spirit. Compete for market share or play competitive sports, but always collaborate with your spouse as your partner in a joint venture of marriage and business. Remember that the love that

**171**

brought you together is worth nurturing in an environment where you both are honored and respected for your respective contributions to that joint venture.

# The American Work Ethic

The American *work ethic* may not be unique to Americans, but it is a defining characteristic of our culture. Deep down inside, every American believes that if they work hard, they can achieve the "American Dream." We all believe in the right to "life, liberty, and the pursuit of happiness," and for many of us that belief includes the right to get rich—more than that, it includes the expectation that we *deserve* to get rich.

Entrepreneurs have bought into the American Dream and thus epitomize the American work ethic. With nothing but an idea and determination, many entrepreneurs and entrepreneurial couples achieve, succeed, and amass great wealth. When it comes time to manage that wealth, as this chapter has demonstrated, most entrepreneurial couples are not well prepared. Not only are they not prepared to handle the money in day-to-day living, but they also are not preparing their children to manage wealth. Often they naively assume that since *they* worked hard to achieve their dream, *their children* will do the same. However, this is often not the case.

Recently I met an heiress of a billion-dollar fortune. This woman, who is now in her forties, has lived in luxury all her life. She attended private schools, of course, and all her friends were from an elite group of exceptionally wealthy families. As a child, she was insulated from the rest of the world by virtue of living in a gated community, being chauffeured to events, and socializing only with other people of her socioeconomic class. In addition, she was reared by a nanny and *visited* with her parents only occasionally.

She recalls being lonely but not realizing that this was a function of her sheltered lifestyle. Then her father fired her nanny after ten years of faithful service. This was devastating to the young woman in more ways than one: She realized her father's extreme power over her life, and she also realized that she loved the nanny more than she loved her parents. As a teenager, she started putting the desperate picture together and became deeply depressed about her life. How was she to make her mark in the world if money was the only measure of one's worth?

By the time the heiress graduated from high school, five of her privileged friends had already committed suicide. She knew that she did not want to take this path, but was unclear about what other options were available to her. After wandering in and out of college for several years, taking sabbaticals to travel around the world, she eventually got a pointless degree after ten years and married. Fortunately for her, her husband was not from a wealthy family and she was forced for the first time to collaborate with a spouse whose values about money were different from her own. After much soul searching, years of therapy, and multiple conflicts with her husband, the heiress went back to graduate school and became a psychotherapist specializing in the treatment of other *inheritors.*

Although children do model their parents, and entrepreneurs often come from families where one or both parents were entrepreneurs, children also develop their identities based on their interpretations of their life experiences. If children grow up in luxury, never having to prove themselves competent because they are insulated by their parent's money, is it really any surprise that many of them do not develop the typical American work ethic? Entrepreneurial couples who do not assess the meaning of money in their lives, who do not plan for the successful psychological management of their wealth and who do not plan for educating their children about wealth will fail their children and ultimately fail the business. Not all entrepreneurial couples will be succeeded in business by their children. Nevertheless, a succession plan is in order. And the succession plan must include not only an orderly transition of power from one generation to the next (whether to your children or to outsiders), but also provisions for raising the children with a healthy money consciousness and a sense of competence in acquiring money of their own.

As you may recall, Rick inherited the restaurant business from his father. Rick learned the business from the ground up starting out as a little boy sweeping up after closing while his grandfather cleared the till. He worked in the business for many years before meeting his wife. Rick even got a taste of life outside the business when he went off to college and worked elsewhere after graduation. He returned to the family business shortly before meeting Chris. Rick was his Dad's right-hand man, but Rick wanted to take the business in a new direction. Because Dad had other interests, he agreed and sold the business to his son. Shortly thereafter the young couple decided to marry. Rick and Chris together have taken the business to a level of prosperity that neither the grandfather nor the father ever dreamed of.

It appears that the work ethic is alive and well in Rick. The reasons are probably quite clear. The family developed a business that could expand with the family. There was room for succession between generations because there was flexibility in how the business evolved. Rick moved out into the world as a young man and demonstrated his competency as an adult *before* taking over his father's business. Also by his buying the business, the restaurants became *his* (and Chris'), not his father's anymore. Whether Rick's family had a conscious succession plan or not, they could not have planned this transition any better.

You may disagree with the American work ethic and want to raise your children with a different set of values about money, but if you are reading this book, that's probably not the case. The very fact of reading this book indicates that you are entrepreneurial or desire to be so someday. To deny your desire to make money, a lot of money, will only sabotage your success and leave your children with low self-esteem. Admit what you want and how much you want. Then design a plan to create the wealth, to manage the wealth, and to teach your children to discover their own ability to create prosperity. Whatever kind of abundance your children ultimately accept, be it money or some other kind of wealth, they will learn from you how to incorporate abundance into a well-balanced life of love and work.

# The Tangled Web

For most entrepreneurial couples, successful money management will be accomplished by conquering desire, developing prosperity consciousness, discovering a reasonable concept of how much is enough, taking competition out of the marriage, and passing along a healthy work ethic to your children. However, if your assessment of your money values includes unethical beliefs or behaviors, you have more work cut out for you. Do not let shame or fear get in your way. If you have erred in the past, clean up your mistakes. If your parents have erred, roll up your sleeves and redesign your life. There's no sense in letting family secrets of improprieties entangle you in a web of lies and unethical behavior that will sabotage your own pursuit of happiness.

Nicholas and Annalisa are copreneurs with a retail furniture business. Nicholas, who is an all-rounder, manages the store, while Annalisa, who is an organizer, lends her talents to customers as an interior design consultant. In spite of being well matched as partners and in spite of their store having great potential, Nicholas and Annalisa have allowed family secrets and improprieties from the past to color their judgment in running the business.

Nicholas was a physically and sexually abused child who ran away from home as a teenager and vowed never to treat his family as he had been treated. However, the ancestral family pattern endured; no one was more surprised than Nicholas when he began abusing his own children. Rather than face the abuse as a sign of emotional distress, Annalisa tried to protect the children from their father without really confronting the problem. Nicholas also ignored the problem, instead pouring himself into the business.

With these family secrets intact, the furniture store prospered—or so Annalisa thought. They had mortgaged the house to invest in the business, and it appeared from what Annalisa and Nicholas were spending that the investment had been a wise one. Yet the secret that Nicholas was an abusive father fostered other secrets. When Annalisa found that the I.R.S. had seized her personal bank account and attached a lien to their house, she learned for the first time that Nicholas had not paid taxes for several years. Thus she also learned that secrets have a way of multiplying—and of catching up with you in the end.

Carol had grown a lot since starting her garden center with Bob. Her greatest growth came with accepting that she was the solo entrepreneur and Bob her supportive spouse. At first, it was difficult accepting the role reversal, but Bob had been so supportive and unthreatened by his wife that Carol felt confident she could handle the responsibility of entrepreneurship and still keep her marriage intact. Bob was a hard worker and a responsible citizen as long as he worked outside the business for another employer, but he never had any desire to achieve great wealth or independence as his wife did. He was happy to let her achieve her dreams.

Bob and Carol did not bother to develop a life plan or to examine their attitudes about money. Adhering to the American work ethic, Carol worked hard growing her business and accumulating wealth. She was so successful financially that she did not notice how Bob handled his income. There was always plenty of money because she lived frugally and Bob paid his own expenses. Still, she began to wonder why she was mismanaging money. There seemed to be an increasing number of "NSF" checks being written on her personal account. She always had enough money in her business account to cover them, but she wondered why she wasn't tracking the cash flow better at home, especially since she ran her business like a tight ship. Thinking herself irresponsible when it came to budgeting, she visited her accountant for advice.

Carol remained puzzled for a long time, until friends started dropping hints that led to her discovery of her husband's addiction to alcohol and gambling. As long as Bob earned only enough money to pay his living expenses, he had not really had a big problem with alcohol. Carol knew when she married him that Bob drank, and she knew that he occasionally entertained himself with gambling, especially on his game at the golf club. But she had no idea how out of control things had become since Bob no longer needed to contribute his income to the family budget. Bob not only bet on his game at the club, but was visiting gaming parlors regularly and losing hundreds of dollars a week.

Carol was so busy managing everything, being an all-rounder type of entrepreneur, that she failed to notice Bob's increasing addictions. Like Karen, the woman who wanted to buy the $5,000 bed, Bob had no outlet for the void in his life that wealth had created, so he turned to drinking and gambling and then writing bad checks to cover his gambling losses. Fortunately, Carol was not willing to keep her husband's problems secret and forced a confrontation with Bob before his behaviors caused a major financial disaster for the couple. Until he got professional treatment for his problems, the couple separated and Bob moved into his own apartment.

Another basic principle of human nature seems to be that once you have violated a boundary in one area of your life, you seem more prone to violate others. Unresolved anger from his childhood led Nicholas to abuse his own children. Once that boundary had been crossed, Nicholas rationalized the crossing of other ethical boundaries, such as lying to his wife and ignoring taxes, until his financial situation became imperiled. In Bob's case, the violation of ethical boundaries was a result of never having established mature boundaries in the first place. His being a laid-back sort of fellow appealed to Carol, who needed a supportive spouse for her driven entrepreneurial personality. Yet Bob's personality was really a cover for an adult who had never properly assessed his strengths and weaknesses and developed a backbone. As a result, Bob never exerted internal control over himself or his behaviors. Rather, his addictive predispositions were managed by the amount of money he earned and his wife's watchful eye. Because Bob did not establish any adult goals for himself, but rather let his wife define his life for him, it was a simple matter to allow his addictions to increase to fill the void that Carol's wealth provided. And Bob had no compunction about lying to conceal his overspending on alcohol and gambling, especially since there was plenty of money to spend.

At this point Nicholas and Annalisa and Carol and Bob are in crisis. This is not a time to assess their money values and redefine a wealth management plan. First, they must face their demons and clean up the considerable mess they have created. Second, they need to decide if the betrayal can be overcome. Trust is a basic in any relationship. If these couples can learn to forgive and trust each other again, they may have a chance to restore their lives to order. In any case, these types of problems are not resolved without professional mental health care and addiction treatment programs.

## Defining Your Wealth Management Plan

You may be further along the path to establishing a healthy relationship with money than some of the couples described in this chapter are. More than likely, however, your relationship with money is a mixed bag, filled with superstition and unresolved conflict. If it hasn't already, your lack of attention to your wealth management plan will cause serious problems in the future. Now is the time to bring this issue out into the light and to discuss with your spouse how you would like to fashion a new approach to money and wealth that fits with the rest of your life plans.

It is important to assess your values about money just as you assessed your values about your relationship, career, and life in general in Chapter Four. The questions in Self-Assessment Exercise 13 may be a good place to start in reeducating yourself about money, redefining your attitudes about wealth, and planning for the healthy management of your wealth. With clear values guiding your life plan, you are in a much better position to accomplish your goals, achieve wealth, and maintain a healthy balance between love and work. If, on the other hand, you are *not* aware of the values that guide you, you can fall into money traps.

Our most important relationships are with our family members, especially our spouse, children, and parents. These relationships provide the greatest source of happiness and misery in our lives. Like it or not, money and the meaning you make of it are intricately woven into those relationships. If you learn to understand your true needs as opposed to your created wants, you will learn how to use money wisely within the family. If you come from a place of prosperity consciousness and recognize that you have always had enough money, you can be ethical in your monetary dealings with your family. By collaborating with your spouse, an open and honest relationship is possible, which will enable you to resolve almost any financial problem that comes your way, even an I.R.S. lien. Furthermore, this spirit of collaboration and prosperity consciousness are the bases for creating a healthy work ethic in your children, who are your greatest legacy. As a consequence of developing healthy values about money within the family, this attitude will generalize to your business and other situations *outside* the family as well, thus creating enough wealth and abundance to meet all your needs.

In other words, it is not *how much* you have, but how you *think about and use* money that creates wealth. This philosophy also applies to maintaining, managing, and passing on wealth. After clarifying the psychological meaning of money in your life, it may be wise to consult with your accountant or financial advisor and your attorney, especially regarding estate planning needs. Putting your new attitude into action will probably require a bit of work and planning. Remember, though, that your plan for abundance and healthy management of your wealth cannot be left up to these professionals. They can design the plan that best fits your values and needs only if you guide them.

## Your Financial Life Plan

Answer the following questions as honestly as you can. There are no right or wrong answers. The purpose of this exercise is to help you clarify your values and beliefs about money so that you can manage your wealth in more appropriate and balanced ways.

1.  What does money mean to you? To your spouse?

2.  What do you want money to mean in your family? In your business?

3.  If you had all the money you needed, how much would that be?

4.  Think of all the ways you would satisfy your wants if you had all the money you needed.

5.  After you have satisfied all your wants, what would you do then?

6.  Is it okay to discuss your salary with others? Why or why not?

7.  To what point is it okay to discuss what things cost?

8.  Is it okay to pay children for getting good grades?

9.  When should your child get a paying job?

10. In the family business, how do you determine what to pay a family member?

11. Is the breadwinner in your family the boss?

12. What did your parents teach you about money?

13. What are you teaching your children about money?

14. What ethical boundaries have you crossed with regard to money that are still "secrets" in the family?

15. How are these secrets costing you, both in dollars and in self-esteem and trust?

## SELF-ASSESSMENT EXERCISE 13 (CONT'D)

## Evaluating Your Responses

Sort through your answers and look for patterns and themes. Are you surprised by your resonses to this exercise? What are the meanings you have made of money? Go back to the beginning of the chapter where I discussed the meaning of money. Do your answers in this self-assessment exercise reflect any of the myths and values of money that are dominant in our culture? Are these values you really want to keep? Think long and hard about the money values you want to pass on to your children. Now rewrite your money values and add to the rest of your life plan a new healthier script for acquiring and utilizing wealth.

## Summarizing Remark

Write one sentence or a brief paragraph summarizing what you learned from this exercise and what you want to change.

# Personal and Professional Growth: Beyond Problem Solving

So much of this book is about resolving problems and handling stress. In this chapter the discussion focuses on a positive aspect of partnering and marriage, that of encouraging the personal and professional growth of each partner. With the love, support, and talents of your spouse, it is possible to accomplish much more with your life than you can accomplish on your own.

Gail had gained so much in her personal psychotherapy that she wanted to share that experience with Nathan so that he could benefit too. Gail had explored the shame of her childhood abuse and moved to a level of forgiveness. She regained the self-esteem she had lost as a child, which prompted her to return to college with the goals of completing two degrees and starting her own entertainment business. When she met Nathan she recognized a kindred spirit just waiting to be nurtured into his own personal strength and talents, so she encouraged him to return to therapy with her. This time the primary goal was to develop the skills necessary for being a successful entrepreneurial couple, but Gail also encouraged Nathan to delve into his past and deal with his own childhood traumas. As a result, Nathan also gained in courage and self-esteem, which led to his return to college with the goal of completing a program in art and graphic design.

A successful marriage for entrepreneurial couples requires room for personal and professional growth. These are couples who are aggressive achievers: They want to leave their mark on the world, and they are determined to live life to the fullest. Even those copreneurial spouses with a traditional sex-role orientation have a desire to be the best they can be. As one traditional wife put it, "My mission is to showcase my husband's talents." With that kind of strength in his corner, how can her husband possibly lose?

There is no room for complacency in an entrepreneurial marriage. The marriage style that worked twenty years ago is unlikely to work today. Couples need to recognize and be alert to the signals that change is needed. For example, Sharon was becoming more and more unhappy in her marriage. She was successful in her business as a realtor/broker and was making more money than she knew what to do with. Likewise her husband, David, turned everything he touched into gold. His multiple enterprises were so successful that he could consider early retirement at forty-five. But money wasn't everything to this couple. They missed companionship. They wanted a "soul mate." Sharon was the first to recognize the lack of spiritual connection between her and David, when she became interested in another man. But rather than allow an affair to be kindled, Sharon recognized this signal for what it was—an indication that it was time to renegotiate the terms of her marriage to David.

Noticing problems at work or home is a surefire way to access the system for change, but it is equally true that *you do not have to be sick to get better.* Even if nothing seems wrong, use your *prosperity consciousness* to motivate you to another level of excellence. As you stay alert and curious, you may discover wonders that would never have come to you had you stuck with a *problem-solving mentality.*

Having an attitude of prosperity consciousness and curiosity about life will enable you to increase your abilities throughout adult life. For example, we now know that intelligence increases with age. In the past, psychologists assumed that intelligence grew until we reached our early twenties and then began to gradually decline over the life span of the adult. This conclusion resulted from comparing the I.Q.s of a cross section of people of varying ages. These studies clearly showed that younger people had higher I.Q.s than older people. What was not considered, however, were the effects of health, education, and lifestyle on I.Q. A young person of eighteen today probably has had access to a better education and higher-quality health care than someone who is currently seventy-five.

To compensate for these other factors, psychologists developed what is known as a *cross-sequential research design.* They studied that same cross section of people, but over many decades. While they found that each succeeding generation of young people has higher I.Q.s than their predecessors, each generation at least maintains their intelligence over time, when death, illness, and other factors detrimental to I.Q. are factored out. Furthermore, although there is finally a small decline in intelligence at extreme old age, as would be expected, it is also true that intelligence actually does grow throughout the adult life span if given the appropriate nurturing (such as an active life and intellectual stimulation).

Considering this phenomenal discovery, why would anyone adhere to the outdated attitude of "If it ain't broke, don't fix it"? Why would you let your intelligence deteriorate from lack of use? Change is constant. Those developing progressions of yours, your partner's, your children's, and your business are on the move even as you're reading this book. The motion may be currently undetected because nothing is noticeably in conflict, but things are moving nonetheless. Instead of seeking homeostasis, recognize that the natural order of things is conflict, chaos, reorganization, and growth. *Seek change* and you will be one step ahead of those *forced to change* when something is finally broken—possibly beyond repair.

## Recognize the Warning Signs of Change

Although change is constant, we often do not recognize that change is happening and even go out of our way to try to stop the inevitable. When we do this, we create more hardship for ourselves than if we simply acknowledged the need for change in the first place. Outright failure is a certain signal that change is needed, but waiting until that point may be so destructive as to be irreparable. Nicholas and Annalisa will never have the same relationship or business partnership again given the destructiveness of Nicholas' anger-motivated behavior and Annalisa's willingness to cover it up.

### Some Warning Signs That Change Is Needed or May Be Coming
- Failure
- Boredom
- Confusion
- Unproductive habitual behavior
- Life's major turning points
- Fatigue
- Weight gain or loss
- Lack of sexual desire
- Forgetfulness

### Boredom

What makes more sense than waiting for outright failure is to learn to pay attention to those subtle wake-up calls that speak to you each day. One such wake-up call is *boredom*. Until Evan examined the differences between himself and Amy, he found that he was bored with life. He had everything that anyone could want because he and Amy had carefully planned for their financial security and the healthy parenting of their two children. But with all the security he had established, Evan still found himself wanting something more exciting in life. He worried, though, that this desire was a throwback to the chaotic lifestyles of his extended kin. After all, his father, an entrepreneur, had shaken the family system a few times with some new venture that did not pan out.

Ignoring the boredom for a while, Evan tried to entertain himself with new hobbies. He went to the bike shop, bought a mountain bike, and explored back-woods trails. He took the family on weekend excursions. He bought himself a new computer and reorganized his work files. He cleaned out the garage and reseeded the yard. He tried to accept that at this stage in life things get pretty routine. Then one day he found himself dialing up an old girlfriend. He justified the call as just wanting to check in with an old friend; he was curious about whatever had happened to her. But when they agreed to meet for lunch, he did not tell Amy and made up an excuse about his plans for that day.

Evan was clever enough to recognize that the guilt he was feeling should be explored. With the help of his therapist, he realized that he had begun to search for answers to his boredom *outside* himself, through a new hobby or an old girl-friend. What he really needed to do, though, was search *within* himself to discover just what the boredom meant. Boredom may be a different signal for each of you, but in Evan's case it covered up his frustration with Amy's poverty consciousness. In attempting to be respectful of Amy's fears, Evan designed his entire life around poverty consciousness, too, which left him little room for creativity. The next step for Evan was to search for a solution to the divergent views toward prosperity that he and Amy held.

## Confusion

Related to boredom is *confusion*. Confusion is another subtle sign that can be easily dismissed by focusing on something that is less confusing. When we are confused, we feel uncomfortable, even incompetent, especially if we are perfectionistic entre-preneurs. But confusion is a valuable signal that a stable pattern has been interrupt-ed. For example, Rhonda found herself confused when her husband of several years seemed to turn on her. Although they had been a classic dual-career couple, dedicated to teamwork, Stan became more and more distant from her as the home remodeling supply business grew. Even when Stan packed up and moved out of their home, Rhonda's confusion did not clear. This behavior was so unlike Stan; what had changed that would make him act this way?

Fortunately for Rhonda, Stan still loved her and had not left her for another woman but for the business. He was eventually willing to return to therapy and resolve their differences. Rhonda's confusion was based in part on her failure to assess her reason for joining her husband in their entrepreneurial venture. While Rhonda viewed the business as another way to partner with Stan as copreneurs, Stan viewed the business as an opportunity to prove himself in a new arena as a solo entrepreneur. He immediately began competing with his wife instead of collaborating with her. In order to resolve her confusion, Rhonda had to take a long look at herself and Stan. She realized that she was not really an entrepreneur, but a supportive spouse. Stan, on the other hand, needed to be left alone to develop the business to prove that he really was an entrepreneur.

### Unproductive Habitual Behavior

A potent warning sign that change is needed is when we engage in *habitual behavior* even though it does not work anymore. For example, Mike and Karla recognized that their usual evening cocktail was leading to drunkenness and fighting because they had not adapted their stressful copreneurial life to adequately cope with a growing business, a brand-new, expensive house, two children, and their new status in the community. They were considered leaders now, but had no model for leadership. Instead, they operated like a young, unfettered married couple, each coming home from a day's work to relax and unwind with a cocktail.

Don and Marla also found themselves pursuing unproductive habitual behavior. For years their marriage worked just fine following the traditional model. Don, as the solo entrepreneur in a professional practice, worked long, hard hours to provide a substantial income for his growing family. He also assisted the Boy Scouts on camping trips and taught his daughter to ski. Marla, on the other hand, attended to the day-to-day affairs of running the household. She managed the household budget on the allowance that Don provided. She cooked, cleaned, gardened, chauffeured the children, and supervised their homework.

The problem for Don and Marla was that everything had worked so well for so long that they were reluctant to change when change was needed. Now that the children were nearly grown, they fought the changes required of them to allow Marla to advance in her career. There was no system for sharing household maintenance or major financial decisions. Neither knew how to include the other in their respective lives, and they were even reluctant to do so. Marla, for example, resented that Don would be home with the teenager, helping him with his schoolwork, while she was at work. Don, for his part, was afraid to relinquish control of the money management because it was such an important part of his identity.

It is a strange fact of life that once we get something working, it doesn't work forever. In fact, just at the point that you get something working really well, it usually starts to decline. Such is the nature of change. Therefore, it is very important to assess your habits. You have developed habits because they are convenient mechanisms for getting things done without having to think too much about them. However, when the habit really does not serve the purpose anymore, *stop doing it.* It is better to do nothing than to continue pursuing a worn-out habit that may have even become counterproductive.

Mike and Karla need to abandon their habitual evening cocktails and develop a more effective method for destressing at the end of the day. Similarly, Don and Marla need to reassess their basic values in order to move beyond their worn out habits regarding the division of responsibilities. If they really want a traditional marriage, perhaps Marla should not work outside the home. On the other hand, if their traditional style was born of convenience when the children were still at home or in school, they may be able to change their style to suit a dual-career life now that the children are grown.

## Turning Points

Life's major *turning points* are another time for important changes. The natural turning points in life, which we have come to expect and accept anyway, are also a time to reevaluate our goals and values. Graduating from high school or college, getting married, the birth of your first child, a job promotion, turning fifty, and the loss of a parent, are all such turning points. Because of acquiring wealth and the leisure time that goes along with it, entrepreneurial couples are often able to take advantage of turning points to enhance their lives personally and professionally. Since these turning points are bound to happen anyway, it seems foolish to deny them. Why not plan ahead? Change is inevitable with each step along the developing progressions of life. Even though you cannot know for certain what each turning point will bring you, you can at least recognize that change is happening and be alert to the phenomenon.

For example, Kevin and Lana were surprised that their lives changed so much with the birth of their first child. Yet it certainly seems reasonable that adding another person to the family will change sleep and eating habits, work schedules, private time for the young couple, and even how the extended family now interacts with them. As we saw in Chapter Two, Kevin's extended family viewed the birth of the baby as a welcome change in the *family* identity, while Lana saw the baby as changing only her *personal* identity.

Similarly, Allison and Chris faced a turning point when it became apparent that Chris' physical disability would require a change of profession. The couple had prepared themselves, though. They viewed the change with some sadness, since Chris loved his work as a chiropratoor; however, the disability insurance and a plan for another entrepreneurial venture helped to launch the couple in a new direction. Allison could continue her work as a massage therapist while Chris and she developed their new bed-and-breakfast establishment.

You may question how one can prepare for the kind of turning point faced by Chris and Allison. If you talk with any insurance agent, you will be amazed to learn the rate of disability that we all face as we age. Planning ahead for disability and death, as Chris and Allison did, only makes sense when you have a business and a family to provide for. If the disability never arrives and death is delayed until you are ninety, you have planned unnecessarily. But what of those of you who are not the exception to the rule?

Boredom, confusion, unproductive habitual behavior, and life's naturally occurring turning points are only some of the subtle wake-up calls that you can strive to tune in to as you and your partner progress both personally and professionally. Others include *fatigue, weight gain or loss, lack of sexual desire,* and *forgetfulness,* among many others. As you pay attention to yourself more and as you come to appreciate change, you will tune in to your own unique signals. This is the kind of self-knowledge that successful people are known for.

## Accessing Purposeful Growth

You have already laid the groundwork for accessing purposeful growth by reading the preceding chapters of this book. Chapter by chapter you have had the opportunity to educate yourself about the lifestyles of entrepreneurial couples and perhaps revise your own life to accommodate this new knowledge. You have learned about the varying types of entrepreneurship available to couples. You have learned that an individual's identity can be known only in relationship to others, especially those with whom your developing progressions intimately intersect. You have learned new skills for communicating with your spouse and business partner. You have undertaken the first steps to life and career planning. You have assessed your relationship or marital style from traditional to egalitarian. You have examined the similarities and differences between male and female entrepreneurs. You filled out

## Five Tools for Accessing Purposeful Growth

**1.** Seek advice.
**2..** Change yourself first.
**3.** Expand your consciousness.
**4.** Get healthy.
**5..** Have a holistic view.

your life plan with a more thorough understanding of your role as a parent. And you have confronted your misconceptions about money to develop a more honest and ethical plan for managing your wealth.

In this chapter already you have learned to recognize the signals of change long before change erupts into conflict. The next step is the difficult one of *accessing purposeful growth* as a result of the inevitable changes that are coming. Although you may now be clear about who you are and just what your values are, and have a detailed life plan to follow, *how* that life will unfold is still a one-day-at-a-time project. The goal now is to recognize and take advantage, as they emerge, of the opportunities that are specific to your needs and plans.

## Seek Advice

It is not always easy to spot those opportunities for accessing purposeful growth, especially those specific to your unique situation, but there are some basic tools that will help. First, *seek advice*. Modern life is much too complicated to do it alone. Although you may take pride in your rugged individualism, which is your birthright as an American, put aside your ego for a while and seek professional help, friendly advice, and even adversarial confrontation. Two heads are better than one, as the saying goes. Even if you feel you cannot use the advice offered, it still might trigger your own thinking to evolve in a constructive direction.

Sheila knew that she was heading into a big unknown reality when she began to consider entrepreneurship. She had been a dutiful daughter and an A student in high school, acquired what she thought was a useful degree in college, and married a loving and supportive man. She was prepared to take her place in the workforce at an entry-level corporate position that would eventually lead to management and perhaps even the executive team. However, she was surprised to find that no one would hire her. As a result of her ensuing crisis of identity, Sheila sought my help, and over the course of a few months we explored her values and built a life plan. Rather than being a conventional employee, Sheila discovered that behind her "good girl" exterior lay dormant a free-spirited, adventurous woman desiring to take charge and make her mark in the world of entrepreneurship. If Sheila had not been willing to seek professional guidance, she might have lost confidence in her employability and might have settled for a position far below her abilities just to have a job. She might have withdrawn into her home life, never really understanding her dreams, let alone fulfilling them. In short, she might have taken the path that Thoreau described as a life of "quiet desperation."

Frank came to a similar conclusion about his life. When I first met Frank, he was already a successful entrepreneur, but he wanted more. He knew that his childhood had inadequately prepared him for adult life. He had already taken a vow of abstinence from alcohol because of the toll alcoholism had taken on his childhood family. He also joined a church because he and his wife felt the need for spiritual support. But Frank also knew he needed a sounding board for his ideas, not only about expanding his business, but about how to do so within the framework of his personal and family values. He asked for my help, not because I was an expert in his industry, but because of my expertise in the area of entrepreneurial couples.

After getting to know Frank and Louise, I worked with them to develop a clearer understanding of their priorities. This was not an easy process, needless to say, since Frank and Louise had to integrate the needs of two intelligent and strong-willed people. Eventually, however, they came up with a basic life plan to guide them. The next step was to gather more information about Frank's specific industry, financial picture, business structure, and so on, so that he and Louise could design a complementary business plan. So I referred the couple to an attorney and an accountant who specialize in family-owned businesses.

Many businesspeople already have their own trusted advisors, so it may not be necessary for you to find a new attorney, accountant, or management consultant. However, it is important that your advisors be familiar with the unique concerns of entrepreneurial couples. If they are not, give them a copy of this book to read, for example. It is also important to remember that entrepreneurial couples are a marital couple *first* and business partners *second*. As we learned in studying the intersecting systems of the individual, couple, family, and business, the entrepreneurial venture is really an expression of the personality and values of the founders. If you are to run a successful business, you will need to attend to the personal, emotional, and psychological aspects of your life and those of the ones you love *before* you can make sound business decisions. As a result, one of your primary consultants needs to be a *psychologist*—preferably one familiar with the inner workings of entrepreneurial couples. Do not let the "shrink" stigma hold you back. Rather, consider the psychologist an extension of your family, a trusted family/business advisor who can help keep you sharp and moving forward, for psychologists are trained to assist you in discovering yourself and helping you to be the best you can be.

## Change Yourself First

When Carol first learned of Bob's addictions, she tried to deal with them the same way she tackled everything else in her life: She took charge and tried to change Bob. She insisted that he seek treatment for his chemical dependency and compulsive gambling. She took the checkbook and credit cards away from him and put him on a cash-only budget. She even demanded that I talk some sense into Bob. The problem with this approach for Carol was that she failed to see the opportunity in this crisis for her own personal growth.

After several months of tears and angry outbursts, Carol realized that Bob's life was not for her to manage. She realized that her own growth had been stagnating as she defined her life more and more around Bob's inexplicable addictive behavior. This style of responding to an addict is known as *codependency*. That is, the addict is dependent on his or her drug (in Bob's case, alcohol and gambling). But the spouse who tries to control the situation becomes dependent on the addict to make problems for the spouse to deal with. Thus the spouse becomes codependent. (For more on these topics, I recommend you go to a bookstore or library, where you are sure to find many titles on addictions and codependency.)

The only problem with the codependent method of problem solving is that it does not work. Even worse, Carol actually made Bob's problems grow more out of control. How is Bob ever going to face sobriety and learn to take charge of his life if Carol is always making decisions for him? Her codependent controlling only *enabled* Bob to remain immature. When Carol realized that the only person she can ever really change is herself, she asked Bob to move out and be responsible for his own recovery. Then she had the arduous task of working on herself and cleaning up her own bad habits, misunderstandings, superstitions, and so on. She also began to realize many dormant strengths that had been overshadowed by her need to protect and control Bob. At this stage in her evolution, Carol began to consider business expansion in a big way. For example, she questioned whether she really wanted to own a nursery and garden supply center, or whether that venture had just been a way to take care of Bob. Then she began to explore some new directions that seemed to fit her unique personality.

## Expand Your Consciousness

As entrepreneurs and business owners, most of you are already well aware of the need to remain competitive by keeping yourself knowledgeable about your industry. You are members of trade associations and attend the annual conventions and shows. You have joined the local chamber of commerce and other business organizations designed to increase your network of business and professional contacts. You may be an officer in these organizations, or perhaps spearhead a committee regarding an industry or community issue. If you prefer to maintain a low profile, you may keep yourself informed by reading the trade journals and newsletters or attending classes to improve your business or professional skills. Usually if one spouse is the behind-the-scenes worker, the other spouse is active and in the public eye. Together you make your business grow by being aware of the changing marketplace and adapting to those changing conditions.

In spite of this devotion to developing their business and keeping themselves informed, many entrepreneurial couples are so busy running their businesses that they do not take the time to *expand their consciousness* in other ways. However, in order to have a balance between love and work, in order for your business life plan to be as successful as your family life plan, for example, it is necessary for you to attend to *all* aspects of your development. Just as you must adapt to the changing marketplace in order to keep your business alive, you must also adapt to the changes in your personal life in order to stay healthy.

Seeking the advice of a psychotherapist is one way to focus on yourself and the changes you personally need to make to create a healthier life, but that method should be augmented by other life-enhancing experiences. You need to expose yourself to new ways of thinking *from many sources*, not just the narrow field in which you work. Read self-help books on personal growth, marital enrichment, and parenting. Attend classes and workshops on assertiveness and communicating with your teenager. Explore alternative health-care options such as naturopathic medicine and acupuncture. Attend a yoga or meditation class or one in tai chi or qi quong.

Becoming psychologically more aware and sensitive is only one aspect of your personal growth. Assess other areas of your life that you have neglected. Perhaps music and art are sorely missing. If so, buy tickets to the local opera season, or take a class in drawing or sculpture at the community college. Study Spanish so that your next trip to Mexico will be more culturally rewarding. Read a novel for a change, or learn fly-fishing—something you have always wanted to do but never felt you had the time for. Developing the creative side of your personality, with no goal in mind except personal expression, will enhance your total well-being.

## Get Healthy

Another area of your life to focus on is your physical health. Science has proven that your eating and exercise habits profoundly affect your intellect and longevity. It is ironic that in a time of accelerating technology and material abundance, Americans are experiencing more and more varied forms of disease. One out of two people today develop cardiovascular disease; one out of three, cancer; one out of five, mental illness; and one out of five, diabetes. Our children will have even worse odds, since the research is showing an increasing rate of birth defects and that today's children are not as strong as children fifty years ago.

As busy as you are, assess your state of physical disrepair and develop a program to correct it. Educate yourself about proper nutrition and physical fitness. Minimize your intake of sugar. Eat more fresh fruits and vegetables and whole foods. Go for a walk every day. During an evening stroll with your spouse, talk about anything but business. If you are more sports-minded, join a basketball team or tennis club. Do your own gardening and housework and build up a few unused muscles. As an added benefit, mindless work sometimes helps to drain the day's stresses and rejuvenate the creative juices for the next day.

## Have a Holistic View

When Arthur turned forty-seven, he was finally able to hear his wife, Leslie. At least he was able to understand that she was unhappy, though what she was unhappy *about* remained a mystery. Arthur began to have an inkling that there was something within himself that needed changing. He loved his wife dearly and only wanted the best for her, but somehow he was not succeeding at meeting her needs. At this stage in his life, with business success already accomplished, he was willing to put his ego aside and examine his flaws. And since this was his third marriage, he could hardly deny that he might have a few weaknesses in the relationship department.

Arthur and Leslie sought professional consultation to assess their interaction problems as a copreneurial couple. During their sessions with me, Arthur and Leslie examined their work relationship and their personal relationship and discovered that most of their conflicts emerged at work. As we learned in Chapter Three, on communication, Arthur kept assuming that Leslie was just like himself, a visionary type of leader, when all Leslie wanted to do was run an efficient office. Leslie was supportive and believed in Arthur's vision, but she did not want to be pushed out into the limelight. For example, every time Arthur rushed off with a new idea and left a project dangling, Leslie was frustrated and bewildered. Nothing seemed to ever get finished, which was very disturbing to Leslie's orderly personality. Arthur, on the other hand, assumed that Leslie would finish the project and was happy to have her do it any way that suited her. When he was finished with something, completed or not, he was finished with it.

Eventually, the patience with which this couple approached their problems paid off. Arthur developed a new admiration for Leslie and allowed her the space to perform at work in just the way that fit her personality. He learned that there are other ways to do things in life besides his own, and that they all work well.

Although Arthur's adaptation to his wife's style restored harmony to their work relationship, it stirred up other disturbing thoughts for Arthur. If there are many ways to be in the world, and they are all appropriate given the stage of development and personality of the individual involved, then Arthur might have been pretty selfish in his assessment of others over the years, perhaps even ruthless. He began to examine his prior marriages, his relationships with his children, his treatment of employees, and many of his business decisions. He questioned *why* he had taken the paths he had taken. He wondered if his selfish way of looking at people, that they should think and be like him, had alienated him unnecessarily from those he loved. He wondered if certain business decisions had been made to protect his narrow view of reality. Had he ignored certain opportunities and dismissed others simply because he wanted things done his way?

All of this speculation depressed Arthur. He did not have the answers to his questions because he could not go back in time and do things differently. What he did have were questions and regrets.

Taking a *holistic view* or understanding the *dialectic of life* makes it possible to grow through such a depression as the one Arthur faced. Allow yourself your regrets. Recognize that there were other options that you might have taken. Make apologies to those you have wronged, if possible. Yet recognize also that you are a changing individual in a changing world: At any moment in time you are making the best choice you know how to, given your level of skill and life experience.

The goal is not to be perfect but to learn and grow with each setback and success. As your developing progression interacts with those of the ones you love as well as the developing progression of your business, there are many opportunities to err and to succeed. Life is a complex process, and most of us pay attention to only a small portion, such as the development of the business. As long as you are making money, you believe you are a success, even though you may have failed at three marriages and your children may have grown up without you.

However tedious and time-consuming this task, it is important to view your life from this holistic and dialectical perspective if you are to keep your mistakes and regrets to a minimum. Arthur was able to pull himself out of his depression and build a quality life with Leslie because he began to see the possibilities for tomorrow once he took a more holistic view of his life. Although he could not bring back those lost years with his children, he could live life from now on by being more open to the warning signs that change is needed, by accessing opportunities for purposeful growth, and by remaining curious about the full range of options that exist for a human being on this planet.

## Crisis Management Versus Long-Term Growth

This chapter has been about change, both personal and professional, for you and your spouse. Change is inevitable and will lead to growth or deterioration, depending on your ability to harness the energy in change and create meaning or purpose out of it. Although most of the time people tend to make adjustments in life only when there is a major crisis, you do not have to be sick to get better. It seems wise then to accept that you are a changing individual in a changing world and to work toward meaningful, purposeful change and growth.

Crises will continue to happen since we cannot accurately predict everything. Yet crises do not have to be the norm if you learn to pay attention to the signals that a change is coming. Some of those signals are subtle, such as feeling bored or confused. Another subtle signal is sticking with a habit that at one time may have been useful but does not now produce the desired results. Turning points in life signal change, so use those developmental milestones to reset your course.

Your goal should be to access purposeful growth instead of just changing for the sake of change. Changing jobs or starting a new business because you are bored will not guarantee success. When the newness wears off, you may find yourself once again in the same predicament, unsatisfied with your life. Accepting change as the norm and being alert to the subtle warning signs of change put you in a better position to recognize the specific opportunities for change that will benefit you, your spouse, and the business. In order to discover the range of opportunities that are available to you, you must seek advice, focus on changing yourself first instead of another, and expand your consciousness through life-enhancing activities and continual education. With the self-awareness that comes from these mind-expanding activities, and with the strength and stability that come from your commitment to getting and staying healthy, you will be in a much better position to resolve immediate problems and move ahead with the new opportunities for growth you discover.

Viewing your life through the lens of dialectical psychology allows you to take a holistic perspective. Seeing your development in the context of your entire life in interaction with the ones you love and in your business enables you to correct past mistakes and hone in on just the right direction to follow from now on. It also enables you to encourage the development of your spouse, partner, employees, children, and so on. When you recognize that change is the norm and you encourage productive change in others, you cannot help but benefit by their changes. For example, I am disconcerted from time to time that with each client couple I work with, I work myself out of a job. As they progress toward self-awareness and more meaningful lives as marital and business partners, they no longer need my guidance. On the other hand, these same clients have assisted me in accomplishing my goal of succeeding in my profession. And that is true collaboration.

Changing from a problem-solving mode to a self-awareness and growth mode may be difficult for some of you. It often seems easier to wait until there is a problem to fix. However, you have been reading this book in order to improve your relationship with your marriage/business partner, hoping for some insights and a few techniques to turn a problem around. It may not have occurred to you until this chapter that you need to expand your consciousness and redesign your outlook on life. In other words, those problems that you want to fix are really signs of a reorganization *that has already started to take place.* You can wait for the inevitable conflict and chaos, or you can take a more proactive approach and explore the territory now, as outlined in this chapter and other chapters in this book.

Changing your perspective in such a dramatic way will not come from reading this book alone. It is also necessary to *make the time* to really evaluate your life, your relationship, and your business; to make a plan for change; and to implement that plan. As busy as most entrepreneurial couples are, you may have a limited schedule for such self-improvement. Only you know how important it is to make the time to reset your course. If you do make the time and your spouse or partner is in agreement with you on what needs to be done, you have a much better chance of succeeding. To start, I would recommend that you arrange a retreat for yourself and your spouse. Go away for a few days to a quiet place where you can think and talk without interruption. Take some time by yourself, too. Sit down with your life plans and compare notes. Get plenty of rest and some exercise and eat nutritious meals. Relax in the shade of a big tree overlooking a lake. In other words, try to make the situation as conducive as possible for the very important work you are doing. It should not take long to reevaluate your priorities and set a new plan in motion if you follow these instructions. The possibilities for your life, your partner's life, and your business are unlimited.

# Stress Management: Taking Care of the Mind-Body-Spirit Connection

As thrilling as it is for the members of entrepreneurial couples to have a partner as dedicated to career and business as they are, this style also produces more stress than other marital styles. Not only do entrepreneurial couples have the normal stressors that plague all career-minded Americans, such as the competing demands of love and work, but they have the added stress of having these domains overlap considerably. Working long hours, working out of your homes, and/or working and living with your business partner/spouse twenty-four hours a day leaves little time to recuperate and replenish inner strength. As the stress increases and the opportunity for recuperation diminishes, many entrepreneurial couples fall victim to stress-related illnesses, mental or emotional problems, chemical dependency, and spiritual despair.

In Chapter Nine I discussed how to design your life for personal and professional growth. Paying attention to the subtle signals that change is approaching, interpreting those signals properly, and learning to make purposeful change will prevent many of the stress-related problems discussed in this chapter. As you educate yourself and begin designing a healthy entrepreneurial couple life, you will naturally make more opportunities for recuperating from the stresses of the day. Each chapter in this book has been leading you toward this goal: to strike a meaningful balance between love and work to create optimum health and happiness.

In this chapter I will introduce you to some couples who postponed attending to a healthy balance in their lives, with devastating results. I hope you will learn from their mistakes. Once you have allowed stress to progress to a serious, even life-threatening problem such as a physical illness, divorce, or drug addiction, it is much harder to restore your system to balance. And you may have created permanent damage. Yet no one is perfect, and undoubtedly every reader of this book has at least one part of their life where this stress process has progressed. If you are going to arrest this deteriorating process, this is no time to be ashamed or to avoid the work you need to do, difficult though it may be. Better to start late on the road toward improving your health and restoring balance in your life than not to start at all.

The process of losing your health (physical, psychological, interpersonal, or otherwise) begins long before symptoms develop and even before you will notice subtle signs such as boredom, confusion, and sticking with useless habits. The stress process begins the moment you allow any part of your interacting systems to be out of alignment. If one system is unattended to or allowed to stay out of healthy alignment for too long, it affects the other systems—which in turn produces stress and deterioration. In order to keep their developing progressions in healthy, productive alignment, entrepreneurial couples need to attend to and take care of the whole person, in relationship to other whole people, in relationship to the whole business entity. In other words, you cannot really separate the mind, body, and spirit. These are not separate, distinct parts of yourself, but rather, interacting developing progressions, just like the other systems of which you are a part.

In a way, so far in this book I have looked at the external lives of entrepreneurial couples, and in this chapter I will look at their internal lives. In addition to looking at the interaction of the entrepreneur with his or her spouse, children, and business, I will explore the interaction within the individual of the basic components that make us human: the *mind*, the *body*, and the life force or essence that some call *spirit*. Unresolved stress in any one of these three areas will affect the others, leading to a breakdown in your functioning as an entrepreneur, a spouse, a parent, a colleague and so on. If you are going to manage the excessive stresses of entrepreneurial life, you actually need more stamina than the average person. To combat the pressures caused by the competing demands of love and work and to build the necessary stamina for this complex lifestyle, you must build a *power plan* to maintain and enhance your health not just physically but mentally and spiritually as well.

Again this chapter is not meant to provide a comprehensive overview of health and stress management. However, I have chosen examples from real-life couples to point out the specific risks entrepreneurial couples face. As you read about some of your contemporaries, you may discover issues that you need to face also. With your life and career plans developed, newly acquired problem-solving and communication skills, a clearer agreement of equity in your marriage/partnership, a wealth-management plan, and goals for personal and professional development, you are in a much better position to tackle the stresses of entrepreneurial couple life and to build a power plan to rebalance your interacting systems.

# The Meaning of *Spirit*

Although I will go into more detail later in the chapter on the effect of stress on spirit, I want to take a moment early on to clarify what I mean when I use this word. *Spirit*, or human *spirituality*, is not synonymous with *religion* or the *religious aspect of life*. Church has nothing to do with spirituality directly. Rather, the *spirit* is that part of each human that makes us a distinctive personality. It is the part of us that defines us and yet connects us to others. It has long been known that a strong, healthy spirit will guide us successfully through adversity, whereas a conquered spirit will succumb to illness and death. It was Mother Teresa's strong spirit that allowed her to transcend her small stature and seemingly insignificant role as a nun to profoundly affect thousands of people for the better. Conversely, it is the conquered spirit that explains the powerful effects of subtle forms of brainwashing in prisoner-of-war camps. In other words, *spirit is that singular life force that directs and shapes our attitudes, beliefs, and behaviors.* Therefore, keeping the spirit or life force healthy is essential to the process of achieving healthy balance in any life. For entrepreneurial couples especially, the key to effective stress management is the proper alignment and interaction of a healthy mind, a healthy body, and a healthy spirit.

# Stress Relief

About 60 to 90 percent of patients who go to their physicians are in the preillness phase, according to Herbert Benson, M.D., of the Harvard Mind-Body Institute. That is, people are experiencing the stress of their unbalanced lives and seeking out help, but they have yet to develop the symptoms of serious illness such as arthritis, hypertension, colitis, cancer, and so on. Because your physician cannot really treat stress, he or she may prescribe antidepressant or antianxiety drugs. Unfortunately, drugs only mask the developing disease. Obviously, what makes more sense is to recognize the stress for what it is, a sign of imbalance in your life (or imbalance in your multiple interacting and developing progressions). Then set out to devise a power plan to reduce the stress.

To try to eliminate stress altogether is unrealistic. The twenty-first century looks to be even more stressful than the twentieth century has been. Even if you reorganize your priorities according to the suggestions in this book, you will still have stress in your life that needs diffusing. With all change comes stress. Diffusing that stress with drugs, however, only compounds the problem. You may get temporary relief, but your mind and body and spirit will continue to be undernourished and out of balance.

The simple solution is to immediately begin to practice some form of healthy *stress relief,* be it floating in a hot tub or practicing transcendental meditation (TM). Benson studied practitioners of TM to learn how it worked to produce greater health. For some time it has been known that TM rests the mind and body, and practitioners of the art report greater health and tranquillity than those who practice no form of relaxation. What Benson discovered is that it is not TM as such that produces the healthful results but the act of bringing the mind back to one word, thought, phrase, prayer, or sound (often referred to as a *mantra*) for a specified period of time—say, twenty to thirty minutes. This is a passive act in terms of physical activity. All it requires is the concentration necessary to bring the mind gently back to the mantra whenever it wanders away.

Whether you practice or use progressive relaxation techniques, TM, Zen, yoga, or hypnosis, the *relaxation response,* as Benson has termed it, is the same. There is a decrease in oxygen consumption, respiratory rate, heart rate, and blood pressure. Furthermore, Benson has found the relaxation response to be effective in treating such problems as hypertension, cardiac arrhythmia, chronic pain, insomnia, side effects of chemotherapy, anxiety, hostility, depression, premenstrual syndrome, even infertility, and in preparing for surgery and X-ray procedures.

With such a simple technique available to us all, it is surprising that there is so much disease in the United States. Yet my research with entrepreneurial couples shows that they are not able to dedicate much time to their personal well-being. First of all, they work more hours each week than other working couples (and copreneurial husbands work the most).

Second, entrepreneurial wives have a great deal of difficulty separating the domains of work and home responsibilities. While their husbands can seem to "turn off" work when they get home or "turn off" home when they get to work, these wives have work thoughts at home and home thoughts at work, so they never rest. Finally, entrepreneurial couples are unwilling to take time from work for their personal needs, though they are willing to take time from home for their work needs. This type of workaholism is characteristic of all entrepreneurs, but when both marital partners evidence the problem, the stress in their lives skyrockets.

All-rounder copreneurs Dennis and Eileen offer an example of how extreme health problems can evolve. These two have spent years ignoring the subtle signals, so now that they are in crisis it is difficult for them to recognize the seriousness of their situation. In spite of being diagnosed with an immune deficiency disease at age thirty, Eileen continued to work as hard as ever. She assumed full responsibility for the home and children, and she reported to work every day at the furniture store to put in a full eight hours as an interior design consultant. She did follow her physician's advice about taking medication, but she did not develop a power plan to de-stress her life or learn to relax.

Dennis is also a hard worker and works even longer hours than Eileen does, sometimes getting home late in the evening after the children are in bed. In order to de-stress, he often goes out for drinks, sometimes with employees, sometimes alone. Dennis has even been known to sleep at the office because he has worked so late. Not only is Dennis fatigued most of the time, but he has developed chronic and incapacitating pain in his back. He is not able to do the heavy lifting he used to do at the store. And his physician has referred him to a specialist to evaluate Dennis for surgery.

This couple needs more than the relaxation response to get them back on track. They ignored or overrode their bodies' warning signs for so long that they have now created a health crisis. Furthermore, they seem out of touch with the seriousness of the situation. Perhaps if they had only taken a break now and then to relax, they could have restored their inner strength periodically and kept a clear head about their priorities.

Similarly, Carol, a solo entrepreneur, kept ignoring the signs of her increasing health problems. At the time her physician finally suggested a hysterectomy, Carol was consuming fifteen ibuprofen a day. Like a workhorse, Carol would plow through each day, seldom stopping to eat, charged by the excitement of developing her garden center. Of course, if she was ignoring her own health problems, she could hardly pay attention to her husband's increasing alcohol use and compulsive gambling.

Chris and Allison are the least likely couple to allow signals of stress to be ignored. After all, Chris is a chiropractor and Allison a massage therapist, dual entrepreneurs who now work together as copreneurs. While Chris was still able to work as a chiropractor, they promoted wellness to their clientele day in and day out. However, it is sometimes hard even for the well intentioned to keep their lives in balance, as Allison and Chris discovered. Since their focus was on monitoring Chris' physical disability and preparing to make the transition to running the bed-and-breakfast, neither of them considered the stress Allison was under. She was the supportive spouse who managed the home front and the office with no complaints. However, when her physician prescribed antianxiety drugs and sleeping pills and suggested a weight-loss diet, Allison knew that she had ignored her own wellness too long.

Incorporating the relaxation response into your daily routine is a simple thing to do. And the benefits seem to far outweigh the minor inconvenience of setting aside twenty minutes a day. However, if like the entrepreneurial couples described in this chapter, you have allowed stress to fully develop into disease, you need more intensive corrective action now. See your physician immediately. You may need medication and/or surgery to correct the damage you have suffered. However, combining the relaxation response with medical procedures will hasten the healing process.

# From Alcoholism to Recovery

Every night at about ten-thirty or eleven o'clock the fighting would start and carry on for two to three hours or more until Jonathan and Brooke got so tired they just fell asleep. This was the culmination of a long day at the office, where the two worked side by side in their advertising business. The business had grown from a small local service business to a thriving international concern, and along with that growth came increasing levels of stress for both partners. By the end of the workday, Brooke frequently wanted to stop off at a bar to "unwind" with a drink before heading home. Jonathan, in a separate car, would go home, relieve the babysitter, and start dinner. When Brooke got home she was relaxed and cheerful, the alcohol having taken the edge off the day's stress. Two more glasses of wine at dinner contributed to her changing personality.

As the evening progressed, Jonathan would busy himself with settling the children down for the evening. He did not mind doing most of the domestic chores because he understood that Brooke did not have as much physical stamina as he did. When it was time to give the children a good-night kiss, he would call to their mother, whom he often found napping on the couch. A couple more drinks later, Brooke was no longer napping and no longer cheerful. Instead, her irritability was growing. Dumbfounded, Jonathan could not figure out why she was mad at him. The accusations started flying, defensive walls shot up, and the arguing would escalate to unreasonable and irrational proportions.

Alcoholism and other forms of substance abuse are an epidemic in our country. We are all aware of the general problem nationwide. There are numerous programs in our schools to prevent drug abuse among our youth. The courts are less tolerant of alcohol-related traffic infractions. And celebrities have established treatment programs to sober up movie stars and politicians. In addition, many employers are taking a hard look at the problems caused by alcoholism and drug abuse. Employers recognize the loss attributable to alcohol and drugs in terms of lowered production, increased accidents, lower quality work, and loss of skilled employees. They have established employee-assistance programs and redesigned insurance benefits to create treatment options for employees. These programs treat not only the addict but the family as well, because it is the strength of the family that determines the addict's successful treatment. The concern reaches to the highest levels in most companies. Whether the employee is the president or a line worker, today's employers are cracking down on alcoholism and drug abuse. No one is allowed to jeopardize the welfare of the company or fellow workers by engaging in dangerous addictive behavior. But the goal is not punishment. Instead, employers want to rehabilitate and return a healthy employee to the job.

Yet among family firms, alcohol abuse and drug addiction are frequently overlooked. Many people who work in family firms but are *not* family members talk about the "secret" at work. The secret that everyone knows about but that no one is willing to mention publicly is that there is a family member who is addicted or engaging in drug or alcohol abuse. Since no one is supposed to talk about it, the family member is protected not only by the family but by all employees as well. For example, Jonathan discovered only after Brooke underwent outpatient treatment for alcoholism that all five of his key executives were aware of her problem, as well as Brooke's entire staff. They had been protecting Jonathan from the truth because they did not want to lose their jobs.

Previously in this book I have explained how this conspiracy of silence and codependency comes to be. The function of the family is to nurture and protect its members. This function is alive and well in a family firm, and usually takes precedence over the welfare of the business or other nonfamily employees. This is a rule that families have followed since the beginning of human civilization, and therefore is not likely to change. If there is an alcoholic in a family firm, be they founder, spouse, son, daughter, or in-law, the family is likely to overlook, condone, deny, rationalize, or minimize the problem in order to keep the family system intact.

Moreover, if the *founder* is or was alcoholic, alcoholism may be a family "tradition" that will be hard to break. That is, drinking may be interwoven into the fabric of family life and corporate life. In the case of Jonathan and Brooke, ordering cases of champagne for every social event was a habit. After their weekly golf game, they would have cocktails. Entertaining business associates always involved drinks at the bar before dinner. Because Jonathan was a social drinker, and because Brooke's drinking had not yet compromised the business's bottom line, it had not occurred to him that his wife might be developing a serious drinking problem.

Leaders in family firms have a tough job. They must weigh the success of the business against the needs of the family. However, allowing alcoholism and other addictions to go untreated is no way to take care of either the business or the family. With others ignoring the problem, the alcoholic or drug addict sees this as tacit approval of his or her behavior. Yet in ignoring the problem, everyone allows the potential threat to the integrity of the family and business to grow. Alcoholism and other addictions lead to the breakdown of the family, which is just what a family firm wants to avoid.

What can help entrepreneurial couples address these problems is to consider that the addict is fortunate to have the backing of both the family and the business. With the support of the two most important systems in his or her life, the addict has increased potential to succeed in treatment. He or she has a loving spouse and family, as well as a supportive employer and a good job to come back to. Another thing to consider is that *everyone in the family* has to support the decisions to confront the addict and to seek family therapy with him or her. If there are dissenters, the addict will solicit allies to defend his or her continued alcohol or drug abuse. While it is painful to acknowledge one's own addiction, it may be even harder to acknowledge the addiction of a loved one. Often family members feel helpless in the face of the overwhelming problems caused by addiction. Therefore, they "enable" the addict rather than face the problem squarely in the eye.

To deal with the humiliation of recognizing that a spouse or other family member is alcoholic, education will help. Professional treatment centers emphasize that alcoholism and drug abuse are best understood as diseases. (In fact, most researchers agree that there are two types of alcoholism. One type is considered genetic and is predominantly seen in men. These men come from families where their fathers and grandfathers were alcoholic. It is unclear what the factors are that predispose a man to alcoholism, but the factors are inherited. The second type of alcoholism is learned and is most probably an inadequate response to stress. Both men and women evidence this type of alcoholism. In any case, whether inherited or learned behavior, once a person begins to drink abusively, he or she may become addicted physiologically.) The disease of alcoholism affects the personality in ways that change the ones we love. While the alcoholic cannot help that he or she has a disease, the person must be held accountable for his or her actions. The alcoholic must be confronted with his or her irresponsible and manipulative behavior so that he or she can change it. With professional treatment and ongoing support that focuses on recovery, the alcoholic can be returned to his or her former productive and loving life.

# From Drug Abuse to Recovery

Although alcohol is the most widely used and abused drug in the United States, Americans are spending millions of dollars on other drugs as well. Legal and illegal drugs can be used abusively and addictively. Furthermore, treatment centers rarely see a "pure" alcoholic anymore. Most patients admitted to these programs are *polydrug* users, such as Jack, who uses alcohol to calm down and methamphetamine to speed up. There are of course major problems in all areas of the mind-body-spirit connection when a person starts mixing drugs and alcohol.

When I met Terri, her life was spiraling out of control. Although Jack (an all-rounder and solo entrepreneur) came to our first meeting and claimed to want help restoring his marriage, he never returned to therapy. Terri was a supportive spouse and worked nearly full-time with Jack in their residential landscaping business. She also held down a full-time job as a paralegal, not only because she loved her profession but also to augment the family income during slow periods for the landscaping business.

When Terri married Jack she knew that he had had a drug problem. He had experimented with a number of common street drugs, including marijuana, LSD, cocaine, and methamphetamines. He also drank alcohol. But he had been in treatment for his drug addiction and was clean and sober for two years when they met. His business was thriving primarily because of Jack's tremendous talent. He seemed to know just what the customer wanted, and he was skilled enough to produce it, on time and within budget. Terri thought that with her help in the office, Jack's time could be freed further to expand the business.

Jack was thrilled about marrying Terri. He felt fortunate that such a bright, educated woman would be interested in him. He had grown up in a poor family, with child abuse and divorced parents. He never finished high school, but he was driven to succeed nonetheless. He wanted more for his life than his parents had. Unfortunately, his driven personality and penchant for the fast life led him into drug use as a teenager. By the time he met Terri he was thirty, divorced twice, behind on child support payments, and struggling to stay clean and sober. Fortunately, he had started his business right out of drug treatment, and because of his considerable charm, was on his way to success rather quickly.

Terri sought my help when Jack's personality started changing about five years and two babies later. He was hostile most of the time and rarely home. She was getting calls from homeowners complaining that Jack had not been out to the work site in days. Employees started complaining too that Jack had not shown up to give them their work assignments. Terri had suspected drug abuse for some time because she found some drug paraphernalia in one of Jack's drawers, but she never asked him about it. She would, however, ask him to roll up his sleeves before he left for work to check for needle marks, a habit she started when they first married. Since Jack always complied, she believed that he was not using drugs intravenously, but she ignored the other signs of drug abuse.

In vain Terri tried to keep her marriage and the business going. However, when Jack became physically violent one evening and threatened to kill her, Terri packed her things, took the two children, and left for a friend's house. The truth is that Jack was once again heavily involved in methamphetamine use and spending his days with drug users and drug dealers. The police had been monitoring Terri's house for a while because of Jack's connection to some very undesirable people. When Terri moved out, Jack just moved his "friends" in. Anything resembling the man Terri first met had been obliterated.

Terri eventually filed for divorce but not before being humiliated thoroughly. Her bank account was garnisheed for bad debts. For a year she was unable to rent a house or even install a phone because she was considered a bad credit risk. She had to explain to teachers and school counselors why she was enrolling her children in schools out of district for their protection. The police even suspected her of drug trafficking since she had lived in Jack's house at one time. They found it hard to believe that she had not known what Jack had been up to for so long. In addition, the legal problems of untangling the family business from debts and customer complaints would take years.

In spite of massive educational campaigns to prevent drug abuse and addiction, like alcoholism, these diseases are very difficult to prevent and treat. Complicating the picture is that people who abuse drugs are not normal when they are on the drugs. The chemicals with which they are flooding their bodies and brains prevent them from thinking rationally. As a result, they make terrible decisions that cost them their health, their livelihoods, their families, and sometimes their freedom. Alcoholics can be arrested for drunk driving, but a cocaine user can be arrested for *possession* of an illegal substance. Moreover, this distinction between legal and illegal drugs increases the likelihood of being involved with criminals when the drug of choice is an illegal one.

If drug abuse is a problem in your entrepreneurial marriage, it *will* affect your business. It is foolish to deny this reality. You or your spouse may be the rare person who does not become addicted. However, why would you want to take that chance? If you are making excuses about your drug use, then you are probably addicted already. It is a simple matter to find out: Most treatment programs, both inpatient and outpatient, offer free screenings to determine your stage of addiction. If you suspect yourself or your partner of being addicted, schedule an interview with a local program.

# Domestic Violence—Get Help Now!

According to a 1997 Gallup Poll report, child abuse is ten times worse than government reports indicate. George Gallup explains that the Gallup Polls reveal more accurate data than some government statistics because the polls go directly into Americans' homes. The questions are anonymous and phrased in such a way that people are more likely to answer honestly. As a result, Gallup finds that Americans are admitting to more child abuse than is reported to government agencies. Furthermore, 70 to 80 percent of child abuse is related to alcohol abuse. Spouse abuse and child abuse indicate an obvious breakdown in the multiple developing progressions of an individual's life, and are evidence of serious mental and spiritual problems. In fact, to allow the stress of entrepreneurial life to become this extreme means that the couple has gone beyond crisis. Chronic problems that have persisted for years are responsible for this total disregard of human values and dignity.

Ray phoned me because he was looking for a psychologist for his wife, Connie. He felt that she was extremely depressed, even suicidal. She would not seek help for herself but agreed to see me if Ray made the appointment. Over the next few weeks, Ray and Connie shared with me a most unique story of two lives nearly destroyed by child abuse, alcoholism, cocaine addiction, and sexual abuse.

Ray and Connie had met as teenagers and had run off to get married without finishing high school. Ray's childhood home life was filled with alcoholism and child abuse, but his parents never divorced. Connie never knew her mother, who died when she was very young. Her father remarried several times, and each time Connie and her sister acquired new stepsiblings. During one of these marriages, Connie and her sister were repeatedly sexually assaulted by older stepbrothers. Probably because they saw in each other a kindred spirit, Ray and Connie were drawn to each other as teenagers. It was from this relationship that they each finally discovered what it was to be loved.

Ray and Connie wanted to be the Romeo and Juliet who got away. They wanted to postpone having children until they could establish themselves financially, so they both went to work at minimum-wage jobs and saved their money. At twenty Connie gave birth to the first of their four children. By the second baby, Ray and Connie had discovered a business that they thought could make them rich. With nothing to lose and everything to gain, they borrowed money from family and started their wholesale health food business. Ray operated the business as a solo entrepreneur, and Connie supported him from home by taking care of the children and doing odd jobs for the business.

Because Connie and Ray were both organizers, over the years the business grew rapidly. The couple felt they were on top of the world. They made very good money, enough to expand the business and hire family members to manage branches in three states. But with the birth of their fourth child, Connie started to demonstrate serious emotional problems. She was irritable and depressed. She stopped caring about her appearance and left the children unwashed and unkempt. She insisted on home schooling the children so she wouldn't have to interact with the outside world. And she rarely left the house, which was never clean.

It was at this point that Ray brought his wife to see me. Just twenty-nine, Connie was underweight and haggard-looking when she revealed to me what she had been living with. Ray was a cocaine addict, spending about $1,000 a week on his drug. In order to keep from being beaten by him, Connie agreed to use cocaine too. She reported that on one occasion when she refused both sex and cocaine, Ray became so angry that he stripped her naked and threw her out the front door, locking it behind her. The children were witness to this and tried to protect their mother, only to be locked in their bedrooms. With increased cocaine use, the couple crossed other moral boundaries. One evening during a poker game with some of his men friends, Ray offered his wife as a sexual prize to the winner of the card game. Ray even went so far as to suggest that the couple each find lovers or "spouse swap" with friends. The loss of control in the relationship seemed to have no end.

Connie shared these horrors as if in a daze. She was deeply depressed, but also not really aware of how extreme things had become in her life. Coming from a childhood of abuse, her boundaries were diffuse. Physical abuse and sexual abuse had always been the norm in her life. Even as an adult, she did not know how to protect herself. Ray, too, was a victim. With no guidance from his parents, he had grown up to be a young man with no values, no ethics. He was ignorant of the devastating effects of drug abuse on the mind, body, and spirit. He was afraid, however. He was afraid of losing his wife, and he was afraid of going to prison. It took a lot of courage to seek my help, considering the potential threat to Ray's freedom.

Some of you may have a difficult time relating to the story of Connie and Ray. Or you may question whether and to what extent their entrepreneurial lifestyle or their own childhood histories contributed to the drug abuse and domestic violence they exhibited in their marriage. Nevertheless, their sad story reveals that stress, ignorance, and drugs definitely do not mix.

Furthermore, just one incident of domestic violence is enough to send a marriage and a business reeling. Jay and Celia thought they were untouchable until Jay allowed mounting stress at work to contribute to alcohol abuse. His very successful auto repair business was starting to go sour because he could no longer compete with a national chain. One night when Celia was still at the espresso cart, Joe came home after having had a few drinks and was annoyed that his wife was not there cooking his dinner. Rather than wait until his wife got home, Jay started an argument with his teenage daughter; before he was through, he had pinned her to the wall and was strangling her, until he stopped in horror. Although Jay was mortified that he got this out of control and immediately apologized to his daughter, he asked her to keep the incident a secret from Celia. Of course, this secret festered and came out two years later when the couple was in marital therapy as part of Jay's alcohol treatment program. Celia was unable to tolerate the betrayal, and the couple separated.

As I have said, at the point that domestic violence erupts, the lives of entrepreneurs are extremely out of control. Stress from the typical workaholic entrepreneurial lifestyle can create health problems, marital problems, drug abuse problems, and ethical problems. As a result of these problems, in combination with the weaknesses of character that evolved years earlier from neglectful and abusive upbringings, the crossing of boundaries into domestic violence is more common than you might think. If you recognize yourself or your partner taking even a small step in this direction, you should seek the help of a psychotherapist immediately.

# Extramarital Affairs Aren't the Problem, Only a Symptom

Steven came to me for help with his anger problem. He reported being easily irritated, and he wanted to nip this problem in the bud before it grew out of control. At fifty, Steven had accomplished his dreams. He had developed a thriving appliance manufacturing firm and was selling his products worldwide. He was currently negotiating a merger with a similar company in Canada. He and his wife of thirty years had just built their dream house, a million-dollar estate on a lake a half-hour from town. The children were nearly grown, with one in graduate school, one working, and one about to graduate from high school. What then could the anger be about?

Steven had always seen himself as a laid-back sort of fellow. Of course, as an entrepreneur this description seems unlikely. Yet his wife and friends all agreed that he was always very affable. Steven and his wife, Susan, worked in the business together as copreneurs, she handling the office and he the operations. They were a good team and complemented each other's strengths. Even as the children got older and became involved in the business themselves, things went smoothly. It appeared that this was a situation where the eventual transfer of the business to a child would go well.

Still, there were secrets that the family did not talk about. Even though the family appeared to be close they never really talked about important things. They played together and gathered the extended kin together for holidays and birthdays. They enjoyed camping and waterskiing in the summer. However, there were never any real heart-to-heart talks. If anyone had personal problems, they took care of them quietly, on their own. This was a family that did not have a mechanism for handling problems and conflicts openly.

The fact that Steven was seeking help was unusual also, but his anger problem was only the tip of the iceberg. Steven revealed that for years he had been having affairs. The affairs never lasted long, perhaps a few months. He was discreet, so neither his wife nor his children suspected him. However, now he was really unhappy in his marriage. He was currently dating a business associate who lived in another state. He would arrange to meet her whenever he had out-of-town business. He found that he was wanting to be with this woman more and more, and regretted that he had to return home from his visits with her. He even started making excuses to his wife for leaving her home on trips she had typically joined him on in the past, such as the annual trade show. But when Susan found two airline tickets charged to the company credit card, and she had not attended the meeting, she became suspicious.

Susan had not really been ignorant of Steven's affairs, but had quietly ignored them because they always passed. This one, however, it was hard to ignore, because the time Steven was spending with this other woman was growing and because Steven was becoming less discreet. The anger and hostility that he demonstrated also gave rise to suspicion. Susan knew that something was dreadfully wrong and needed to change, but like her husband had no way to talk about or attempt to resolve such a problem.

After I brought Susan and Steven together in the same room, we were able to discuss the problems. Steven felt confined by his lifestyle. He had always been a "nice" person, a good husband and provider, a doting father. He resented that he had never had a chance to "let his hair down." Susan, on the other hand, was quite content with her life. She wanted nothing more than to be a mother and supportive spouse, as her mother and grandmother had been before her. She raised her three daughters with these same values. She assumed that Steven felt the same way, and was shocked to learn otherwise.

Too often people turn to sex as a way to escape the stresses of entrepreneurial life. For some reason, another partner with no connection to the busy world of the workaholic often seems appealing, refreshing. Once this pattern of elicit affairs is begun, it is a difficult pattern to break. Like drug addiction, it is immediately satisfying to find relief in the arms of a stranger, someone who will let you escape temporarily from your ordinary life. Soon, however, what was temporary escape becomes a habitual need. The real problems have been so long overlooked that they cannot be recognized. In Steven and Susan's case, it took several months to identify just what was troubling them, and then only after a trial separation.

Once ethical boundaries are crossed, it becomes increasingly easier to cross other boundaries. Susan and Steven made the mistake of ignoring their problems and allowing his unfaithful behavior to continue too long. They needed to be brave and to admit with the first indiscretion that there was a problem in either their marriage or their business partnership or both. As a result of their delay, they created a lot of confusion and hardship for themselves, their children, and the rest of the family. When Steven moved out and began openly dating this other woman, his children were horrified and his wife humiliated. Needless to say, working together became a nightmare. On more than one occasion the couple engaged in yelling at each other in front of employees.

Fortunately, after a few months Steven recognized his mistake and wanted to work things out with Susan. He had created much hurt and animosity with his recent behavior, but Susan was willing to work with him to uncover solutions in therapy. With some exploration, they discovered that Steven especially needed more room to grow. While he still loved his wife, he did not want to run a copreneurial venture anymore; he wanted to expand the business on his own. Susan was happy keeping the business relatively small and low-key. She was not up to the merger and multimillion-dollar status that her pioneering husband was aiming for. But if Susan was to remain in the business, she would have to change her attitude, for Susan was holding Steven back. Rather than have affairs, Steven needed to put his energy to more creative use and develop the business to the level he was really capable of.

When Franklin Roosevelt was president, the public did not know of his numerous extramarital liaisons. There was a *code* at the time that the president's reputation would not be tarnished by gossip. Today, however, as the numerous news stories about Gennifer Flowers, Paula Jones, and Monica Lewinsky amply illustrate, our presidents are not protected by that code. Extramarital affairs are viewed as a weak person's way of resolving personal problems, and Americans do not want a weak president. Whether you agree with the current mentality or not, it is clear

**211**

that extramarital affairs cause serious dysfunction in a marriage and weaken the ability of an entrepreneurial couple to make good business decisions. Trust between business partners is vital. Without it, your business and/or your life may wander in a meaningless direction for years, as life did for Steven.

## Rising out of the Ashes of Financial Disaster

Chapter Eight offered an in-depth look at wealth management and how money issues can trap entrepreneurial couples. It is not money in itself that is the problem, but how we think or what we believe about money and how we in turn use it based on those beliefs. In situations of extreme dysfunction, such as those I have described in this chapter, it is not surprising that money problems surface along with addictions and domestic violence. As I have said several times, once one ethical boundary is crossed, it becomes easier to cross others. Yet it is equally true that not all problems in an entrepreneurial relationship eventually cause money problems. Some couples retain their financial wealth in spite of problems in other areas of their business and life. Still other couples are able to keep a problem isolated long enough to work it out so that the balance is restored before the consequences affect the pocketbook. In the case of dual entrepreneurs Jay and Celia, however, money trouble was the triggering event that upset the balance of their lives and business.

There is not an entrepreneurial couple reading this book that has not experienced financial problems. Perhaps your first venture fizzled out. Perhaps a change in the industry forced you to seek diversification. You may have had to borrow money to make payroll on at least one occasion. You may even have faced bankruptcy. The American Dream is not as easy to achieve as the naive may think. It takes hard work and resilience—often a lot of resilience to fight back when the cash flow has dried up. When entrepreneurial couples have life and business plans, and when they have been attending to their stress level and keeping their developing progressions in a healthy balance, they can face money troubles with determination and creativity. Unpleasant as the task may be, healthy couples do what they need to do. Still, you never know just exactly how you will survive a financial disaster until you face one.

Jay and Celia felt confident that their lives were on track, having established a comfortable dual-entrepreneurial life that was low-key enough to still foster family life with their two teenagers. But slowly and insidiously, Jay's business was falling apart. A combination of factors came into play. Jay's two partners were not as

**212**

eager to work as he was, and Jay found himself carrying them more and more. Second, Jay had miscalculated the market. Although he was a good auto mechanic and ran an efficient shop, his small homegrown business was being overshadowed by a corporate chain. Third, as Jay's business failed, Celia's business was taking off. She received offers from two other malls to set up espresso carts, which would mean she needed to buy more equipment and hire employees.

Jay was envious of Celia's success and showed it by making increasing demands on her. It was not good enough that Celia was developing a successful small business; she also had to be home in time to fix Jay's dinner each night. The children also started feeling Jay's control. They not only had to be the best players on the sports team but had to come home with perfect grades. The couple who had never openly fought before started having long arguments late into the night.

Finally, the day of truth came and Jay lost his business. His partners bailed out on him, so he was left with the entire debt to pay. He owed the bank more than the business was worth by then. Jay was thoroughly demoralized. He had lost his dream and a great deal of money, and he would be paying for his failure for years to come. Rather than seek help for his depression, and rather than turn to Celia for support, Jay began to drink. Eventually the drinking led to Jay trying to strangle his teenage daughter, which, when she found out about it, led Celia to leave him.

Jim and Lynn faced a similar situation when Jim lost a major contract, but they handled it very differently. Jim is a solo entrepreneur and Lynn his supportive spouse. They have worked well together for many years in their traditional marriage. The couple never viewed their construction business as a way to make a million dollars; they were happy that the business did well enough to support the family and provide a comfortable middle-class lifestyle. Like Don and Marla, they are routineers, which means that they are a hardworking entrepreneurial couple who are self-employed as a way to make a living.

As a result of this style, however, Jim was not very creative about exploring the marketplace. Expansion was never on his mind, so once he found a comfortable niche, he kept working it. Lynn took care of the home and children, and handled the billing for the business. Unfortunately, Jim had his "eggs all in one basket." Although he had other small contracts, 50 percent of his business was subcontracting for a large residential builder. When the builder declared bankruptcy, Jim was left owing money to customers whose projects he could not complete because the builder could not pay Jim.

Jim and Lynn began talking about the problem as soon as it became apparent in what direction the large builder was going. Although Lynn had always left business management to her husband, she rolled up her sleeves and pitched in making phone calls. Some customers were willing to work with Jim until he could line up a new builder for their projects. Jim got busy and found other work for his employees, but still had to let a few go. The couple had to get practical and decided to sell a piece of land on which they had intended to build their dream house. They looked at their household budget to see what else they could trim. As it turned out, Jim and Lynn managed to squeak by this financial crisis by pulling together and tightening their belts. The construction industry as a whole was still hale and hearty, even if one residential builder had miscalculated and failed. Jim figured that it would take three years to reestablish himself. As well, he learned a valuable lesson about diversification and staying on top of the changing marketplace.

Jim and Lynn did one more thing that helped save their business and their marriage: They sought the advice of a relationship consultant. In spite of having very few discretionary dollars to spend, they felt it best to seek the advice of a consultant familiar with entrepreneurial couples. They were able to recognize that this crisis could cause friction between them, especially since Lynn was not working outside the home and had little way to help Jim directly save the business. In their counseling with me, Jim and Lynn were able to become aware of their values and priorities and devise their life and business plans accordingly. Without this advice, this entrepreneurial couple might have rushed into the crisis, solving it in a manner that would disrupt the other developing progressions in their lives. For example, both agreed that they wanted to preserve their traditional marriage and keep Lynn at home with the children if possible. Lynn was actively involved in the local school as a volunteer. She coached her son's soccer team and was also a Girl Scout leader. These are contributions to the family and the community that the couple wanted to maintain. However, Lynn also had to become more knowledgeable about the business. The current crisis got the couple thinking about possible future crises, such as what would happen if Jim were killed. In his line of work, injury and disability are common. And Jim had lost one friend to a cave-in at a work site. If such a disaster should occur, Jim and Lynn wanted to have a plan to carry on the business and provide for the family. So, despite their traditional marriage, Jim began training Lynn to be his *successor* in managing the business.

Financial problems cannot always be avoided, but disasters can be prevented with wise planning and an understanding of the dialectic of life. Money ebbs and flows just like the tide. When it is flowing, it is foolish to consider that it will always do so. Preparing for the inevitable shortfall is a necessary part of entrepreneurial life. In addition to focusing on money specifically, entrepreneurial couples need to have well-thought-out life and business plans so that they have the wisdom and tools to deal with a financial crisis. But even more important is checking out each individual's personal mental and physical health. Jay did not attend to his mental health and as a result created more than financial disaster. Jim and Lynn, however, recognized that financial problems are only the tip of the iceberg. They chose to assess their personal strengths and weaknesses as part of developing a power plan to attack the financial problems, and this strategy proved to be quite effective.

# If Divorce Is Your Only Alternative[1]

Since six out of ten marriages in America end in divorce, it is probably wise for entrepreneurial couples to take this fact into consideration when developing their life and business plans. Remember, planning for the worst does not mean you will create the worst; it simply means that you have developed contingencies should the worst happen. Planning for the possibility of divorce can have the opposite effect, too: If an entrepreneurial couple knows the full ramifications of divorce, this may give them incentive to keep their developing progressions in healthy interaction.

In this section I will lead you through the steps of dissolving a business partnership with your spouse in the event of divorce. I am only highlighting things you should know, not going into depth. Obviously, if you have reached the stage of divorce you should contact a qualified attorney, especially one familiar with entrepreneurial couples. Recognizing how complicated it can be to sever a partnership with your spouse should alert most entrepreneurial couples. I would rather you developed your life, business, and power plans from a positive, proactive position, but sometimes a little fear makes the best incentive. Don't ignore this section because your marriage is stable. Read on and be advised of the preparations *now* that could save you hours, days, weeks, and months of anguish should a divorce occur down the road.

When things have deteriorated to the point of divorce, an entrepreneurial couple probably faces dissolution of the business partnership as well. I have seen cases in which a divorced couple manages the business together after the divorce, but this is really rare and quite a strain. People in this latter situation either are very

---

[1] In this section I have relied heavily on the advice of matrimonial attorney Howard Marshack. Mr. Marshack is a seasoned professional licensed in both Oregon and Washington and is familiar with issues of matrimonial law throughout the United States. In addition to having advised numerous entrepreneurs, Mr. Marshack, as my husband, helps me to keep my personal and business boundaries clear and our interacting developing progressions in healthy alignment.

advanced souls or just have a difficult time letting go. The more typical scenario is that one partner gets the business and the other gets compensated for his or her interest in the business. Before this simple solution is reached, however, there is usually a time-consuming and costly legal battle involving at least two attorneys, business appraisers, witnesses, and other experts. In addition to all of this is the emotional and physical strain on each individual, the children, employees, customers, and so on. If you are in partnership with your spouse, read on and be advised.

If you and your spouse have come to a point of wanting a divorce, the trust between the two of you is undoubtedly as low as it will ever get. If you cannot trust each other as spouses, how can you continue to trust each other as business partners? It is at this point that entrepreneurial couples start entangling themselves in a money trap. Without trust, they often become controlling and secretive. After all, you have a financial interest to preserve and you may not trust your partner to conduct the business and preserve the assets for your common benefit. To combat this lack of trust, the court can determine which spouse will have the management responsibilities of the business until the divorce is decided. The court can impose upon the managing spouse specific duties to account to the other. The nonmanaging spouse may be granted regular rights to inspect the business premises and regular access to the financial records. Often the spouse granted this interim right to manage the business is in the best position to be awarded the business in the final settlement. (Things can get stickier if there are partners in the business other than the entrepreneurial couple. Certainly the court must consider the rights of these partners as well. For simplification in this section, I will assume that the divorcing entrepreneurial couple has no other partners. However, if this is not true for you, you should also consult your family/business attorney about other considerations.)

The attorney's fees and costs in a dissolution of an entrepreneurial marriage can be very expensive. One of the most expensive aspects of a divorce is hiring the professional business appraisers to appraise the value of the business. If possible, it is best to have the spouses agree on a neutral business appraiser. If each party hires their own business appraiser, you can imagine how that further complicates things. Often two experts have significantly different opinions as to the value of the business, even under the best of circumstances. Because each spouse hires their own expert, the experts may be viewed as an extension of the advocates themselves, thus increasing the likelihood of widely divergent opinions as to the value of the business.

Not all businesses require an appraisal, especially if the net worth of the business is less than the possible costs it would entail to appraise it in a nonadversarial context. When a modest business is involved, entrepreneurial couples can take a practical approach of valuing the used equipment and accounts receivable. Although this method does not determine the value of goodwill, reputation, or position in the market, it is a relatively inexpensive way to value a business. Fighting over the intangible assets of the business such as goodwill can increase your costs immeasurably and just may not be worth it in the long run.

Many divorcing entrepreneurs are surprised to learn that the business is a marital asset whether or not they are copreneurs, dual entrepreneurs, or a solo entrepreneur with a supportive spouse. The marital interest in the business includes inventory, equipment, bank accounts, investments, real estate holdings, and other tangible assets. The nontangible value of the business is also a marital asset. Such things as accounts receivable and the reasonable expectation of future patronage or goodwill are other marital assets. Another surprise is to learn that you are also both responsible for the business debt. Such business debt includes obligations to pay leases, loans and promissory notes, unpaid taxes, suppliers, professionals for their services, payroll, utilities, and other unpaid costs that have accrued as part of doing business.

The big question for entrepreneurial couples is who will get the business. If you have been a solo entrepreneur with a supportive spouse or perhaps dual entrepreneurs, this question may be fairly easily solved. But if you are copreneurs, who have both actively put your heart and soul (as well as other talents and money) into the business, the decision is not so easy. If the two of you can make this decision before you go to court, you will save yourself a lot of money and emotional wear and tear. Typically, one spouse is awarded the entire marital interest in the business. This person also acquires the marital responsibility for the business debts. The other spouse is awarded an equitable share (usually one half) of the net value of the marital interest in the business. The specific value of the business and business debts and the specific amount to be paid to the spouse leaving the business are either negotiated by the parties before trial or determined by the court.

As we saw in Chapter Eight, Jonathan insisted on rewriting the old prenuptial agreement between himself and his wife, Brooke, years after they had successfully grown their advertising agency to international status. His reasoning was that he and Brooke need a way to part amicably if that time should ever arise. Although Jonathan had the right idea in terms of planning ahead for the worst, these types of marital agreements are not always helpful in defining the respective spouses' rights and obligations in the event of a divorce.

Marital agreements may be prenuptial agreements, postnuptial agreements, or separation agreements. The validity of the agreement depends on how well it is

**217**

written and, in many jurisdictions, whether procedures are followed. For example, some agreements have been set aside because one of the spouses did not have adequate opportunity to consult an attorney. Another common reason for an agreement being set aside is that a spouse was given very little time to consider a prenuptial agreement before the wedding. This is considered giving an unfair ultimatum.

Marital agreements, even if valid when signed with proper procedures, are often of little use, especially if the agreement was prepared before the business enterprise was begun or became a copreneurial venture. If the agreement was signed before the business venture was begun, it is likely the agreement did not adequately contemplate the mutual efforts the parties would put into the joint venture. The agreement may not be adequate for the same reasons if it was signed *after* the business venture was begun but *before* the parties contemplated working together.

Rarely is an agreement between spouses the functional equivalent of a partnership agreement between unrelated people. The mutual responsibilities husbands and wives share are far more multidimensional and complex than a mere business partnership. Nevertheless, an agreement between spouses prepared after or in contemplation of an entrepreneurial venture can go a long way to define the parties' mutual rights and obligations in the event of a divorce and dissolution of the partnership. The agreement may specify which spouse will carry on the business. The agreement may define the spouses' respective contributions to the business, especially those that predated the marriage. The agreement may define how much compensation the husband has to pay the wife for her interest in the business or vice versa, though this aspect of the agreement may be the most difficult to enforce.

Many entrepreneurial couples are shocked when I suggest that they consult an attorney about a partnership agreement, including an agreement for future dissolution of the partnership. However, I firmly believe that ignorance is no excuse for falling on bad times. If you as an entrepreneurial couple are well informed about the worst possibilities as well as curious about advantageous opportunities, and if you build your power plan to include a well-written partnership agreement with your spouse, you will be in a much better position to manage the change that will inevitably come into your life. Life is becoming ever more stressful as we move into the twenty-first century. Monitoring your life for signals alerting you to changes that could lead to divorce is a reasonable way to help keep the developing progressions of your entrepreneurial life flowing smoothly.

Finally, I might add that hiring an experienced matrimonial attorney is essential to drafting such a partnership agreement. Later, if your marriage should dissolve, an attorney is also essential for determining the validity of the agreement given the passage of time and the changes that have taken place. Do not cut corners here. Just as you should hire the best family/business consultants for other aspects of your entrepreneurial lifestyle, so should you hire the best professional advisors when it comes to keeping your business in shape. Your business is an extension of the two of you and represents years of commitment. Furthermore, your business may be an important part of the legacy you pass on to your children and grandchildren. The least you can do is buy a little insurance by hiring a competent attorney and drafting a healthy agreement.

## Spirit Defines the Meaning of Life

Viktor Frankl, a survivor of a Nazi concentration camp, wrote, "Man is not diminished by suffering but by suffering without meaning." In this chapter you have read about the suffering of some entrepreneurial couples. Their suffering is a result of having allowed their lives to become unbalanced, of crossing boundaries in unhealthy ways, and of denying the inevitability of change. In order to restore balance, you must create a healthy lifestyle for yourself and the ones you love and work with. If you have been attending to the *mind* and the *body*, you are well on your way to a healthy integration of intimacy, family life, and meaningful work. However, until you assess and address the strength of your *spirit*, you will not achieve true balance or prosperity.

Remember that spirit is not bound by religion, but as Frankl suggests, it defines the *meaning of life*. Many successful entrepreneurial couples do not belong to a church or any religion, but they do have a strong sense of spirit and they do believe in God. According to Gallup Polls as recent as 1997, 90 percent of Americans believe in God. The *spirit connection* is not just a belief in God but the ability to relate to God, often through communities such as churches provide. The healthiest Americans are often members of those religious groups that have a strong identity with their church. For example, Matthews and Koenig reported in 1997 that even if you control for dietary practices, Mormons, Jews, and Seventh Day Adventists are healthier than other Americans. These three religious groups are known for their strong sense of religious community. Therefore, it is not the religion per se that contributes to overall health, but the *intensity of the commitment to spirit*, whether by being a member of a religious community or by maintaining a spiritual practice or connection in some other way.

Although most Americans believe in God, many of us are prone to have fragmented and impersonal lives, which leads to hedonism, increasing drug addiction, and other health problems. Spirituality in the sense of the expression of our spirit, is not a regular part of our lives because so many of us have abandoned religion. According to Kabbani, a physician and author on Islamic spiritual healing practices, religion gives us something to believe in, an identity, a way to know ourselves in relation to others. Churches, therefore, provide a community within which to know ourselves, to belong, and to repair our fragmented lives.

Many entrepreneurial couples list church attendance as one of the last things on their list of things to do. After all, you are busy, busy people, working fifty to sixty hours a week. When would you find the time? You barely have a few moments to eat a quick meal and watch television before falling into bed at the end of your day. However, just as you have reevaluated other aspects of your life and business plans, you need to reevaluate your spirit connection. If you really want to create a balance among intimacy, family life, and meaningful work, you need to repair the third leg of the mind-body-spirit connection. (Furthermore, if you want to live long enough to enjoy the fruits of your labors, you might want to reconsider the use of television as an expedient stress reliever. According to a review of the research by Dale Matthews, M.D., and Herb Koenig, Ph.D., there is a positive correlation between television watching and mortality: In other words, the more you watch TV, the shorter your life.)

Einstein once said, "Religion without science is blind. Science without religion is lame." As we move into the twenty-first century, we are realizing the truth of this statement more and more. Entrepreneurial couples are not different from other people on the planet. We are part of something much more than the sum of the parts. Those who embrace their spirit connection are finding greater health and prosperity—and even science is starting to prove this. For example, in a Duke University study by Herb Koenig (as yet unpublished), elderly patients who were regular church attenders stayed in the hospital a shorter length of time (ten days, on average) than those patients who did not attend church (twenty-five days). In another study (Graham, Kaplan, Coroni-Huntley, James, Becker, Hames, and Heyden, 1978), researchers compared smokers' blood pressure among participants who were two-pack-a-day smokers. Those who attended church had lower blood pressure than those who did not; indeed, the church attenders had blood pressure that was not different from those who did not smoke. In a third study (Desmond and Maddox, 1981), this one of heroin addicts, researchers reported that 45 percent of participants in a religiously oriented treatment program were still abstinent at the time of a one-year follow-up, compared to only 5 percent who participated in a nonreligious program.

It is true that you cannot always prevent pain. Although change is constant, you cannot always predict accurately what those changes will be, and pain may be a natural by-product of the interaction of your developing progressions. Yet if you have a healthy spiritual connection, your suffering may be minimized, as the previously mentioned studies indicate. For Viktor Frankl, a Jew confined in a Nazi concentration camp, pain was constant, but by discovering the meaning of his life through his spirituality, his suffering was reduced.

Florence Nightingale, the founder of modern nursing, was another healer who found the balance between mind, body, and spirit to be essential to health. According to Nightingale, pain relief comes from attending to the body through medicine such as analgesics and surgery, attending to the mind through stress-management methods, and attending to the spirit through prayer or inner contemplation. Nightingale suggested that prayer was more than mind calming: Because the universe is orderly, she argued, inner contemplation invokes order or balance within, thereby creating healing.

When Benson studied the relaxation response, one of the methods of relaxation he studied was prayer. While those who prayed did not achieve any greater relaxation than did those practicing TM, other research has indeed shown the healing (not just relaxing) power of prayer. In fact, those who are prayed for, even though they do not pray for themselves, heal faster. Byrd reported in 1988 that hospitalized cardiac patients who were prayed for had, as a group, less congestive heart failure, used less diuretics, had fewer cardiopulmonary arrests, had less pneumonia, used fewer antibiotics, and were less frequently intubated than a similarly matched group of hospitalized cardiac patients who were *not* prayed for. Furthermore, the patients did not know they were being prayed for and the religions of the patient or the person praying were not relevant. In other words, it is not religion per se that heals, nor is religion the direct connection to spirit, but there is a *spirit-to-spirit connection* between people.

If you review the stories of the couples I have described in this chapter, you may be able to see how some of their suffering could have been avoided if they had a stronger sense of self, a sense of self as belonging to something larger than just this earthly existence, and if they had made a commitment to that higher self (i.e., through prayer or inner contemplation). If working hard to make an entrepreneurial business successful and profitable results in workaholism, drug addiction, financial problems, domestic violence, extramarital affairs, and divorce, what's the point? Even with the couples who sank to such depths as I have described in this chapter, the point is to make *meaning* of the experience, to put the disaster into the context of one's life and reorient that life to meet your true values. If one of those values is a belief in God yet you are not attending to that spiritual relationship, the balance in your life is compromised and will inevitably lead you to some form of personal or interpersonal dysfunction.

## Building Your Power Plan

After reading this chapter, you may already be assessing the state of your own mind-body-spirit connection. Even though your life may not be as out of control as the lives of some, you still may be alarmed by the stories you have read and are alerted to the changes you need to make in your own life. The questions in Self-Assessment Exercise 14 offer a review of the subjects discussed in this chapter. Use them as a guide to your own personal assessment of the state of your mind-body-spirit connection. Then ask yourself how you plan to correct the problems you have identified, and begin to build your own personal and couple *power plan* for total mental, physical, and spiritual health and well-being.

## Your Power Plan

Answer the following questions as honestly as you can. There are no right or wrong answers. The purpose of this exercise is to help focus your attention on your mental, physical, and spiritual health so that you can manage the excessive stresses in your life more effectively and avoid some of the worst crises and breakdowns that entrepreneurial couples are likely to face.

1. In comparison to some of the couples described in this chapter, what similar problems are you in the process of developing?

2. How can you begin today to devote more time to personal stress management, such as the relaxation response?

3. What physical health problems, including any addictions, need attending to *now*?

4. If there is any form of domestic violence occurring in your life, what is your plan to stop it?

5. If you are using extramarital affairs to solve or avoid couple, family, or business problems, what is your plan to revamp your style to be consistent with your true values?

6. If you have a history of financial improprieties and misfortune, what are these signals telling you about the imbalance in your life?

7. If you are considering divorce, first ask yourself if divorce is a result of imbalance in the mind-body-spirit connection. If so, what alternatives to restoring balance are there other than divorce?

8. What plans have you made with your spouse to discuss a healthy partnership and dissolution agreement with an attorney?

9. Take the time to really evaluate your spiritual commitment. If that aspect of your life has been on hold, what's keeping you from exploring your spiritual commitment now?

10. Who are the professionals you rely on to help you build your power plan? Make sure your medical doctor, naturopath, chiropractor, psychologist, and so on are in healthy balance themselves so that you all work together to build a power plan that successfully manages the excessive stresses of entrepreneurial couple life.

## Evaluating Your Responses

With the experience you have gained by working the other self-assessment exercises in this book, you are better prepared to confront the serious stresses uncovered by this exercise. It takes courage and good communication skills to remedy infidelity, drug abuse, financial problems, and other personal inadequacies. Try to remember that you and your partner are human beings, both doing the best you know how to do, given your level of knowledge and experience at the time. Now, however, after reading this chapter, you have more knowledge than before, and it is time to build a more sophisticated power plan than you have ever had.

If you have uncovered even only one of the problems alluded to in this exercise, it may take a long time and a lot of work to correct it, but get started. Cleaning up old business paves the way to implementing a more healthy lifestyle in the future. You cannot build a life on shaky ground. Once you have reordered your life by cleaning up mistakes, begin attending to the many stresses that plague the entrepreneurial couple life, and have a plan to defuse stress on a daily basis.

## Summarizing Remark

Write one sentence or a brief paragraph summarizing what you learned from this exercise and what you want to change.

# Constructing a Master Life Plan:
# How to Be Successful in
# the Twenty-First Century

The man on the other end of the line was speaking softly, so I had to listen carefully. "I don't know if you can help me," he said. "My wife and I are having problems. She doesn't even know I'm calling you, and I'm not sure she will even agree to see you." I reassured him that I was willing to help even if his wife was a little reluctant to seek consultation. "But I am not even sure you *can* help," he said, "because our situation is kind of unique."

"How's that?" I inquired. "Let me know what your special concerns are, and together we will decide if it is something I can help you with."

The man paused, composing his thoughts so that he could succinctly describe his "unique" situation to me. "Well, it's just that we work together and it is causing a lot of problems. I really love my wife, but employees are complaining about her to me and that puts me in the middle. And at home, things are pretty tense too. She doesn't seem happy with me at all. I think maybe there's a kind of competition thing going on. So you see, this is kind of an unusual situation, and I am not sure you know much about this sort of thing, or if anyone does."

More often than not, this is how my first conversation with a member of an entrepreneurial couple goes. One spouse or the other calls, with trepidation about whether anyone can help. The isolation of entrepreneurial couple life has led them to believe that their situation is unique, when in fact, entrepreneurial couples are quite common. In addition, the assumption that the other spouse is reluctant to seek consultation is also common. This assumption, however, is often incorrect. Entrepreneurs are usually so busy working and not communicating intimately with their business partner/spouse, that they don't realize that he or she is just as concerned about their problems as is the caller.

I hope that after reading this book you no longer have concerns that you are alone. Even though each person and couple is unique in many ways, and no one style or solution works for everyone, there is much that you have in common with other entrepreneurial couples. My goal in writing this book is to bring you the awareness that you are one couple in a growing sea of entrepreneurial couples in this country. Furthermore, you are not alone in your search for a way to balance and integrate intimacy, family life, and meaningful work.

To be effective in balancing and integrating intimacy, family life, and meaningful work, you need knowledge and skills in three areas: (1) self-awareness, (2) planning, and (3) what I like to think of as the laws of the universe. The couples I have described in this book have this knowledge and these skills to a lesser or greater extent than yourself, depending on just where they (and you) are in terms of their interacting developing progressions. However, if you are thorough in your research of entrepreneurial life, and if you are diligent in working through the Self-Assessment Exercises included in this book, you will be well on your way to a more satisfying relationship with your business partner/spouse.

## Self-Awareness

Making the phone call to me was a first step toward self-awareness for that entrepreneurial husband. Realizing that you are not alone is a powerful thing. Knowing that others have gone before you somehow makes it easier to explore the challenging territory of couple entrepreneurship. In reading this book, you have acquired a great deal of knowledge about other entrepreneurial couples, and I hope learned many things about yourself in the process. Self-awareness in this context really means *self-awareness in relationship to others.* Certainly among the twenty types of entrepreneurial couples, you can see yourself and your spouse. Are you an entrepreneurial spirit yourself, a supportive spouse, or both? Are you dual entrepreneurs, copreneurs, or a solo entrepreneur with a supportive spouse? Is your enterprise structured as a family business? Finally, what style of entrepreneur are you and your spouse—all-rounder, organizer, routineer, or pioneer?

In comparing yourself to the couples described in the book, realize that these couples are not representative of all entrepreneurial couples. Rather, they represent a range of styles. I have chosen examples of each style, but really there are more than twenty. The variety is infinite if you take into consideration the diversity in personality and talents among entrepreneurs. For example, you may be an all-rounder but nothing like Carol or Anton or Howard in terms of personality or type of business. Also, you may be a copreneurial couple but have a pioneering style, regardless of the fact that most copreneurs are all-rounders.

Your self-awareness and your awareness of your partner have no doubt increased as you practiced the communication attitudes and skills outlined in Chapter Three. Using your senses instead of just following worn-out beliefs makes it easier to read your partner and the situation better. Acquiring the skills of listening and respectful confrontation enables you to avoid compromise and come to healthy win-win solutions. Recognizing that each person is doing the best he or she know how relieves you of the burden of blame and guilt so that you can work as a team toward solutions. Developing your flexibility in communicating allows you to use whatever tool is necessary to create a winning situation. Finally, knowing when to quit, when the situation has deteriorated beyond repair, is far better than persisting in a foolish consistency.

If you are like most entrepreneurial couples, you chose this lifestyle because it fits you. Entrepreneurial life is rewarding to you both personally and as a couple. It is equally important to be sure that your marital style fits you too. Are you and your spouse more characteristic of a traditional or an egalitarian couple? Your sex-role orientation and work/home self-concept have a powerful influence on each and every decision in your life, from the type of business you own to how you manage it to how you parent your children to how you interact with your spouse.

Are you comfortable with your traditional marriage in a dual-entrepreneurial relationship, for example? Or do you want to renegotiate the terms? For another couple, is your egalitarian relationship getting in the way of taking proper care of the children? Or does this style provide the kind of role models you want to give your children? Are you really satisfied with your style, or is it causing you extreme stress to maintain an unconscious habit? It is possible to renegotiate the terms of your marriage even if you have been operating with a certain marital style for decades. Sex-role orientation and work/home self-concept are not innate, but learned behaviors.

Perhaps your awareness grew as you read about women entrepreneurs. While there has been much written about men, it is only fairly recently that women entrepreneurs have been studied. A husband and wife, as co-owners of a business, certainly need to be informed about issues that affect entrepreneurial women if they are to navigate the waters of male-female relationships at home and at work. Although women entrepreneurs want many of the same things men entrepreneurs do, they tend to approach business differently. Coming from the heart of the holistic perspective, entrepreneurial women achieve success in the business world through an interconnected web of relationships, one of which is with their spouse.

It may be for this reason that the number of entrepreneurial couples is growing as rapidly as the number of female solo entrepreneurships.

Being a parent offers many opportunities for self-reflection. In Chapter Seven you were given the opportunity to assess your level of parenting savvy. Are you an authoritarian, permissive, or authoritative parent? Have you been properly educated to undertake this important responsibility? Do you need to seek guidance now to insure that you are preparing your children properly for their future? Even more than knowing the latest advice on proper parenting is having the right attitude. Getting to know your child complements getting to know yourself. As you assist your child in discovering himself or herself, you are opening discoveries about yourself as well. As you and your spouse face adversity openly and honestly, you are modeling for your child how to handle troubling times in a positive way. When you allow your child the room to advance only as quickly as his or her developmental timetable will allow, you are teaching respect for the individual. As tempting as it is to teach obedience instead of encourage independence, your ultimate goal as an achieving parent is to have achieving children who are high in self-esteem. And finally, what more wonderful gift can you give yourself and your children than the gift of fond memories of their childhood?

Money is one of the main triggers for conflict between a husband and wife, yet money is seldom the real issue. Demystifying the topic of money has probably opened your eyes. Now that you are more aware of the meaning you and your spouse make of money, you are in a better position to handle it wisely. If you are stuck in the money traps of desire or poverty consciousness, what will it take right now to move you in the direction of prosperity consciousness? If you have been competing with your spouse, or defining your self-worth by accumulating dollars, your entrepreneurial relationship is sorely lacking in creative collaboration. If your children are to grow into healthy, achieving, responsible managers of their wealth, they need your help in modeling the spirit of abundance.

Self-awareness is too important to be left to moments of crisis. Since change is inevitable and nothing lasts forever, people who seek out change and opportunities for purposeful growth will be one step ahead of others. What are your plans to expand your consciousness about the world of relationships in which you live?

Those of you brave enough to really look at the serious dysfunction in your lives can still develop a meaningful entrepreneurial life with your spouse and family. If you listen to the internal and external signals that change is needed, many of these traumas can be avoided, but if you have let them creep into your lives, don't allow yourself to be victimized. Face your mistakes and a make a power plan to correct them. Even the most serious heartache you have ever faced—be it an extramarital affair, financial loss, drug addiction, physical disease, or divorce—can provide an opportunity for growth and add to your wisdom.

## Planning

With the work of expanding self-awareness well under way for you and your spouse, the next step is to apply this new knowledge of self and others by developing your life and business plans. Instead of just winging it, you can actually plot a course that best suits yourself, your spouse, your family, and your business. Your master plan will keep evolving over time, as does your personal awareness, but you have tools now to revamp your master life plan as your life expands. Those basic tools include (1) planning with your spouse, (2) using your newfound communication skills, (3) brainstorming, (4) being open to all possibilities, (5) shooting for the moon, (6) preparing for the worst, and (7) remaining flexible. Approaching each change in life with these planning tools will enable you to revise your master life plan to fit the latest integration of your developing progressions.

In Chapter Four, which focuses on planning, you assess your personal goals in life, your relationship goals, and your business goals; but until you included parenting (discussed in Chapter Seven), wealth management (Chapter Eight), and stress management (Chapter Ten), your master plan was not yet complete and in balance. Take a moment now to review those six plans as well as the results of the other exercises in the book. If all you have are notes on scraps of paper, turn to the appendix where the exercises are repeated for your convenience. First, reevaluate your responses to all fourteen exercises. Write a brief statement of your discoveries and decisions under *Summarizing Remark* at the end of each exercise. If you follow the instructions in the appendix, you will eventually create a holistic life plan from these summaries, encompassing a *master life plan*, an *action plan*, and a *mission statement*. Work with your partner (and your children or other significant people who are ultimately involved in your life) in developing your plan so that you can compose a life that is harmonious at work and at home.

The bulk of the work you do in the self-assessment exercises will result in the development of a *master life plan*, which encompasses your personal life plan, relationship life plan, business life plan, family life plan, financial life plan, and power plan. In the *action plan* you will list the steps you will take to accomplish the goals outlined in your master plan. Many of the action plan steps will come from the other exercises in the book, such as your satisfaction with the division of household and work-related responsibilities. The *mission statement* is the underlying principle that will guide all future decisions regarding your life/business plan. Your mission statement needs to reflect your concern with how to balance and integrate every important developing progression in your life. For Frank and Louise, the mission statement involves developing a successful entrepreneurial venture that will contribute to continuing good health, loving relationships, and spiritual growth. For Don and Marla, it is the awareness that the business should benefit the family as a whole. For Marty and Gisela, it is always shoot for the moon and never settle for second best. For Jonathan and Brooke, it is to preserve their independence while still operating as a team. And for Sharon and David, it is abundance in all relationships—intimate, family, and business.

As your master life plan takes shape, you may feel a sense of pride that you are restoring order to your life. It may surprise you to find how much of your life already makes sense. That is, unconsciously you have been following a meaningful plan, although perhaps with a few detours. By becoming conscious of your under-lying master plan and mission statement, you have the opportunity to streamline your progress by developing a specific action plan, and to finally accomplish your goal of finding balance among intimacy, family life, and meaningful work.

# The Laws of the Universe

It may seem a bit presumptuous of me to claim that I have introduced you to the laws of the universe, especially in one short book on the specialized topic of entre-preneurial couples. However, the laws of the universe are simple really and apply to all human realms, whether those realms are astrophysics or an entrepreneurial ven-ture. Now that you and your spouse have acquired self-awareness and you have a master plan by which to navigate your lives together in entrepreneurship, you need to understand your place in the greater scheme of things to keep the progress going.

That greater scheme of things has been summed up by Desmond Tutu as *ubuntu*. Tutu is a former archbishop, a Nobel Peace Prize recipient, and chair of the South African Truth and Reconciliation Commission. According to Tutu, *"Ubuntu* speaks to the essence of being human and our understanding that the human per-son is corporate. The solitary individual is, in our understanding, a contradiction in terms. You are a person through persons." (Desmond Tutu is quoted by Eric Sirotkin on page 7 in the Summer 1997 *Noetic Sciences Review*.)

*Ubuntu* is demonstrated by dialectical psychology and the theories that emanate from it, such as social exchange theory, life cycle theory, and systems theory, all of which were discussed in Chapter Two. This holistic perspective teaches us that each individual is a changing person in a changing world, that the domains of love and work are not separate but intricately intertwined, that all human development is the result of dynamic, spiraling, developing progressions in interaction with other spiraling, developing progressions. In other words, people *are* relationships. That is one of the most basic laws of the universe. Entrepreneurial couples represent this philosophy in the material world through their dynamic interaction as couples, as parents, and as business partners.

It is one thing to become more self-aware, to enhance your personal reality. It is advantageous to have a master life plan so that you can be true to your values and your growing self-awareness. And it is remarkable that some entrepreneurial couples can face so many hardships with such resiliency and come to restore the mind-body-spirit connection. However, the real success of your entrepreneurial venture as a couple is the *reality you create as your developing progressions collide*—not only with each other's developing progressions, but also with those of your children, your business associates, your employees, your customers, your friends, and your neighbors.

This is another very important law of the universe, that *reality is our personal construction.* As much help as reading this book may be to you in understanding the nature of entrepreneurial couple life, as much as professional guidance may augment your learning of how to balance the competing demands of love and work, the real power lies *within each individual* to create a healthy integration of intimacy, family life, and meaningful work that meets his or her unique qualifications. In the process of *making your whole life work, at the business and at home,* keep in mind that you are creating and reshaping reality with each decision and step you take. This is an awesome responsibility requiring the highest of ethical standards.

For your convenience, all of the self-assessment exercises in the book are repeated here. Grab your notes and review each exercise. Now that you have read the entire book, you may want to change some of your answers so they fit better into a holistic concept of a master plan. This is your chance to do that. Copy the following pages so that you can share the results with your partner. Self-Assessment Exercise 15 is a final exercise to help you pull together all of this material into your mission statement, master plan, and action plan.

SELF-ASSESSMENT EXERCISE 1

# What's Your Entrepreneurial Couple Style?

Check the boxes that apply to yourself and your partner. Choose just one box to check in each category, even if you have a blend of styles, because you probably have one dominant style. It is easier to plan around your dominant style. You may also wish to note your less dominant style and determine what that message is all about.

**Type of entrepreneurial couple**

❑ Solo entrepreneur  ❑ Dual entrepreneurs  ❑ Copreneurs
   with a supportive spouse

**Your personality**            **Your partner's personality**

❑ All-Rounder                   ❑ All-Rounder

❑ Organizer                     ❑ Organizer

❑ Routineer                     ❑ Routineer

❑ Pioneer                       ❑ Pioneer

**Family firm**                 **Names of family members (if a family firm)**

❑ Yes                           1. _____

❑ No                            2. _____

                                3. _____

## Evaluating Your Responses

Take note of the style you have chosen. Does your partner see it differently? Has the style changed over time? Why? Is your personality compatible with that of your partner? What are the strengths and weaknesses of your respective styles and as a team? Now that you are consciously aware of your style you are in a position to make the most of it for the success of your business and your partnership.

## Summarizing Remark

In one sentence or a brief paragraph, summarize (1) What is your style?, and (2) Who are the significant players?

## SELF-ASSESSMENT EXERCISE 2

# Examining the Dialectic of Your Relationship

Answer the following questions as honestly as you can. There are no right or wrong answers. The purpose of this exercise is to help you gain insight into yourself and your relationship.

1. With regard to how you live your life (including your business, your marriage, and your family), what is the single most important thing you learned from your father? From your mother?

2. Why did you choose your spouse or partner? Why did he or she choose you? What do you do to keep the relationship alive?

3. Where do you want to be in five years? In ten?

4. Are you and your partner on the same wavelength when it comes to goals in life? For the business? For the children?

5. Are your personal goals, couple goals, and business goals in line with your goals for the children? For the extended family?

6. What one accomplishment would you like to be known for after you are dead?

SELF-ASSESSMENT EXERCISE 2 (CONT'D)

## Evaluating Your Responses

The answers to these questions will help you determine the stages of development for yourself, your partner, your family, and your business. Perhaps you will notice discrepancies in developmental goals among the systems. Some of your current values may be different from those you held when you started the business or the relationship. Take note of these discrepancies and differences and discuss them with your partner. You will take the insights from this exercise into the next few chapters of the book as you revamp your entrepreneurial couple lifestyle to fit your unique personalities and developmental requirements.

## Summarizing Remark

Summarize in one sentence or a brief paragraph what you learned in this chapter and in this exercise. Then use that summary as a lens through which to view each succeeding chapter and exercise.

## SELF-ASSESSMENT EXERCISE 3

## Your Personal Life Plan

Answer the following questions as honestly as you can. There are no right or wrong answers. The purpose of this exercise is to help you identify your personal values and goals, so that you can plan for yourself a life that is consistent with them.

1. Make a list of the fifty things that you have always wanted to do but have not yet done.

2. Make a list of ten to twenty of your most prized accomplishments. Rank your list in order of most prized to least prized.

3. Make a list of your worst habits. Rank this list, too, from worst bad habit to least bad habit.

4. Shop in a store that does not necessarily appeal to you, and buy something there. Eat in a restaurant that serves food you have always claimed to dislike.

5. Ask people what they think of you. Ask if they think you are smart, if they like your clothes, or if they would choose you for a friend or relative if they had a choice.

6. Be honest for an entire day. Notice how you feel about that.

7. Go to church (any church will do). Or, if you do this already, go to church on a day you normally would not go.

8. Describe three people—real or fictional, current or historical—that you most admire. Describe them in detail, and indicate why you admire them.

9. If you had $10 million, what would you do next with your life?

10. If you could change anything about your childhood, what would you change?

## SELF-ASSESSMENT EXERCISE 3 (CONT'D)

11. What was the most important value you learned from your father as you were growing up? From your mother? From another significant relative or friend?

12. If you could live anywhere, where would you live, and in what kind of house?

13. If you could do your life over again, what would be the most significant change you would make?

14. Write down one thing you are so ashamed of you have never told anyone. If you are brave enough to share it with someone, do so. If you are not yet brave enough, seal the piece of paper in an envelope and hide it from others until you are ready.

15. After you are dead, what one thing would you most like to be remembered for?

## Evaluating Your Responses

If you have truly applied yourself to the questions and tasks above, you should have acquired a great deal of information about yourself. Now gather up your notes and begin sifting through them. Read them over and over several times until you begin to see patterns, both in your behavior and in your thoughts and beliefs. These patterns are the foundation of your new life plan. Share your notes with others to see what patterns they notice. You will be surprised how often someone tells you that he or she knew about this or that pattern all along.

Many of your life decisions have been made out of habit or because your parents told you to do something or because of a foolish consistency. Look past these patterns to the patterns that truly reflect the inner you. If $10 million would allow you to go back to school to study zoology, and you won several 4-H awards as a child, and you would live on a ranch in Wyoming if you could live anywhere, and you wear cowboy boots with your three-piece suits and donate liberally to the Humane Society, what are you doing living in an apartment in New York and running an advertising agency? What are the patterns here?

After developing a list of patterns and priorities in your life, play with different possibilities for a while. Perhaps you can continue living in New York, running your ad agency, and wearing cowboy boots, but now you can also develop a plan to attract Wyoming clients. Or you can develop a specialty in advertising for nonprofits that support animal rights. And on holidays and vacations, you can head out to your ranch and ride your favorite horse.

## Summarizing Remark

Write one sentence or a brief paragraph summarizing what you learned from this exercise and what you want to change.

## Your Relationship Life Plan

Answer the following questions as honestly as you can. There are no right or wrong answers. The purpose of this exercise is to help you identify your values and goals for a primary relationship, so that you can build one that reflects them.

1. How did you and your partner meet? What attracted you to him or her?

2. Why did your partner choose you?

3. What did you learn about marriage from your parents?

4. What did your partner learn about marriage from his or her parents?

5. If you could do it all over again, would you choose this same partner? List your reasons.

6. What would you change in your partner to make the relationship better?

7. What do you need to change in yourself that would improve the relationship?

8. What are your partner's most deeply held beliefs? His or her most prized accomplishments? His or her most cherished dreams?

9. The people whom you dated before getting involved with your current partner—what were they like? Why did these relationships not work out?

10. The people whom your partner dated before getting involved with you—what were they like? Why did these relationships not work out?

## SELF-ASSESSMENT EXERCISE 4 (CONT'D)

11. What is your favorite recreational activity? Your partner's?

12. Name three important lessons you have learned from your partner.

13. Describe how you feel about sex with your partner.

14. Describe the ideal marriage. Describe your ideal mate.

15. Describe one important way you have disappointed your partner and one way she or he has disappointed you.

16. How do your children or other significant family members view your primary relationship?

## Evaluating Your Responses

You have come a long way if you have done these exercises honestly. You may have had some sleepless nights and long talks with your partner. Ideally, your partner is working on these exercises too. The goal here is to build and/or rewrite a life plan that encompasses the individual life plans for each of you as well as a relationship plan that you create together.

As with the exercise on your personal life plan, sift through the information you have gathered here. Look for patterns, themes, and foolish consistency. Begin to ask why and why not. Explore new forms of commitment with your partner. If there are areas in your relationship, such as intimacy and sex, that are no longer working, begin problem solving with your partner.

## Summarizing Remark

Write one sentence or a brief paragraph summarizing what you learned from this exercise and what you want to change.

## Your Business Life Plan

Answer the following questions as honestly as you can. There are no right or wrong answers. The purpose of this exercise is to help you identify your business/career values and goals so that you can pursue and develop a business or career that embodies them.

1. **Describe why you and your partner chose to work together as an entrepreneurial couple.**

2. **Whose idea was it to start the business?**

3. **How did you pick the service or product to market?**

4. **Who is the boss? Why?**

5. **How did your parents make decisions, especially if they were an entrepreneurial couple?**

6. **If you had a million dollars, would you sell your business? Ten million? A hundred million?**

7. **Describe your business goals in terms of their meaning to you, your partner, and your family.**

8. **What plans have you made for your business when you retire?**

9. **Could your partner step in and run things if you were disabled or deceased?**

10. **In what ways have you prepared your children for participating in the business?**

11. **Describe one of your greatest business failures and what you learned from it.**

12. **What are you most proud of with regard to your business?**

13. How are you and your partner viewed in the community as a business couple?

14. What image or reputation does your business have in the community? What image or reputation would you like it to have?

15. If you could start all over again, how would you design your business differently?

## Evaluating Your Responses

There are many more questions that I could ask you, but if you have been honest, you are off to a good start on brainstorming for your business life plan. Notice patterns and themes. Notice contradictions and inconsistencies. Marvel at and appreciate the ways in which you and your partner are "in sync." The questions and directives given here may spur you to many discussions. I hope so. Notice where you and your partner agree and disagree. You may be even more confused before you are finished. Do not be discouraged. Confusion often indicates that old, encrusted foolish consistencies have been knocked loose and are rattling around until you can find a new organization or framework for your life.

## Summarizing Remark

Write one sentence or a brief paragraph summarizing what you learned from this exercise and what you want to change.

## SELF-ASSESSMENT EXERCISE 6

# Your Sex-Role Orientation

From the following three columns of words, check the ones that best describe your personality. Check only those words that describe you *most* of the time, not the words that describe you only sometimes. For example, if you are cool in a crisis most of the time, but once in a while excitable in a crisis, check only the first description. However, if the words or terms from the first two columns really do apply equally, check "Both."

| | | |
|---|---|---|
| Aggressive _____ | Passive _____ | Both _____ |
| Independent _____ | Dependent _____ | Both _____ |
| Unemotional _____ | Emotional _____ | Both _____ |
| Dominant _____ | Submissive _____ | Both _____ |
| Cool in a crisis _____ | Excitable in a crisis _____ | Both _____ |
| Active _____ | Kind _____ | Both _____ |
| Rough _____ | Gentle _____ | Both _____ |
| Competitive _____ | Noncompetitive _____ | Both _____ |
| Worldly _____ | Home oriented _____ | Both _____ |
| Decision maker _____ | Helpful _____ | Both _____ |
| Tenacious _____ | Understanding _____ | Both _____ |
| Stoic _____ | Strong need for security _____ | Both _____ |
| Self-confident _____ | Need approval _____ | Both _____ |
| Superior _____ | Inferior _____ | Both _____ |

## SELF-ASSESSMENT EXERCISE 6 (CONT'D)

| | | | | | |
|---|---|---|---|---|---|
| Reserved | _____ | Warm | _____ | Both | _____ |
| Stress-resistant | _____ | Low stress tolerance | _____ | Both | _____ |
| Selfish | _____ | Selfless | _____ | Both | _____ |
| Feelings seldom hurt | _____ | Feelings easily hurt | _____ | Both | _____ |
| Totals: | _____ | | _____ | | _____ |

## Evaluating Your Responses

Although this exercise is not scientific, it is loosely based on the instrument I used in my study and asks about the traits or qualities stereotypically associated with masculinity and femininity. Tally your responses from each column. The more qualities you have from column one, the more masculine your orientation. The more qualities you have from column two, the more feminine your orientation. The more qualities you have from column three, the more androgynous is your sex-role orientation.

## Summarizing Remark

Note whether you are predominantly masculine, feminine, or androgynous in your orientation. What is your partner?

## Your Work/Home Self-Concept

Get two pens, one with red ink and the other with black ink. From the following list of word pairs, circle the words that most describe you *at work* in black, and then those that most describe you *at home* in red. It is okay to circle the same word with both black and red ink if that is your self-concept both at work and at home. Remember to circle the word that *most* describes you, not the word that describes you only sometimes. It is highly unlikely that anyone is *always* formal at work or *always* ineffective at home, for example, but if these are your tendencies, circle those words.

| | |
|---|---|
| **Formal/Informal** | **Participative/Autocratic** |
| **Active/Passive** | **Producing/Developing** |
| **Leader/Follower** | **Demanding/Allowing** |
| **Powerful/Powerless** | **Directive/Nondirective** |
| **Contribute/Receive** | **Unemotional/Emotional** |
| **Impatient/Patient** | **Extrovert/Introvert** |
| **Task-oriented/Person-oriented** | **Confrontive/Supportive** |
| **Relaxed/Tense** | **Advising/Directing** |
| **Covert/Overt** | **Relaxed/Focused** |
| **Collegial/Hierarchical** | **Unilateral/Bilateral*** |
| **Serious/Fun** | |

*\*Bilateral* means that you share duties and responsibilities with your partner, whereas *unilateral* means that you handle the duties and responsibilities yourself.

## SELF-ASSESSMENT EXERCISE 7 (CONT'D)

Next, list the word pairs where you *changed* from work to home. That is, if you circled "Focused" in black ink but "Relaxed" in red ink, then list that word pair below.

Finally, compare the word pairs where you changed with those of the participants in my study.

1. **If you changed from black to red on the following word pairs (the first term in each pair being black), you more resemble the** *copreneurial husbands* **in my study:**

   Formal / Informal                Active / Passive

   Producing / Developing           Leader / Follower

   Demanding / Allowing             Powerful / Powerless

   Contribute / Receive             Impatient / Patient

   Directive / Nondirective         Tense / Relaxed

   Extrovert / Introvert            Serious / Fun

   Focused / Relaxed

2. **If you changed from black to red on the following word pairs (the first term in each pair being black), you more resemble the** *copreneurial wives* **in my study:**

   Formal / Informal                Tense / Relaxed

   Advising / Directing             Focused / Relaxed

   Bilateral / Unilateral           Serious / Fun

## SELF-ASSESSMENT EXERCISE 7 (CONT'D)

3. If you changed from black to red on the following word pairs (the first term in each pair being black), you more resemble the *husbands* in *dual-career couples* in my study:

Formal / Informal                   Active / Passive

Leader / Follower                   Contribute / Receive

Unemotional / Emotional             Task-oriented / Person-oriented

Extrovert / Introvert               Tense / Relaxed

Focused / Relaxed                   Serious / Fun

4. If you changed from black to red on the following word pairs (the first term in each pair being black), you more resemble the *wives* in *dual-career couples* in my study:

Formal / Informal                   Active / Passive

Leader / Follower                   Powerful / Powerless

Tense / Relaxed                     Focused / Relaxed

Unilateral / Bilateral              Serious / Fun

## Evaluating Your Responses

Again, this exercise is not scientific, but the variables it asks about are similar to those used in my study. Of course, you may not resemble any of the four types in my study. Remember, these are statistical averages, so you may be one of the exceptions to the rule that got swallowed up in the averaging process. For example you may look like a leader at work but more like a copreneurial wife at home. Or perhaps you do not consider yourself a leader at all because your company consists of only you, but you do

## Evaluating Your Responses (cont'd)

not resemble a copreneurial wife at work either. Nevertheless, even if you do not score identically to one of the four types, you probably look similar to one of them. Look for a pattern or dominant theme.

## Summarizing Remark

In a nutshell, how would you say your self-concept changes from work to home?

# How You Divide Household Responsibilities

Complete the following questionnaire to determine if your division of household responsibilities more resembles that of dual-career couples or copreneurs. Circle the appropriate answer. Remember to circle the answer that most resembles your situation. For example, if the husband usually washes the dishes, circle "Husband." However, if you typically share the task, circle "Both."

| | | | |
|---|---|---|---|
| **Who washes the dishes?** | Husband | Wife | Both |
| **Who shops for food?** | Husband | Wife | Both |
| **Who does the laundry?** | Husband | Wife | Both |
| **Who cooks or prepares breakfast?** | Husband | Wife | Both |
| **Who cooks or prepares lunch?** | Husband | Wife | Both |
| **Who cooks or prepares dinner?** | Husband | Wife | Both |
| **Who does the yard work?** | Husband | Wife | Both |
| **Who makes small household repairs?** | Husband | Wife | Both |
| **Who does the general housework?** | Husband | Wife | Both |
| **Who handles car maintenance?** | Husband | Wife | Both |
| **Who chauffeurs the children?** | Husband | Wife | Both |
| **Who supervises the children's homework?** | Husband | Wife | Both |
| **Who plays with the children?** | Husband | Wife | Both |

## Evaluating Your Responses

Are household responsibilities fairly evenly distributed, as for most dual-career couples? Or are they assumed mostly by the wife, as for most copreneurial couples?

## Summarizing Remark

Note how it is and what you want to change.

# How You Divide Work-Related Responsibilities

Complete the following questionnaire to determine if your division of work-related responsibilities more resembles that of dual-career couples or copreneurs. Circle the answer that most closely resembles your situation. For example, if the husband usually handles customer service, circle "Husband." If you typically share the task, circle "Both."

| | | | |
|---|---|---|---|
| Who is responsible for bookkeeping, billing and collection, and payroll? | Husband | Wife | Both |
| Who is responsible for front office and secretarial functions? | Husband | Wife | Both |
| Who is responsible for budget planning? | Husband | Wife | Both |
| Who is responsible for business and market planning? | Husband | Wife | Both |
| Who handles customer service? | Husband | Wife | Both |
| Who handles sales? | Husband | Wife | Both |
| Who supervises employees? | Husband | Wife | Both |
| Who is responsible for quality control? | Husband | Wife | Both |
| Who makes major purchasing decisions? | Husband | Wife | Both |
| Who is responsible for building maintenance? | Husband | Wife | Both |
| Who handles stocking and shipping? | Husband | Wife | Both |
| Who maintains equipment? | Husband | Wife | Both |
| Who is responsible for product development? | Husband | Wife | Both |
| Who handles contract negotiation? | Husband | Wife | Both |
| Who manages paraprofessional services? | Husband | Wife | Both |
| Who manages professional services? | Husband | Wife | Both |

## SELF-ASSESSMENT EXERCISE 9 (CONT'D)

# Evaluating Your Responses

Are work-related responsibilities divided along traditional gender lines as for most copreneurial couples? Or are they distributed between husband and wife according to who is best suited to the task?

# Summarizing Remark

Note how it is and what you want to change.

# Your Satisfaction with the Division of Household Responsibilities in Your Marriage/Personal Relationship

The following is a list of responsibilities that are common in running a household. For each area of responsibility, circle whether you are "Satisfied" or "Dissatisfied" with the arrangement you and your spouse have made with regard to who is responsible for each item.

1. **Control in decision making**      Satisfied      Dissatisfied

2. **Household money management**      Satisfied      Dissatisfied

3. **Personal investment management**      Satisfied      Dissatisfied

4. **Housekeeping responsibilities**      Satisfied      Dissatisfied

5. **Child-care responsibilities**      Satisfied      Dissatisfied

6. **Arrangements for leisure activities**      Satisfied      Dissatisfied

7. **Balance of household responsibilities**      Satisfied      Dissatisfied

## Evaluating Your Responses

Notice where you are satisfied and dissatisfied. In my study all categories of couples (copreneurs, dual-career employed couples, dual entrepreneurs, and solo entrepreneurs with a supportive spouse who is employed full-time) were satisfied with the division of household responsibilities even if the division was inequitable. How do you compare? Obviously, if there is some dissatisfaction it may be useful to discuss your feelings with your spouse so that you can avoid unresolved power struggles.

## Summarizing Remark

Write one sentence or a brief paragraph summarizing what you learned from this exercise and what you want to change.

Appendix

# Your Satisfaction with the Division of Work Responsibilities in Your Business Relationship

The following is a list of tasks and responsibilities that are common in running a business. Even if you are not involved in running a business with your spouse, you may find the questionnaire helpful in assessing your satisfaction within your entrepreneurial venture or in a business partnership with someone else. For each area of responsibility, circle whether you are "Satisfied" or "Dissatisfied" with the arrangement you and your spouse (or other business partner) have made with regard to who actually handles each item.

1. **Control in decision making**     Satisfied     Dissatisfied

2. **Day-to-day operations**     Satisfied     Dissatisfied

3. **Financial management**     Satisfied     Dissatisfied

4. **Investment management**     Satisfied     Dissatisfied

5. **Product/service development**     Satisfied     Dissatisfied

6. **Personnel Management**     Satisfied     Dissatisfied

7. **Balance of work responsibilities**     Satisfied     Dissatisfied

## Evaluating Your Responses

Notice where you are satisfied and dissatisfied. In my study all copreneurs were satisfied with the division of work responsibilities even if the division was inequitable. How do you compare? Obviously, if there is some dissatisfaction it may be useful to discuss your feelings with your spouse or other business partner so that you can avoid unresolved power struggles.

## Summarizing Remark

Write one sentence or a brief paragraph summarizing what you learned from this exercise and what you want to change.

254

# Your Family Life Plan

Answer the following questions as honestly as you can. There are no right or wrong answers. The purpose of this exercise is to help you identify your parenting and family values and goals, so that you can plan for yourself, your partner, and your children a life that is consistent with those values.

1. Make a list of the people who were most significant to you as a child and indicate what you learned from them or how they influenced you.

2. Make two lists for each of your parents. In the first column, list those parenting qualities you most admire about that parent. In the second column, indicate those parenting qualities you least admire. Which parent are you most like and least like? Which of their parenting qualities do you possess? What would you like to change?

3. Repeat step 2 with grandparents, teachers, and other significant adults from your childhood.

4. What are your fondest memories from childhood? Why?

5. What do you think your children would recount as their fondest memories? Ask them.

6. How would your children describe you if asked about you as a parent and as a person?

7. What do your really know about your children? What do they like? What makes them laugh? Do they have opinions about anything? Who are their heroes?

8. Sit down and have a meaningful conversation with each child and let her or him take the lead.

9. Have a family meeting with all family members and discuss how the family might reorganize itself and raise everyone's consciousness about healthy family relations.

10. What are the qualities you believe are responsible for your successes in life? Are you teaching those qualities to your children?

11. Do you and your partner share the same parenting philosophy? If not, what is your plan to get on the same track?

12. Pick up a good book on parenting and begin educating yourself. With your partner, read and discuss one chapter each week. Then apply what you are learning.

## Evaluating Your Responses

By now you are probably getting pretty good at sifting through your responses and those of your partner. You have been evaluating and reevaluating other aspects of your life plan. Now it is time to reorganize your parenting priorities too. Look for the patterns in your answers. Really listen to what your children and your partner are telling you. Notice where the discrepancies are between your good intentions and your actual behaviors. How can you bring them together? If you are continuing in an unhealthy pattern, now is the time to change it. Notice, too, what you are doing right, and build on those successes.

Taking into account all that you have learned from this exercise and from each other, including the children, what will it take for you to become an authoritative parent who takes time to get to know your children, who takes seriously the responsibility to foster resilience and independence in your children, who understands that children need time to make changes, and who wants your children to remember their childhood fondly?

## Summarizing Remark

Write one sentence or a brief paragraph summarizing what you learned from this exercise and what you want to change.

## SELF-ASSESSMENT EXERCISE 13

# Your Financial Life Plan

Answer the following questions as honestly as you can. There are no right or wrong answers. The purpose of this exercise is to help you clarify your values and beliefs about money so that you can manage your wealth in more appropriate and balanced ways.

1. What does money mean to you? To your spouse?

2. What do you want money to mean in your family? In your business?

3. If you had all the money you needed, how much would that be?

4. Think of all the ways you would satisfy your wants if you had all the money you needed.

5. After you have satisfied all your wants, what would you do then?

6. Is it okay to discuss your salary with others? Why or why not?

7. To what point is it okay to discuss what things cost?

8. Is it okay to pay children for getting good grades?

9. When should your child get a paying job?

10. In the family business, how do you determine what to pay a family member?

11. Is the breadwinner in your family the boss?

12. What did your parents teach you about money?

13. What are you teaching your children about money?

14. What ethical boundaries have you crossed with regard to money that are still "secrets" in the family?

15. How are these secrets costing you, both in dollars and in self-esteem and trust?

## Evaluating Your Responses

Sort through your answers and look for patterns and themes. Are you surprised by your resonses to this exercise? What are the meanings you have made of money? Go back to the beginning of the chapter where I discussed the meaning of money. Do your answers in this self-assessment exercise reflect any of the myths and values of money that are dominant in our culture? Are these values you really want to keep? Think long and hard about the money values you want to pass on to your children. Now rewrite your money values and add to the rest of your life plan a new healthier script for acquiring and utilizing wealth.

## Summarizing Remark

Write one sentence or a brief paragraph summarizing what you learned from this exercise and what you want to change.

# Your Power Plan

Answer the following questions as honestly as you can. There are no right or wrong answers. The purpose of this exercise is to help focus your attention on your mental, physical, and spiritual health so that you can manage the excessive stresses in your life more effectively and avoid some of the worst crises and breakdowns that entrepreneurial couples are likely to face.

1. In comparison to some of the couples described in this chapter, what similar problems are you in the process of developing?

2. How can you begin today to devote more time to personal stress management, such as the relaxation response?

3. What physical health problems, including any addictions, need attending to *now*?

4. If there is any form of domestic violence occurring in your life, what is your plan to stop it?

5. If you are using extramarital affairs to solve or avoid couple, family, or business problems, what is your plan to revamp your style to be consistent with your true values?

6. If you have a history of financial improprieties and misfortune, what are these signals telling you about the imbalance in your life?

7. If you are considering divorce, first ask yourself if divorce is a result of imbalance in the mind-body-spirit connection. If so, what alternatives to restoring balance are there other than divorce?

8. What plans have you made with your spouse to discuss a healthy partnership and dissolution agreement with an attorney?

9. Take the time to really evaluate your spiritual commitment. If that aspect of your life has been on hold, what's keeping you from exploring your spiritual commitment now?

10. **Who are the professionals you rely on to help you build your power plan? Make sure your medical doctor, naturopath, chiropractor, psychologist, and so on are in healthy balance themselves so that you all work together to build a power plan that successfully manages the excessive stresses of entrepreneurial couple life.**

## Evaluating Your Responses

With the experience you have gained by working the other self-assessment exercises in this book, you are better prepared to confront the serious stresses uncovered by this exercise. It takes courage and good communication skills to remedy infidelity, drug abuse, financial problems, and other personal inadequacies. Try to remember that you and your partner are human beings, both doing the best you know how to do, given your level of knowledge and experience at the time. Now, however, after reading this chapter, you have more knowledge than before, and it is time to build a more sophisticated power plan than you have ever had.

If you have uncovered even only one of the problems alluded to in this exercise, it may take a long time and a lot of work to correct it, but get started. Cleaning up old business paves the way to implementing a more healthy lifestyle in the future. You cannot build a life on shaky ground. Once you have reordered your life by cleaning up mistakes, begin attending to the many stresses that plague the entrepreneurial couple life, and have a plan to defuse stress on a daily basis.

## Summarizing Remark

Write one sentence or a brief paragraph summarizing what you learned from this exercise and what you want to change.

## SELF-ASSESSMENT EXERCISE 15

# Your Master Life Plan

Pull the summarizing remarks from each exercise and enter them in the spaces provided. First you will gather remarks from the self-awareness exercises, and then from the planning exercises. This will enable you to draft a master plan with items from your action plan. There are five parts to this exercise.

**PART ONE:** Self-awareness exercises

1.  **Self-Assessment Exercise 1:**
    *What's your entrepreneurial couple style?*

2.  **Self-Assessment Exercise 2:**
    *Examining the dialectic of your relationship*

3.  **Self-Assessment Exercise 6:**
    *Your sex-role orientation*

4.  **Self-Assessment Exercise 7:**
    *Your work/home self-concept*

5.  **Self-Assessment Exercise 8:**
    *How you divide household responsibilities*

6.  **Self-Assessment Exercise 9:**
    *How you divide work-related responsibilities*

7.  **Self-Assessment Exercise 10:**
    *Your satisfaction with the division of household responsibilities in your marriage/personal relationship*

8.  **Self-Assessment Exercise 11:**
    *Your satisfaction with the division of work responsibilities in your business relationship*

## SELF-ASSESSMENT EXERCISE 15 (CONT'D)

**PART TWO: Planning exercises**

1. **Self-Assessment Exercise 3:**
   *Your personal life plan*

2. **Self-Assessment Exercise 4:**
   *Your relationship life plan*

3. **Self-Assessment Exercise 5:**
   *Your business life plan*

4. **Self-Assessment Exercise 12:**
   *Your family life plan*

5. **Self-Assessment Exercise 13:**
   *Your financial life plan*

6. **Self-Assessment Exercise 14:**
   *Your power plan*

**PART THREE: Your Master Life Plan**

From Part Two take all the summarizing remarks and write one or two pages that reflect your vision for the future. Be sure to include each area of your life—personal, relationship, business, family, financial, and health/stress management.

**PART FOUR: Your Action Plan**

Now that you have a vision of your master life plan, make a list of the steps you will take to accomplish your goals. The summarizing remarks in Part One contain much material for the changes you want to make. Review the summarizing remarks from all of the exercises in Part One and Part Two and list the changes you will be making under the headings below. Be so brave as to even estimate date of completion.

## SELF-ASSESSMENT EXERCISE 15 (CONT'D)

**Action Steps to Accomplish Your Personal Life Plan**

1.

2.

3.

4.

5.

**Action Steps to Accomplish Your Relationship Life Plan**

1.

2.

3.

4.

5.

**Action Steps to Accomplish Your Business Life Plan**

1.

2.

3.

4.

5.

**Action Steps to Accomplish Your Family Life Plan**

1.

2.

3.

4.

5.

## SELF-ASSESSMENT EXERCISE 15 (CONT'D)

**Action Steps to Accomplish Your Financial Life Plan**

1.

2.

3.

4.

5.

**Action Steps to Accomplish Your Power Plan**

1.

2.

3.

4.

5.

**PART FIVE: Your Mission Statement**

You have worked hard to investigate your life and your goals. You now have a vision of the future—a master life plan and action steps to accomplish that plan. Take the time to distill your work into one succinct guiding principle. Think of the work you have just done as the body of a newspaper article and the mission statement as the headline. How do you want the headline to read? What is the defining quality of your entrepreneurial couple life? How do you make it work at work and at home?

# REFERENCES

Adler, A. (1927). *Understanding Human Nature.* New York: Greenberg.

Barnett, F., and Barnett, S. (1988). *Working Together: Entrepreneurial Couples.* Berkeley, CA: Ten Speed Press.

Benson, H. (1975). *The Relaxation Response.* New York: Morrow.

Bernard, J. (1972). *The Future of Marriage.* New York: World.

Biernat, M., and Wortman, C. (1991). Sharing of home responsibilities between professionally employed women and their husbands. *Journal of Personality and Social Psychology* 60 (6), 844–860.

Bryson, R., Bryson, J., Licht, M., and Licht, B. (1976). The professional pair. *American Psychologist* 31, 10–16.

Byrd, R. (1988). Positive therapeutic effects of intercessory prayer in a coronary care unit population. *Southern Medical Journal* 81, 826–829.

Carland, J., Hoy, F., Boulton, W., and Carland, J. (1984). Differentiating entrepreneurs from small business owners: A conceptualization. *Academy of Management Review* 9 (2), 354–359.

Danco, L. (1976). *Beyond Survival: A Business Owner's Guide for Success.* Cleveland, OH: University Press.

Davis, J., and Taguiri, R. (1989). The influence of life stage on father-son work relationships in family companies. *Family Business Review* 2 (1), 47–76.

de Beauvoir, S. (1952). *The Second Sex.* New York: Vintage.

Desmund, D., and Maddux, J. (1981). Religious programs and careers of chronic heroin users. *American Journal of Drug and Alcohol Abuse* 8 (1), 71–83.

Donckels, R., and Frohlich, E. (1991). Are family businesses really different? European experiences from STRATOS. *Family Business Review* 4 (2), 149–160.

Dumas, C. (1988). *Daughters in Family-Owned Businesses.* Doctoral dissertation, Fielding Institute, Santa Barbara, CA.

Durkheim, E. (1947). *Division of Labor in Society* (G. Simpson, trans.). Glencoe, IL: Free Press.

Emerson, R. (1983). *Self-Reliance.* Calistoga, CA: Illumination Press.

Epstein, C. (1971). Law partners and marital partners: Strains and solutions in the dual-career family enterprise. *Human Relations* 24 (6), 549–564.

Erikson, E. (1950). *Childhood and Society.* New York: Norton.

Flemmons, D., and Cole, P. (1992). Connecting and separating family and business: A relational approach to consultation. *Family Business Review* V (3), 257–269.

Frankl, V. (1992). *Man's Search for Meaning.* Boston: Beacon Press.

Freud, S. (1923). The ego and the id. *The Major Works of Sigmund Freud.* Chicago, IL: Encyclopedia Britannica, 1952, 697–717.

Friedlander, F. (1990). *Work-Home Identity Scale.* Unpublished manuscript, Fielding Institute, Santa Barbara, CA.

Galbraith, J. (1984). *The Affluent Society.* New York: New American Library.

Gallup, G., Jr. (March 1997). The epidemiology of spirituality. Presentation made at the Spirituality and Healing in Medicine II conference. Los Angeles, CA.

Gove, W. (1972). The relationship between sex roles, marital status and mental illness. *Social Forces* 51, 34–45.

Graham, T., Kaplan, B., Coroni-Huntley, J., James, S., Becker, C., Hames, C., and Heyden, S. (1978). Frequency of church attendance and blood pressure elevation. *Journal of Behavioral Medicine* I, 37–43.

Gray, J. (1992). *Men Are from Mars, Women Are from Venus: A Practical Guide for Improving Communication and Getting What You Want in Your Relationships.* New York: HarperCollins.

Hoffman, L. (1981). *Foundations of Family Therapy: A Conceptual Framework for Systems Change.* New York: Basic Books.

Jensen, A. (1969). How much can we boost I.Q. and scholastic achievement? *Harvard Educational Review* 39, 1–123.

Kabbani, S. (March 1997). Islamic spiritual healing practices. Presentation made at the Spirituality and Healing in Medicine II conference. Los Angeles, CA.

Kanter, E. (1977). *Work and Family in the United States: A Critical Review and Agenda for Research and Policy.* New York: Russell Sage Foundation.

Kelley, H., and Thibaut, J. (1978). *Interpersonal Relations: A Theory of Interdependence.* New York: Wiley.

Knocke, A. (Sept. 1988). Hidden figures on women. *Nation's Business,* p. 40.

Lankton, S., and Lankton, C. (1983). *The Answer Within: A Clinical Framework of Ericksonian Hypnotherapy.* New York: Brunner/Mazel.

Levinson, H. (Nov. I, 1983). *Levinson Letter.* Greebrae, CA: Ivan Levinson & Associates.

Marshack, K. (1994). *Love and Work: How Co-Entrepreneurial Couples Manage the Boundaries and Transitions in Personal Relationship and Business Partnership.* Doctoral dissertation, Fielding Institute, Santa Barbara, CA.

Marx, K., and Engels, F. (1939). *The German Ideology.* New York: International Publishers.

Matthews, D., and Koenig, H. (1997). Spirituality and medical outcomes. Presentation made at the Spirituality and Healing in Medicine II conference. Los Angeles, CA.

McKinley, M. (1984). *A Study of Adult Development of Wives in Family-Owned Businesses.* Doctoral dissertation, University of Pittsburgh, Pittsburgh, PA.

McWhinney, W. (1986). Entrepreneurs, owners, and stewards: The conduct of family business. *New Management,* 4–II.

Nightingale, F. (1994). *Suggestions for Thought: Selections and Commentaries.* (M. Calabria and J. Macrae, eds.). Philadelphia: University of Pennsylvania Press.

Piaget, J. (1967). *The Child's Conception of the World.* Totowa, NJ: Littlefield Adams.

Ponthieu, L., and Caudill, H. (1993). Who's the boss? Responsibility and decision making in copreneurial ventures. *Family Business Review* VI (I), 3–17.

Putnam, C. (1993). *A Conceptual Model of Women Entrepreneurs.* Doctoral dissertation, Oregon State University, Corvallis, OR.

Quinn, R., and Cameron, K. (January 1983). Organizational life cycles and shifting criteria of effectiveness: Some preliminary evidence. *Management Science* 29.

Rapoport, R., and Rapoport, R. (1979). The dual-career family: A variant pattern and social change. *Human Relations* 22, 3–29.

Rapoport, R., and Rapoport, R. (1969). *Dual-Career Families.* Middlesex, England: Penguin.

Rapoport, R., and Rapoport, R. (1965). Work and family in contemporary society. *American Sociological Review* 30 (3), 381–394.

Riegel, K. (1976). The dialectics of human development. *American Psychologist* 31, 689–700.

Salganicoff, M. (1990). Clarifying the present and creating options for the future. *Family Business Review* 3 (2), 121–124.

Salganicoff, M. (1990). Women in family businesses: Challenges and opportunities. *Family Business Review* 3 (2), 125–137.

Satir, V. (1988). *New Peoplemaking.* Palo Alto, CA: Science and Behavior Books.

Spence, J., and Helmreich, R. (1978). *Masculinity and Femininity: Their Psychological Dimensions, Correlates, and Antecedents.* Austin, TX: University of Texas Press.

Stevenson, L. (October 1986). Against all odds: The entrepreneurship of women. *Journal of Small Business Management,* 30–36.

Thoreau, H. (1992). *Walden, or Life in the Woods.* New York: Knopf.

U.S. Bureau of Labor Statistics (1989). *Special Labor Forces Reports* (reports nos. 13, 130, 134; bulletins 2163, 2307). Washington, DC: Government Printing Office.

U.S. Commerce Department. (1987). *Economic Censuses: Women-Owned Businesses.* Washington, DC: Government Printing Office.

U.S. Department of Labor (1977). *Working Mothers and Their Children.* Washington, DC: Employment Standards Administration, Women's Bureau.

U.S. Small Business Administration (1997). Facsimile transmittal from the Office of Advocacy, Washington, DC.

von Bertalanffy, L. (1951). General systems theory: A new approach to unity of science. *Human Biology* 23, 302–312.

Weber, M. (1947). *The Theory of Social Economic Organization* (A. M. Henderson and T. Parsons, trans.). Glencoe, IL: Free Press.

Wicker, A., and Burley, K. (1991). Close coupling in work-family relationships: Making and implementing decisions in a new family business and at home. *Human Relations* 44 (1), 77–92.